Strategic conversations on **the euro at the vanguard of global integration**

Edited by
Albert Bressand

Forewords by
Jacques Santer and Rolf-E. Breuer

With the participation of
ABN AMRO Bank N.V., Amsterdam Exchanges N.V., Cedel Bank, Deutsche Bank, Deutsche Börse AG, Euroclear, European Investment Bank, Eurostat, MATIF SA, REUTERS Holdings PLC, SBF - Bourse de Paris, Société Générale Asset Management, SWX Swiss Exchange, Eurex.

PROMETHEE   ERNST & YOUNG

Published by
PROMETHEE
30, rue d'Astorg – 75008 Paris – France
thinknet@promethee.grolier.fr

ISBN 2-907587-01-3

France/Copyright: January 1998 / Printed in France

Illustration: "PlaNet euro", painted by Victor Krotov to illustrate the ThinkNet process of strategic conversations around the euro.
Victor Krotov is a surrealist painter born and living in Moscow.

Design / Production : BRIEF (www.brief.fr)

The euro
at the vanguard of global integration

About the ThinkNet collection 7
Jean-Charles Raufast and Albert Bressand

PROLOGUE

The euro, Europe and the world 9
foreword by Jacques Santer, President, European Union Commission

The euro, markets and the State 13
foreword by Rolf-E. Breuer, Spokesman of the Board of Managing Directors of Deutsche Bank AG.

An eventful non-event 18
Overview by Albert Bressand, Managing Director, PROMETHEE
Editor's acknowledgment and note 35

PART I - ONE CURRENCY, MANY STOCK EXCHANGES, ONE MARKET

I. **The euro "Big Bang" and Europe's place in the new geography of global capital markets** 38
Strategic Conversation with Jean-François Théodore, Chairman & CEO, SBF-Bourse de Paris
The Networked Market Study Group (PROMETHEE insert) 62

II. **The euro and beyond: financial markets and the search for renewed economic dynamism in Europe** 68
Strategic Conversation with Werner Seifert, CEO, Deutsche Börse AG

III. **Close to the euro and close to the world: a Swiss perspective on the global networks of exchanges of the future** 88
Strategic Conversation with Jörg Fischer, President, SWX Swiss Exchange, Eurex

IV. **The "European big board" of the euro era and its implications for the Amsterdam financial center** 102
Strategic Conversation with George Möller, Chairman & President, Amsterdam Exchanges N.V.

V. **Beyond country risks: derivatives markets and risks taking in the euro era** 116
Strategic Conversation with Gérard Pfauwadel, Chairman & CEO, MATIF SA

PART II - EUROPEAN HUBS FOR GLOBAL FINANCE

VI. **Euroclear in the age of euro-clearing: quality of information and risk management** 130
Strategic Conversation with Luc Bomans, Managing Director & General Manager, Euroclear

VII. **The euro: the catalyst for entrepreneurial change in Europe?** 140
Strategic Conversation with André Lussi, CEO, Cedel Bank

VIII. **The U.K may or may not join, but the City of London will be in the euro!** 156
Strategic Conversation with André Villeneuve, Executive Director, REUTERS Holdings PLC.

Part III - European banking and the euro challenge

IX. Perspective from a global, universal, network bank **172**
Strategic Conversation with Dolf van den Brink, Member of the Managing Board, ABN AMRO Bank N.V.

X. Asset managers already live with the euro: Société Générale and the "Club Europe" initiative .. **184**
Strategic Conversation with Philippe Collas, CEO, Société Générale Asset Management (SGAM)

XI. A large issuer promoting markets in euro: the European Investment Bank perspective **196**
Strategic Conversation with René Karsenti, Director General of Finance, European Investment Bank

Part IV - The global integration frontier and the euro

XII. Convergence at the intersection of interdependence and governance: the euro and the multi-tier globalization map **222**
Presentation of the analytical framework by Catherine Distler and Albert Bressand.
Short Conversations with Jean Saint-Geours (IASC Advisory Board) and with René de La Serre (Chairman, Conseil des Marchés Financiers – CMF) and Bertrand de Mazières (Secretary General, CMF)

XIII. Measuring economic convergence: the euro as catalyst of global trends and the need for certified information **244**
Strategic Conversation with Yves Franchet, Director General of Eurostat

XIV. Europe, convergence and the world: a quantitative overview, in co-operation with Eurostat ... **256**
Financial markets of the Union: capitalisation, returns and pension funds. 288
Section and text by Thomas Rabe, Cedel Bank

Promethee and Ernst & Young associates **300**

Index **302**

About the ThinkNet Collection

"Rapid change" has become a cliché. But the expression conceals more than it reveals: after all, it was Charles Péguy who wrote: "the world had changed less since Jesus Christ than it has changed over the last thirty years". This view of a tremendous acceleration of time was put forward in 1913, three quarters of a century *before* the theme found its contemporary expression under Alvin Toffler's pen... And yet, three quarters of a century *earlier,* Chateaubriand had already described "a land expanded by the power of ubiquity, and yet shrunk to the small proportions of a globe thoroughly explored".

The challenge is not change *per se* but the discrepancy between the speed at which we learn and the speed at which our knowledge becomes obsolete. Accessing information is only an appetizer in the effort to prepare for change. To call English poetry to the rescue, the information age will find us often in the situation of wondering like T.S. Eliot "where is the knowledge we lost in information, and where is the wisdom we lost in knowledge ?".

The strategic conversations in this ThinkNet Collection are an effort to share the knowledge and to work toward some at least of the wisdom needed to put information into its meaningful perspective. We endeavour to mix the Ernst & Young emphasis on "ideas, solutions and results" with the PROMETHEE enthusiasm for long-term visions and for intellectual debates. Inviting our guests to "think aloud", listening and learning, we have tried to combine the discipline of strategy and the art of conversation.

This first volume is about one of the most spectacular changes about to happen in this century: a dozen sovereign countries joining forces to create a new currency as a stronger foundation for their common relation to the global economy.

We are most grateful to the prominent financial decision makers who have accepted to take part in this first set of open dialogues and to share some of the visions that guide their action. We also want to thank Eurostat for their insightful help with data and Dan Newman, Cécile Le Moigne, Sabine d'Armau de Bernède and Marie-France Boudet for their decisive contributions in making this project happen.

We are also most grateful to Ivan Wagner, chairman of the Ernst & Young Banking and Financial Services worldwide practice, who has supported this first book focused on the euro and the global financial scene with a rare combination of openness and steadfastness. We are also indebted to the Ersnt & Young associates in the various national practices who have mobilized for this important project.

It is a great pleasure to invite each and every reader to join in this network, in these efforts and to share in this search, if not for wisdom at least for insights. Welcome to the ThinkNet !

Jean-Charles Raufast
Vice Chairman,
Ernst & Young International

Albert Bressand
Managing Director,
PROMETHEE

Prologue

Foreword by Jacques Santer,
President of the European Commission

The euro, Europe and the world

> The European Union is indeed "at the vanguard" of economic integration

Since more than a decade, the process of globalisation has deeply affected economic relationships between countries, regions, and economic actors. Following rapid technological change, the progressive elimination of tariff barriers to trade, falling costs of transport and communication and the development of global financial markets, trade and investment links between countries have intensified considerably. Economic integration has become a shared goal for governments and policy makers, and it is not confined to Europe.

However, never before has any regional grouping of countries succeeded in taking economic integration as far as Europe has done. Customs duties between European countries came down steadily in the 1950s and disappeared completely in 1968 with the completion of the customs union. The completion of the single market on January 1, 1993 was aimed at eliminating non-tariff barriers to trade between Member States. The creation of the euro will now push this process even further. It is no coincidence that historically, a single market and a single currency are observed to go together. The efficiency gains from market integration are amplified by monetary integration through various effects.

"The euro at the vanguard of European integration" is thus a theme which lies at the very heart of the basic goals of the European Union, as the introduction of the euro will be an additional – and major – step in the ongoing process of European integration. The advantages of Economic and Monetary Union and the euro are manifold.

> Monetary integration complements the single market

The Maastricht Treaty lays down a number of conditions for participation in Economic and Monetary Union (EMU). In order to prepare for EMU, and once it is in place, Member States need to follow sound economic policies, based on low inflation, healthy public finances, and stable monetary conditions. These rules of good economic management are the recipe for lower interest rates and stronger economic growth.

Inflation expectations have already been reduced substantially in a large number of Member States as a result of the successes that have been booked in the fight against inflation. The continuation of economic policies geared towards low inflation is guaranteed by the Treaty provisions relating to the mandate of the European Central Bank, whose objective is price stability, as well as by the pursuit of healthy policies with regard to public finances. The countries participating in the monetary union will already have made a substantial effort towards fiscal stability, as this is one of the convergence criteria of the Maastricht Treaty. In EMU, they will continue their endeavour to bring public finances close to equilibrium. This will be beneficial for economic growth and employment through a reduction in interest rates, which will stimulate investment, and through an increase in consumer confidence and in consumption.

The move towards monetary union on January 1, 1999 will reduce the overall uncertainty for exporters and investors associated with the existence of national currencies and independent monetary policies. This will lead to an increase in intra-Union trade and foreign direct investment, and, consequently, economic growth. Also, a reduction in exchange rate uncertainty could lower the risk premium firms have to pay on equity and would therefore greatly benefit investment. Estimates have shown that even a reduction in the risk premium of only 0.5 percentage points could raise income significantly.

The introduction of the euro will also lead to a reduction of the costs associated with the trade between participating Member States. A recent study for the European Commission shows that the transaction costs of intra-EU trade – foreign exchange commissions, the difference between buying and selling rates, and the costs for foreign exchange management – amounted to roughly 1% of GDP per year over the years 1986-95. Economic research suggests that even small transaction costs can have significant economic effects. This implies that the overall economic losses from exchange rate transaction costs are larger than the direct costs alone.

For consumers, one direct effect of the introduction of the euro will be to increase price transparency: it will be possible to compare prices in different member countries directly, which should benefit competition and lead to price reductions. EMU will also enable importers, exporters, and investors to make more accurate calculations of the costs and returns of their activities. This will in particular be beneficial to small and medium-sized enterprises, who are at a disadvantage compared with large companies as regards their possibilities to manage exchange rate variations.

The introduction of the euro will mark the emergence of a major new international currency. Its scale will imply that financial markets in euro will have greater depth and liquidity compared with existing national currencies, and this is likely to lead to the development of new financial instruments. Enhanced liquidity and the availability of new financial instruments will lead to a reduction of financing costs for enterprises.

The creation of the euro-zone will make its economies less vulnerable to external exchange rate fluctuations. This follows from the reduction of the share of international trade which is conducted in third currencies in the euro-zone as compared to its composing Member States. This implies that the euro area will be less sensitive to external shocks.

The euro-zone will be a large pole of stability in the international economy. It will abolish all exchange rate fluctuations between the former currencies of the participating countries. The stability of the euro area will also be guaranteed by the pursuit of a monetary policy aimed at price stability by an independent central bank and by fiscal policies aimed at budgetary consolidation and continued discipline. The stability of the euro area will not only be beneficial for the European Union, but will also benefit third countries.

> Employment is a major concern

The euro, albeit a milestone in the European integration process, is only an instrument for achieving a more prosperous and efficient economy.

The issue of employment is central to the concerns of Europe's citizens, and every effort must be made to combat unemployment, the unacceptable level of which poses a threat to the cohesion of our societies. The Luxembourg European Council has accordingly decided that the relevant provisions of the new Title on employment in the Treaty of Amsterdam are to be put into effect immediately. This decision makes it possible in practice to implement the provisions on co-ordination of Member States' employment policies as from 1998. Such co-ordination will be based on "employment guidelines", which are common lines of approach for both objectives and means that draw directly on the experience built up in the multilateral surveillance of economic policies. The idea is to create for employment the same resolve to achieve convergence towards jointly set, verifiable, and regularly updated targets, while respecting the differences between the situations of individual Member States.

Here too, European efforts are taking shape in a framework of co-operation and dialogue with our partners. Within the G7, world leaders have also recognised the need to create the conditions for sustainable employment growth through appropriate macro-economic policies and well-functioning labour markets. Strong growth will help to reduce unemployment, by creating a virtuous circle, but there is a need to address the structural problems which impede job creation and income growth. Subsequent G7 Job Conferences have resulted in strong commitments for close co-operation on these issues.

> Challenges for the future

As President of the European Commission, I look with satisfaction on the enormous progress that has been made in the field of further integration, but there are still enormous challenges facing us.

Being "at the vanguard" as this book rightly says, is not a comfortable position to be in, but we welcome this challenge, and we look forward to an intensification of our dialogue with the other parts of the world. With Asia, notably through the ASEM process, with the America's, and with our close partners in the ACP countries, as well as with the Mediterranean region. The major challenge for the years to come is of course the enlargement with the countries of central and eastern Europe and Cyprus. This has to be seen against the background of a positive review of European integration, stretching from the 1986 Single Act to the Treaty of Amsterdam in June 1997, which comprises two enlargements, three major reviews of the Treaties, and two significant financial packages. These developments, as well as changes in the outside world, and in particular the end of the Cold War and the collapse of the Soviet Union, have given a new impetus for integration, both at the European and at the global level.

I therefore gladly support the initiative taken by the PROMETHEE think-tank in Paris in engaging key actors of the European financial scene in this open dialogue about the implications of the introduction of the euro for their institutions, for Europe, and for the world.

Jacques Santer

Foreword by Dr. Rolf-E. Breuer,
Spokesman of the Board of Managing
Directors of Deutsche Bank AG.

The euro, markets and the State

At the end of the 20th century, European Monetary Union and the global integration of national economies are confronting Europe with new social, political and economic challenges. The introduction of the euro in 1999 will take Europe to a new level of integration that will have a global economic impact. Supported by modern technology, the 21st century will be an era of electronic and virtual networking in which the ongoing globalization process will lead to a new capital market structure. What developments are in store for the capital market in Europe and globally?

> Capital markets

Today's capital markets are among the fastest growing of all markets. They transform savings efficiently into the investment capital needed for economic expansion. Capital markets distribute opportunities and risks among investors, companies and intermediaries. Efficient capital markets are a key factor for growth and prosperity.

Europe's prospect is to create a much more efficient and larger capital market than the markets of member states with exchange rate risks and national (over-) regulation could ever have achieved. The fragmentation of European capital markets stems from divergent taxation and accounting law, different currencies, regulated access to capital and stock markets and different market systems. Much of the euro's attraction will depend on whether it will be possible to create a European capital market as a level playing field in line with the principles of competition.

Today, on the eve of monetary union, it is clear that the money, bond and equities markets will grow together, though at different paces. All market participants will benefit from an inexpensive, liquid and safe market which is easy to access and is not tied to location. But there will also be changes in competitive conditions to be tackled by European exchanges, banks, payment and clearing systems.

The greater irrelevance of national boundaries in Europe will lead to capital flowing more easily to investment projects with optimum yield/risk structures. National interests can no longer be upheld in this environment without economic justification. Companies will then be able to choose between a much broader range of capital offerings and finance growth increasingly through equity capital markets.

This will increase demands on European stock markets, which will have to grow beyond their national regulative regimes into a European dimension so as to be able to offer attractive and inexpensive services for investors, traders and issuers. By cooperating and concentrating they will instal networked market structures in Europe with remote membership. The most efficient market architectures will dominate the others and replace them over time.

> Networked markets, and shareholder value

The emergence of a European networked stock market system will become the basis of global competitiveness. The contributions from leading stock market representatives in the first part of this book highlight their strategies and the underlying dynamic changes in the stock market scene. As pan-European integration of stock markets proceeds, clearing and settlement systems will also coalesce. Cross-border real-time settlement will be the norm in Europe. As Europe liberalizes, back-office financial services will become a commodity, bringing immense economies of scale within reach through the use of modern information technology. The second part shows how European market leaders view developments in this segment.

For stock corporations, the yardsticks for success or failure in Europe will in future be set more strongly by the capital market. Growing institutionalization of assets will raise the importance of shareholder value. Share markets will differentiate more strongly between value-creating and value-destroying companies. European yield comparisons reveal structural weaknesses, the elimination of which will be all the more painful the longer structural change is postponed. National inefficient industrial structures must be replaced, and historical privileges removed. This should improve companies' competitiveness and increase their innovation and productivity potential.

Banks will follow this trend and consider what changes they must make to achieve major added value in future. There is not much time left to answer this question, which makes adjustment all the more urgent. The January 1, 1999 deadline is a spur to change, as confirmed with different emphases by the authors of the third part of this book.

> Citizens, the State and the needs of future generations

What are the implications of these trends for government action? In the last 50 years, government influence on markets has gradually increased. While the share of government spending in Germany was still 25% in 1920, it reached 32.4% by 1960 and is more than 50% today. The share of tax revenues in Europe's GDP was 41.3% in 1980, 43.8% in 1990 and 45.4% last year. Despite much effort, state activity is not receding, which suggests that globalization only appears at first sight to have led to more market. Due to the complex and obscure mechanism of transfer payments between different parts of society, higher government spending can no longer be shown to mean better social conditions. People know that a rising government share of national income means greater misallocation. And yet, citizens and politicians continue to demand more and more of the state.

The state must review its role. We must demand less state involvement. Government in a developed, open and technologically advanced information society must play a regulative role. Economic, political and social objectives must be harmonized without stifling personal initiative and efficient market processes. The danger lies in former national concepts being projected into the European or global future.

Labour markets are an example of how overregulation, without heed for economic principles, leads to inadequate market flexibility and higher unemployment. The tendency to fulfil expanding state obligations at the expense of future generations must be nipped in the bud. Initial, though often only short-term, steps to reduce government involvement have been taken by European states in their efforts to meet the EMU convergence criteria. Taking into account social and economic constraints, the state must focus in the long term on a small number of core activities.

One of the main future challenges to European society lies in the structuring of social security systems, which are unsustainable in their present form. Today's state social security schemes induce high costs, low productivity, capital misallocation, and also, owing to their increasing misuse, are reducing the competitiveness of Europe's economy. The system motivates individuals to make personally rational decisions which have negative effects on society and are often not subject to market control mechanisms.
The share of social security expenditure in GDP is today about one-third; it will probably rise by 2030 to 50%, unless market-oriented and socially acceptable incentive and sanction mechanisms are introduced to stop this trend in Europe. To curb the growth in the number of state pension recipients in relation to the working population, supplementary private pension instruments are needed, or state schemes must be put on a funded basis.

> The euro, and the competitiveness of Europe

How will EMU affect Europe's position in the world economy? How far Europe's global competitiveness can be increased depends on how well the government can resist the probable calls for regulation and protection of markets. Protectionism will be hard to prevent in the European Union in the short term. Whatever the intentions of protectionist action, in the long term it must capitulate before economic necessity.
More beneficial mechanisms or structures bred by competition will predominate and in the long term replace old structures. The EMU-driven restructuring momentum in European capital and goods markets is an opportunity for market participants that dominate in the European Union to improve their global competitiveness.

In the last decade, international trade has expanded twice, foreign direct investment three times, and cross-border equities trading ten times as fast as global goods production. The globalization trend in these markets is immense.

The use of technology and the ability of capital markets to differentiate between risks, separate them and trade them worldwide with new financial instruments will continue to grow. Greater global availability of capital in conjunction with leading-edge computer and information technology will stimulate globalization in the next ten years on a far bigger scale than hitherto. For Europe, therefore, the euro is only one more step in this direction. But it's the milestone triggering the change to improved market structures.

This volume describes the coming changes in Europe and highlights strategic alternatives, but also visions. Experienced practitioners present

in detail their view of future developments and actions needed.
The contributions by practitioners from banking, the stock markets and clearing organizations offer interested readers greater insight into future market changes. The final part of this book then sets out modern views and studies by Promethee and Ernst & Young International on the economic, regulatory and technological transformation process. **Rolf-E. Breuer**

The long march to the euro

Latin monetary Union	1865
Shift to Gold Standard	1876-78
Bretton Woods	July 1944
Adoption of the Werner Plan	March 1971
End of dollar convertibility in gold	Aug. 1971
Monetary Snake	1972
Start of the EMS	March 1979
Second oil crisis	1979-1981
Plaza Accord on stability of global exchange rates	Sept. 1985
Louvre Accord on stability of global exchange rates	Jan. 1987
Basle/Nyborg agreement on measures to strengthen EMS	Sept. 1987
Stage 1 of EMU begins with full freedom of capital flows	July 1990
European Union ("Maastricht") Treaty signed	Feb. 1992
First Danish referendum on Maastricht	June 1992
Sterling exit from ERM	Sept. 1992
French referendum on Maastricht	Sept. 1992
Swiss reject participation in EEA	Dec. 1992
Second Danish referendum on Maastricht	May 1993
ERM bands widened to 15%; House of Commons ratifies Maastricht	Aug. 1993
Stage 2 of EMU begins, creation of EMI	Jan. 1994
Madrid summit confirms 1999 as the start of EMU, adopts a detailed "scenario" for transition to the single currency and the name "euro"	Dec. 1995
Dublin summit proposals for Stability and Growth pact	Dec. 1996
Florence agreement on ERM-II for "out" countries	June 1996
Amsterdam summit adopts Stability and Growth Pact and launches employment initiative	June 1997
Luxembourg summit on employment	Nov. 1997

Countries for the euro to be identified and parity grid among them adopted	May 1998
European Central Bank to come into existence	July, 1, 1998
Euro created. Euro used for all capital market operations and, optionally, for many others	January 1, 1999
Euro bank notes and coins introduced, to co-exist with national currencies for 6 months at most	January 1, 2002

Overview by Albert Bressand,
Managing Director, PROMETHEE

An eventful non-event

There are events that capture the headlines – matters of war and peace, elections, market crashes, athletic events... There are also events that capture the imagination – first views of Pathfinder on Mars, new drugs to cure stubborn diseases, princely marriages and deaths, walls falling down in Berlin... And then there are events that look very much like non-events. The sort of things that take time, that come in complex stages, that are forgotten after being celebrated only to be rediscovered again in a different form. The euro is one of these eventful non-events.

> Around the corner

A fundamental reason for this paradox is the way in which European integration fits in the historical and geographic complexity of a continent so many times torn and re-drawn by war and peace, by religions and languages, by empires and cultures.

The euro is both about the short term deadlines of the Maastricht agenda *and* about the long term history of the continent. The financial geography of the euro reflects the immediate results of macroeconomic convergence *and* the long succession of unions and dis-unions that have led to the present borders and to the present desire to live together.

Like prosperity, the euro has been "around the corner" for quite a while, even if under other names. Since 1865 when Belgium, France, Italy and Switzerland got together in the Latin Union on the assumption that the rapid development of trade that they were witnessing could not coexist for very long with unpredictable changes in exchange rates. Fixed exchanges rates, or even a common currency, such was the stated objective of this "monetary union" based on common definitions of the value of currencies, in silver and gold. Twelve years later, however, the common parity grid between silver and gold revealed itself unsustainable in the face of global trends in supply and demand, and this early monetary union quietly dissolved in the disciplines of the emerging Gold Standard... before war and nationalism rendered such co-operation unthinkable for long, dark decades.

But ideas have a life of their own. The monetary instability that followed the collapse of the Bretton Woods System was seen, notably in France, as hard to reconcile with trade openness. Calls for a return to "a monetary order" could be heard again, with increasing strength, in countries where it had become almost a *cliché* to refer to the post Bretton Woods monetary system as "the international monetary disorder".

Defensive feelings about global monetary instabilities went hand-in-hand with *positive* objectives regarding the construction of "an ever closer union" among all European countries willing and able to take part. The type of integration set in motion by the six founding members of the European Community and by many of those countries that joined in the following decades has never been limited to free trade. The "common market" and the Economic Community established by the 1957 Treaty of Rome followed upon the 1951 Coal and Steel Community that allowed to pool resources in sectors then essential for war and peace matters. And it went together with the Euratom treaty aimed at the development of joint research on atomic energy, then seen as *the* energy of the future.

In this context, the fact that economic integration could extend to monetary integration was seen as natural. Indeed, the "common market" had barely been put in place in July 1968 by the six EEC member-countries when the Werner report put forward this objective as the new guiding beacon. Maastricht and Amsterdam had not yet lent their names to some hard-to-read treaties but the special influence of Dutch cities on the mood of European heads of State was already at work at the Hague in March 1971. The European Community, as it was bravely announced at that conference, would implement the Werner plan and become a true Economic and Monetary Union (EMU) at the beginning of the 1980s. Combining deepening with widening, as Europe has done since the beginning, the conference also gave the green light for a new round of negotiations with the U.K. as the latter was now intent on joining the Community more or less as it had developed.

A couple of oil shocks and many currency crises later, the Werner plan was still just a plan, and EMU still "around the corner". Meanwhile, however, the giant European "common market" had been "gulliverised" by the countless little chains of invisible trade barriers, incompatible norms, health regulations, exchange rates controls, long queues of trucks at customs stations and diverging economic policies. Monetary co-operation, in those years, seemed to have been invented mostly to provide students of European integration with a reservoir of paradoxes on which to comment wittily before addressing the serious issues of agricultural policy and regional subsidies.

First came the days when the (monetary) "snake" would pop in and out of a "tunnel", losing a few of its member currencies here and there but still hopeful of recreating an island of relative stability for Europe in a global ocean of volatility. Greased, as sceptics saw it, with snake oil, European monetary co-operation gave rise to creative pseudo-currencies like "green guilders" and to yet another type of transfer toward the farm lobbies called "Monetary Compensatory Amounts". The purpose seemed to be to protect the ideal of European integration from sobering realities that appeared more like dis-integration.

Then came ERM and EMS. Almost as Laurel and Hardy, it seemed that the former was bound to remain forever thin, as few countries would be able to live up for very long to the Germanic disciplines of the Exchange Rate Mechanism (ERM) while the latter was born fat, as any EC country could be a member of the institutional arrangements and the decision process of the European Monetary System (EMS).

Defining who was "in" and who was "out" of the EMS has always been a matter of shades of greys rather than of black-and-white contrast. While all EC countries had the right to belong to the EMS, the ERM only included those that were ready for its discipline. Within the ERM itself, there was the "normal" band of fluctuation (2.5% on both sides of the grid until the market crisis of 1993) but there was also a group of countries with a "broad band" of 5%, and one country (the Netherlands) with a super-narrow band of 1% toward the Deutsche Mark. As with the euro now, the geography of monetary integration was anything but straightforward.

> Fixed and flexible, with pragmatic obstinacy…

The pragmatic arrangements behind EMS and ERM worked surprisingly well during their first ten years. A key reason was that countries did not hesitate to adjust the ERM parity-grid as often as needed. The exchange rate regime was "fixed but adjustable" as in the old Bretton Woods years and flexibility was put to good use. The EMS rules of *decision by consensus* prevented beggar-thy-neighbour devaluations.

These arrangements clearly worked less well in the wake of the 1992 Maastricht Treaty as governments put the cart before the horse by behaving as if any adjustment in parities would distract them from the monetary union now in sight. Hence, like the familiar character running in so many cartoons, the fixed-parity grid continued for a while beyond the cliff... before falling twice into oceans of market disbelief in the summers of 1992 and 1993.

Even mild optimists could see than the Danish "no" to Maastricht of June 1992 had been followed by a hotly contested and narrowly won French referendum. With good eyes, they could see that Banque de France found itself for a while in a situation of *negative* reserves (net of short term EMS loans and swaps) and that meeting the Maastricht criteria in the face of bad spending habits in many countries would be made even more difficult by slow growth in all of them and by the after-shock of German reunification. The more so as Germans appeared to have second thoughts about giving up the Deutsche mark for some "Club Med" currency extravaganza.

Markets began to burn the EMU convergence they had adored. Fluctuations bands were broadened from 2.5% to an almost meaningless 15% both ways. The international financial press pronounced the single currency dead. As Mark Twain once observed of reports about his own death, it turned out, however, that these pronouncements "were greatly exaggerated".

The one thing that remained was the Treaty in which 13 countries had committed themselves to the single currency. That Treaty, however, was a fundamental building block for Europe after the German re-unification of 1990. The fact that market forces had removed all the bells and whistles around EMU (fluctuation bands, media blessings and even French foreign-exchange reserves) actually exacerbated the political willingness to make the single currency happen, even if it had to be under the streamlined appearance of what we called at the time the Franmark [1].

With the EMS, Europe had clearly moved beyond the puzzling world of snakes and pseudo-currencies. The depth of consultation and co-operation established in those years was a foundation solid enough to support the objective of the single currency even in the absence of the "bands" that had come to symbolise it. Rather than denouncing the George Soroses of this world, the attitude of European central bankers was to make it more likely that speculators too could get their fingers burnt if they confused fluctuation bands with the political resolve that had created them in the first place. Gradually, without fuss, all currencies came back to the original parity grid...

1. Albert Bressand, "How the Franmark could save the day", *International Economy Magazine*, Washington D.C., december 1992.

The flexible fixed-parity grid

	BEF Belgium	DKK Denmark	DEM Germany	ESP Spain	FRF France	IEP Ireland	ITL Italy	LUF Luxbrg	NLG Netherland	PTE Portugal	GBP U.K.
24/09/79	-	-3%	+2%		-	-	-	-	-		*
30/11/79	-	-5%	-		-	-	-	-	-	-	*
23/03/81	-	-	-		-	-	-6%	-	-	-	*
05/10/81	-	-	+5.5%		-3%	-	-3%	-	+5.5%		*
22/02/82	-8.5%	-3%	-		-	-	-	-8.5%	-		*
14/06/82	-	-	+4.25%		-5.75%	-	-2.75%	-	+4.25%		*
21/03/83	+1.5%	+2.5%	+5.5%		-2.5%	-3.5%	-2.5%	+1.5%	+3.5%		*
18/05/83	-1.9%	-1.9%	-1.9%		-1.9%	-1.9%	-1.9%	-1.9%			*
17/09/84	-	-	-		-	-	-	-	-		*
22/07/85	+2%	+2%	+2%		+2%	+2%	-6%	+2%	+2%		*
07/04/86	+1%	+1%	+3%		-3%	-	-	+1%	+3%		*
04/08/86	-	-	-		-	-8%	-	-	-		*
12/01/87	+2%	-	+3%		-	-	-	+2%	+3%		*
21/09/89	-	-	-		-	-	-	-	-		*
08/01/90	-	-	-	-	-	-	-3.68%	-	-		*
08/10/90	-	-	-	-	-	-	-	-	-	-	*
14/09/92	+3.5%	+3.5%	+3.5%	+3.5%	+3.5%	+3.5%	-3.5%	+3.5%	+3.5%	+3.5%	+3.5%
17/09/92	-	-	-	-5%	-	-	-	-	-	-	-
23/11/92	-	-	-	-6%	-	-	*	-	-	-6%	*
01/02/93	-	-	-	-	-	-10%	*	-	-	-	*
14/05/93	-	-	-	-8%	-	-	-	-	-	-6.5%	*
03/03/95	-	-	-	-7%	-	-	*	-	-	-3.5%	*

** Some currencies are component currencies of the ECU but are not participating in the exchange rate mechanism (ERM). Presently, these include the Greek Drachma, the Portuguese Escudo and the British Pound*

> The Monnet method and the political economy of self-fulfilment

As President Jacques Santer points out in his introductory remarks, “historically, a single market and a single currency are observed to go together”. Actually, the common market and the common currency have come about as a result of the same type of political and economic interactions. The same “method”. The Monnet method.

As can be seen in the following diagram, the pragmatic approach adopted by Jean Monnet and the founding fathers of the Union allowed European countries to progress, step by step, into two different directions: that of a wider market, and that of deeper economic and political integration. Five successful rounds of enlargement in 1973 (U.K, Ireland, Denmark), 1980 (Greece), 1986 (Spain, Portugal), 1990 (Eastern Germany) and 1995 (Austria, Sweden, Finland) have illustrated that the geography of European integration is still an open one. The Union of 21 is already at the negotiation stage, and a Union of 24, 25 or 26 members is one or two decades down the road. As a result, pre-membership association agreements, transitory periods and the like will remain on the map for a long time, as they have since the early 1980s. Again, "in" and "out" is a question of degree and of time horizon. The U.K. in this respect is merely a more spectacular case, as its exceptions and transition periods - including that with regard to the euro - tend to be slightly more emotional and entail major economic and geopolitical repercussions.

One small step after another... the Monnet method

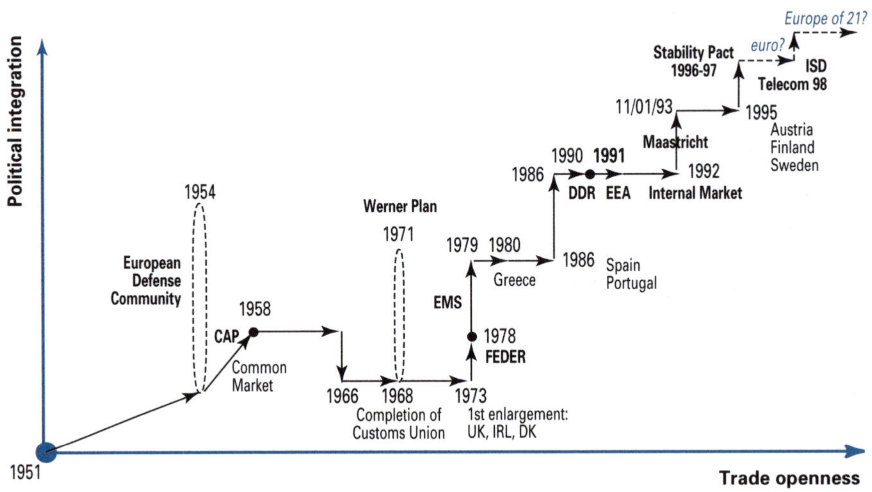

© PROMETHEE, 1997

But this complex geography goes well with straightforward deadlines – whether 1968, 1992 or 1999 – as it allows to adapt to very diverse situations. It is part of the pragmatic "Monnet method" whereby the process of moving forward is more important than the capacity – still almost non-existent – to agree on the ultimate destination.

What was poorly understood beyond the relatively small circle of "true believers" in European integration was that EMS and ERM were not so much about fixed rates as about tighter and tighter co-ordination.
An ongoing *process* rather than a specific *outcome*. This emphasis on process was also to become a fundamental aspect of the self-fulfilling prophecy known as the euro.

> A networked geography

The relationship to *time* is clearly the most straightforward aspect of this process. None of our guests in these "strategic conversations" harbored the slightest doubt about the fact that the euro would happen, that it would happen on January 1st, 1999 and that appropriate solution would be found to deal with whatever problem might still arise within shooting distance of the "Maastricht criteria".

The relationship to *space*, however, is more complex, and our conversations offer many examples of the various levels of integration, interconnection and co-operation that will shape the financial geography of the euro.

Jean-François Théodore, in our first conversation, presents a number of essential clues to decipher this geography-in-the-making. His description of various types of agreements entered into by SBF-Bourse de Paris illustrates a combination of global market forces, of European integration and of intense competition within Europe as well as among "time zones". To reduce cost, exchanges are led to share or co-develop the costly *technologies* behind today's markets. To preserve their identities, they are doing so within specific *networks* and with a full menu of *strategic options* to choose from. While exchanges compete and co-operate, the new geography for investors, traders and issuers is increasingly that of one European "networked market" that they can access through one single screen but that build on a set of separate national institutions and markets.

The links between global forces and their European expressions at the time of the euro are also vividly illustrated by Jörg Fischer as he describes why the seven Swiss markets of the 1980s joined forces in the field of derivatives and how electronic technology enabled them to do so. It is clear that this early experience with cross-market integration has allowed the Swiss Exchange to position themselves very closely to the center of what will be the cash and derivatives markets in euros.

That geographic paradox is all the more interesting as Switzerland is an "out-out" country (*out* of the euro and *out* of the Union) and yet, that it has built strategic links and positions more swiftly than the U.K. The latter, one might say, is an "in-out-in" country as she is *in* the union, with an opting *out* clause from the euro but also with the stated objective to be *in* sometime around 2002. As several of our guests suggest, the British posture might be hard to sustain for long without harming London.

For the next few years, however, the consensus is clearly that *London* will remain the only European financial center able to prosper without some alliance or joint venture with other centers. In André Villeneuve's words, London Achilles' heel could be complacency as the continental financial centers have modernized rapidly and as Paris, for instance, has already taken the advantage over London in the important field of settlement. Whether the continental alliance taking shape will really help the non German financial centers is a matter, however, on which André Villeneuve is still very cautious...

> Technology... and liquidity

Our conversations allow to explore the euro-geography in more detail than simply in terms of "continent vs. London". In Rolf-E Breuer's words "the 21st century will be an era of electronic and virtual networking in which the ongoing globalization process will lead to a new capital market structure".

Inside the euro zone, the perspective of the Amsterdam exchange brings to light the importance of "centers of excellence" in such fields as oil and energy related markets. It also illustrates the possibilities of technology to reach beyond Europe itself as well as the limits of what used to be described with enthusiasm, a few years ago, "round the world, round the clock trading". George Möller brings to light the importance of timing as well as the essential role of liquidity in sorting out useful technology from simply excellent technology and in reshaping flows among markets.

Discussions with Gérard Pfauwadel and Jörg Fischer also help understand why the key differences between *derivatives* and *cash* markets do not lead to two different patterns of integration but, rather, to the search for some "critical mass" by each financial center as a prelude to various types of alliances and integration with other centers. Over the long term, the competition taking shape between the "euro-euro center" in London and the "networked euro-center" on the continent may evolve, as Jörg Fischer and George Möller suggest, toward competition between two types of market *structures* rather than between two market *places*... Hence these conversations also deal with the different ways in which technology can be used to modify market structures, from the radical changes that happened with Soffex in Switzerland

and that extended all the way to the regulatory and legal framework to more complex patchworks of legal and technical connections as can be seen between France and the Swiss-German Eurex.

We are also privileged to look at the euro from the stand-point of three major global network operators that happen to be *based in Europe* but that play a critical role in the working of *global* capital markets: Euroclear, Cedel Bank and REUTERS. All three of them are what Luc Bomans call "hubs for cross-border services". As he observes, they will contribute to a new geography of investment by accelerating capital flows *toward* the euro countries but also *from* them toward the rest of the world as the euro triggers a massive reallocation of portfolios inside as well as outside of Europe.

> Taking risk

Seen from one of these powerful networks, the euro is, here too, both a non-event *and* a major transformation in the nature of risks in which markets will deal. As observed by Rolf-E Breuer, "the greater irrelevance of national boundaries in Europe will lead to capital flowing more easily to investment projects with optimum yield/risk structure"; economic development, however, entails many other dimensions and "the danger lies in former national concepts being projected into the European or global future".

For André Lussi, globalization is too often equated with the removal of barriers when it also reflects the new power of information technology to shape and reshape relations. The *competitiveness* of Europe must then be seen as a combination of its integration – with the euro a major step – and of its capacity for seizing the opportunities open by technology "without undue interference from cartels of all types".

The new barriers may well be cultural rather than legal, and several of our guests, like Werner Seifert, discuss the impact that the euro can have not simply in accelerating the shift from a bond culture toward an *equity culture*, but, also, in generating different attitudes toward risk taking and entrepreneurship. Speaking in defense of the derivatives markets, Gérard Pfauwadel makes clear that they provide some of the tools needed to enable companies to take risks and that this willingness to look risk in the eyes will remain necessary in Europe long after the last futures contract among euro-currencies has been traded.

Indeed, at many different levels, *risk* and *risk taking* is a central theme running through these conversations. This is true in the sense of *eliminating* the risk that can be avoided, beginning with currency risk among euro countries but including also the huge "pipeline risks" in the clearing and settlement networks essential to the smooth working of markets. This is true also in the sense of using the higher degree of certainty thus acquired to *take the risks worth taking.* All our guests seem to agree that the euro is not a defensive insurance policy against currency volatility but, more importantly, an open invitation to Europeans to take entrepreneurial risks. The conversation with René Karsenti allows to see how the European Investment Bank, better known for its funding of infrastructural projects, will channel up to 1 billion ECUs of its profits toward venture capital as part of the Amsterdam action plan.

Many of our guests have been led, at one time or another in these conversations, to look at the force of demography behind financial flows and to express worries about the time lost in Europe to draw the full implications of a rapidly ageing population. *Pension funds*, it seems, are one essential contact point between the world of markets and the world of basic social needs. In René Karsenti's words, "Europe has been lent to us by our children". Intermediating between generations, such is also one of the challenges well hidden behind the euro. The tendency to look at the issue in the rear mirror (except in the Netherlands and the U.K. where pension liabilities are funded) raises deeper issues of governance.

> Interdependence *and* governance

As we attempt to show in the last part of this book, the integration frontier involves a combination of *interdependence* – free flows of goods and services as well as of capital – and a set of institutional and behavioral patterns better understood as part of *governance.* An essential aspect of the convergence process behind the euro is that it has developed at the intersect between these two realms.

The market forces of interdependence have played a very strong role, as all governments can measure the cost to them of following free-spending policies that markets "punish" with much higher interest rates. But the *policy* decisions have also been very important as the political legitimacy of the single currency on the continent allowed governments to take difficult decisions that lobbies would have blocked easily in their national settings.

At a time when markets in euros do not exist yet, the conversation with René Karsenti offers a rare opportunity to reflect on the ways and means whereby markets can be *created.* After all, the European Investment Bank (EIB) was already a key force behind the emergence of markets in ECUs; the ways in which it is using its 24 billion ECUs issuing power to help markets in euro take shape should be of interest to many. Already, present issues in national currencies are being managed so as to be "euro-tributaries" designed to dovetail into euro issues on the day the euro will come to life.

But governance is not just about anticipating and steering, it is also about *social acceptability.* In this respect, the role of the EIB in helping the poorer regions of Europe catch up is an important part of the long, invisible process that will render the euro possible. Optimal currency zones, as the old economic literature used to call them, do not just happen, they are built, including in the very concrete sense of roads and bridges!

As observed by René Karsenti, however, Europe is "a continent of 18 million unemployed still looking for the appropriate division of labor between the public and private sectors". Many of our guests seemed to share Rolf-E Breuer's view that this division of labor has been tilted too far toward the State and that "due to the complex and obscure mechanism of transfer payments between different parts of society, higher government spending can no longer be shown to mean better social conditions". As the euro countries begin to look at tax and fiscal matters as relevant to their convergence process, discussions of *the role of the State*[2] can be expected to become central to the post-euro policy dialogue – and this time London is not asking for its usual opt-out, wait-and-see clause...

> A fortress, a vanguard or a pace setter?

Interdependence is global in nature. And governance too is not limited to the European level, although the latter involves much more precise and effective mechanisms. The monetary co-operation that intensified among the G7 countries through the Plaza agreement of 1985 and the Le Louvre agreement of 1987 added international respectability to this European undertaking. They illustrated, once again, that European integration develops well *in conjunction with* global integration, rather than as an *alternative to* global market realities too easily derided as "international dis-order".

The same has been obvious in trade matters. While non-Europeans are tempted to search for "fortresses" in the ruins of trade walls dismantled, and while some Europeans believe that the common market is really about

2. For in depth discussion of the post euro challenges, see *Europe 2012, globalisation et cohésion sociale : les scenarios luxembourgeois*, Albert Bressand, Bruce Scott (editors), Manuel Baldauff, Léon Helbach, Gérard Hoffmann, Thierry Wolter, rapport de la Fondation Alphonse Weicker, Economica, Paris et Luxembourg, 1997.

"préférences communautaires", the fact is that each major step toward free trade in Europe has found an echo and a facilitator in a similar step at world level, even if with smaller ambitions.

The Treaty of Rome went very well with the Dillon round that took place at GATT from 1958 to 1962, and so did the "common market" put in place in 1968 with the Kennedy Round that concluded in 1967. The same held true of the "Europe 1992" program which was a major catalyst for – and influence upon – the Uruguay Round and notably its important agreement on services. Synergies developed to the point where the U.S. ambassador in Brussels had even found natural to ask for "a seat at the table" for internal market negotiations, only to be asked in return whether the U.S. was interested in becoming the thirteenth EC member...

Third countries, and not just the U.S., feared being excluded from some of the huge benefits of the market opening of 1992. "Fortress Europe" was a popular concept. But the reality is overwhelmingly that the cosy national arrangements between government and business or among businesses are increasingly difficult to perpetuate in a framework where any of fourteen other countries can see and challenge them. Regionalism and globalism are different brands of openness with much more in common among them than any of them with nationalism. In addition, unlike in the case of the North American Free Trade Agreement (NAFTA), no European country is disproportionately more powerful than the other members, which means that agreements have to be reached through the power of persuasion rather than through the persuasion of power.

What is coming therefore is not "Fortress euro" but a vanguard, a pace setting event that other regions and global players will gradually incorporate into their thinking and, why not, into their aspirations.

Mexicans after the peso crisis and Asians in the wake of the 1997 currency free falls have probably begun to look at their power over national currencies with a more discriminating eye. Many years ago, Richard Cooper wondered in *Foreign Affairs* about a single currency for the world [3].
The view is still futuristic, first of all because countries that stop to adjust to one another via currency movements need elaborate systems of governance to insure the necessary convergence, something that does not seem to exist yet even among such close countries as the U.S. and Japan. But, as our brief summary of the EMS may have shown, there are intermediate steps.

---

3. Richard N. Cooper, "A Monetary System for the Future", *Foreign Affairs*, Vol. 63, No 1, Fall 1984. See also Albert Bressand, "Mastering the 'Worldeconomy'", *Foreign Affairs*, Vol. 61, No 4, Spring 1983.

Indeed, in one of these "strategic conversations", Dolf van den Brink presents a strong and convincing argument that "a global currency pact" will come quite naturally to the agenda of G7, G8 or other global meetings such as IMF meetings shortly after the year 2002.

As in Europe, even the economists most opposed to government intervention in markets will come to realize that *interdependence* and *governance* cannot develop for very long in separate trajectories. Global markets call for global governance.

Already, in a market perspective, readers of the conversations with Luc Bomans and André Lussi will find concrete examples of what it takes to keep "systemic risks" and "technical risks" in check in the global bond markets as well as in cross-border equity trading. They will also hear pressing calls for stronger co-ordination across countries, including for important aspects of the transition to the euro such as securities denomination that do not seem to have received all the attention they deserve. It is nice to have "global capital markets", but when one needs to use securities held in one country as collateral for financial operations in another country, one can see the need for stronger regulatory convergence and for adaptation of national laws to international realities.

In these respect, by its efforts to adapt governance to interdependence, the Europe of the euro is not a "special part" of the global economy, it is merely a vanguard.

> Currencies as catalysts

Indeed, if there is one theme common to all our guests, it is that the euro is not an isolated cause for change but a catalyst, an accelerator of a deeper and broader transformation.

A catalyst is both very little and very much depending on the scope of one's vision. Again, the euro is a non-event *and* what Jean-François Théodore calls "a historic opportunity, perhaps the greatest opportunity of this century for the financial markets of Europe and for those who rely on them for their economic development".

Much of what our guests describe would have happened anyway, even if more slowly. This is true of the *strategic alliances* among stock exchanges, which could have developed simply a response to the competition with London's SEAQ International and with private trading systems ("PTS") and over-the-counter markets. This is true also of the *concentration* among asset management firms that Philippe Collas describes, of the concentration among banks upon which Dolf van den Brink and André Villeneuve comment and it is also true of the *interconnection* of national Central Securities Depositories (CSDs) that is blurring the border between these *national* market infrastructures and the two "international" CSDs, Euroclear and Cedel, that play a critical role in the eurobond markets (CSDs are important players that keep, transfer and pledge everybody else's securities).

In that sense, nothing might appear really "different" to an observer focusing on the global economy. Yet, anyone listening to Dolf van den Brink, Philippe Collas or Gérard Pfauwadel will realize that the pace of change is accelerating tremendously, with major qualitative changes already under way.

The perspectives of ABN AMRO and Société Générale Asset Management illustrate, again, the critical importance of global rather than "merely" European strategic positioning. Similarly, in Werner Seifert's words, one should adopt a "bottom up" approach to the euro "because the financial community has been exposed to many changes that predate the euro, reflecting (...) financial globalization and technological change". His key question is then "how the euro will influence this ongoing process of change".

What is true in the markets is also true in the realm of economic policy. Having described the amazing speed at which countries have converged toward the Maastricht criteria, Yves Franchet wonders "convergence towards what?". The truth of the matter is that the U.S. also has been "converging toward Maastricht" if that means giving up the bad habits of excessive public deficits and the false hopes of just-enough-inflation.

> Learning, leap-frogging and leading

The euro is the European way of navigating these strong global currents. And yet, in doing so, Europe is also setting the pace and is giving globalization new dimensions that other regions will address later. Even if "merely" a catalyst, the euro is providing Europe with a major opportunity at least to catch up and, in a number of cases, to learn, to leapfrog and to lead.

Learning is what each member country does as the internal market challenges established ways of doing things. As in telecoms where full competition has become the rule since the beginning of 1998 or in banking where in André Villeneuve's words, banks that believe "that their domestic branch network will adequately protect them are placing their faith in a new Maginot line". In that sense, the European integration process is a more powerful source of learning than any other regional or global agreement. In all other cases, whether NAFTA, ASEAN or the World Trade Organization, there are ways for a country to protect its vested interests and its ways of doing things while the European Court of Justice and the European competition authorities are able to knock them down in the EU. If the U.S. were a member of the EU, it would have been requested to outgrow its Glass Steagall Act earlier and more swiftly than U.S. domestic lobbies have let it happen…

Leapfrogging occurs when those catching up can have the benefits of more advanced technologies. One example is mobile telephony: Europe was clearly behind in the late 1980s but managed to develop a standard for digital cellular phones (GSM) that now allows the same phone to be used from Lisbon to Moscow at much higher levels of quality and security than the still predominantly analog and incompatible U.S. mobile phone networks. The same may become true, as suggested in the first part of this book, for securities trading: a fragmented Europe is seeking rejuvenation through a combination of electronic networking and of the rules of *mutual recognition* and *cross-market* access.

Leading is more delicate as it involves a capacity to act together vis-à-vis the rest of the world which, as we said, is bound to remain the exception rather than the rule for quite a while. Yet, leading can happen. Mutual recognition is one good example: the freedoms granted by the "single banking passport" or by the Investment Services Directive could certainly be shared more widely provided nations accept to hold as legitimate the decisions taken by other countries. At this stage, mutual recognition has begun to extend outside of Europe but only in the narrower field of technical tests. As we saw with Dolf van den Brink's remark, the beginning of the next decade could see discussions on some type of "currency pact" for which the European learning experience could be an accelerator of global learning.

We hope that the "strategic conversations" in this book will help our readers – whether financial experts or interested laymen and laywomen – better understand the "invisible work" that has led Europe from the Coal and Steel Community to the Common Market, from the Common Market to the "internal market" of 1992, from a Europe of 6 to a Europe of 15 on its way to a Europe of 21 and, last but not least, from a Europe of currency barriers to the Europe of the euro.

The journey is not over, language barriers and cultural differences will remain very strong and the *subsidiarity* principle implies that national strategies will still play an important role. This is not a borderless utopia but a community of real men and women with their roots, their hopes and their fears. But the move is clearly toward a "European way" in globalization. And that "European way" is bringing national communities much closer to one another than globalization has done anywhere else in the world. In that sense, the end of the present decade may well be remembered by people all over the world as *the years of Internet and the euro.*

Again, a first aspect of this invisible work is a pragmatic relationship to time and to geography. A second aspect is a process-driven self fulfilling prophecy in which being "self-fulfilling" becomes more important than being prophetic. A third aspect is a set of synergies with global transformations that push Europe sometimes to leapfrog, always to learn and, in some cases, to lead.

As editor, let me add that it has been a privilege for my colleagues at PROMETHEE and Ernst & Young to share views, visions, sometimes doubts and always excitement and enthusiasm with our eminent guests. We hope these "strategic conversations" – for which we claim the responsibility for remaining inaccuracies or shortcomings– will help Europeans and non-Europeans in their understanding of this eventful non-event that is grounded in European history as well as in the immediate pressures of global bond markets, in high politics as well as in myriad of implementation processes, in the need to open and to catch up as well as in the will to unite and invent... **Albert Bressand.**

Editor's acknowledgement and note

The practitioners who have kindly accepted to open their doors and their minds for these conversations invite the readers to share their visions of what the euro will mean for their firms, for their countries, for Europe and for the world. They do so from the standpoint of their practical experience with capital markets, at home and abroad.

This book is not a sales pitch for the euro or for any specific company, neither is it written to support one's national perspective. It is a dialogue among free minds. All opinions are expressed in an individual capacity and, more importantly, in a spirit of informed discussion, of research and of sharing. Behind each chapter are long hours of free wheeling discussions between the eminent person at the center of the conversation and two or three members of the "ThinkNet" team put together by PROMETHEE and Ernst & Young. Short profiles of the associates involved are provided at the end of the book. Conversations have taken place in English, each one of us using in his or her own words and with no effort to standardize language: we are all speaking our mind.

A short statistical annex has been developed in co-operation with Eurostat and some focused inserts provided, including a much needed glossary of clearing and settlement. We are indebted for their help to Albert Geiger, Denis Peters, Thomas Rabe, Bruno Rossignol and Stephan Schuster. Our thanks also go to Antoinette Hunziker-Ebneter, CEO of SWX.

My personal gratitude goes also to Jean Saint-Geours, René de la Serre and Bertrand de Mazières for their help in bridging the gap between practitioners and regulators, and to the associates of Ernst & Young who have contributed so kindly and efficiently, notably to Patrick Gounelle and Patrick Flochel, Pierre Hurstel, Lionel Lavigne, Bernard Nivollet, Christian Mouillon here in Paris and, all over Europe, to Joachim Epperlein, Michael Gardiner, Hans de Haan, Kenneth Hayes, Dan Newman and, of course, to Antoine Bracchi, Jean-Charles Raufast and Ivan Wagner.

A.B.

Part I

One currency, **many stock exchanges,** *one market.*

Chapter I

The strategic issues *behind the conversation*

A powerful "second big bang". A major change for global financial markets as a whole. A world of two currencies. A new wave of expectations leading to a succession of integration waves... the view presented by Jean-François Théodore on the coming of the euro is clearly not that of a few countries merely changing their units of account! What is discussed here is a combination of transition and transformation, of technology and organization, of mundane efforts to reduce costs and of fresh looks at the role of markets in society at large.

The quality of coordination during the transition to the euro is the more pressing issue. The search for new benchmarks is a more lasting challenge, for issuers and intermediaries as well as for each financial center.

Competition will intensify, within and across time zones, with the powerful New York Stock Exchange an increasingly close competitor for listing and global intermediation. and yet, this will also be a time of intense cooperation among stock exchanges as they join forces to reduce costs, to upgrade technology and to pursue the Holy Grail of unsurpassed liquidity...

A new financial geography is taking shape. Beyond the famous London/Continent divide, various levels of cooperation are identified for a detailed mapping of the emerging continental financial hub as well as of its links with other regions.

Our conversation explored many different types of very concrete undertakings - be they common electronic trading platforms or the more ambitious and difficult Franco-German strategic interconnection. In the background was the global "network of financial networks" already reshaping financial geography.

A.B.

conversation with

JEAN-FRANÇOIS THÉODORE,

SBF - BOURSE DE PARIS

This conversation with Jean-François Théodore, Chairman and CEO of SBF - Bourse de Paris, Chairman of SICOVAM and Chairman of the Steering Committee of the Paris Europlace Association, was conducted by Albert Bressand and Catherine Distler (PROMETHEE) and by Joachim Epperlein (Schitag Ernst & Young, Dusseldorf) in Paris.

The euro "Big Bang" and Europe's place in the new geography of global capital markets

Seen from the Paris Bourse, is the euro a threat or an opportunity? And is it a back-office matter, or a radical change? **Jean-François Théodore:** We certainly do not see the euro as a "threat"! Actually, "opportunity" may not be too strong a word to describe the strategic implications of moving from national currencies to a common currency. The euro represents an historic opportunity, perhaps the greatest opportunity of this century, for the financial markets of Europe and for those who rely on them for their economic development.

Of course the euro is also a fantastic challenge, and it will translate into much higher levels of competition. But the changes that our financial markets are about to undergo are of historic proportions. We should think of the euro as a *beginning* rather than as an end, as the fuse that will start the real unification of the European financial markets.

We have already witnessed a substantial amount of unification in the European financial markets as a result of deregulation and technology and of the Big Bang that they have made possible. But the markets nevertheless have remained fragmented, especially from the perspective of non-European financiers who are less at ease in crossing currency lines.

The euro will be a powerful second Big Bang that will sweep many countries simultaneously, and it will have far-reaching implications for the man in the street as well as for corporations, for entrepreneurs as well as for investors, for Europeans as well as for non-Europeans. It will be only a couple of years after the Big Bang of 1999 before people stop talking of "French" or "German" securities and begin to look at the various financial instruments in a different light.

As for the second part of your question, the euro is both a radical change and a source of thorough re-organisation for almost everybody's back-office. At the present time, the second aspect is the most visible one. It is clear that the euro does have a strong back-office dimension, and not a simple one! The transition to the euro is a very big project indeed, and a project which entails at least two specific difficulties.

First, everything must be done against one fixed deadline, which means that unlike what can be done in many other projects, one will not be able to simply "take an extra three weeks" if need be. Just think of it as being a boat that we simply cannot afford to miss. I say a boat, but in terms of the control that a given actor can have over the date, it is more like a tide! A second special difficulty is that the project cannot be neatly confined within the limits of one central back-office organization – SICOVAM in our case – and that it involves about fifty key players in a very direct manner.

But this back-office work finds its meaning and purpose in a broader process of change affecting the overall working of the European capital markets.

So, altogether, the euro is a radical change, a secular opportunity and an overarching deadline. A very big bang indeed!

> A big bang for Europe, a big bang for global finance

What about the impact of this big bang outside of Europe? Will there be a "before" and "after the euro" for financial globalization at large? **JFT:** It will be, in my opinion, a major change for the global financial market as a whole. Already, when my colleagues and myself are in the U.S., we can see two things: market participants on the other side of the Atlantic believe that the euro will happen, and they look at it as a watershed change. And this impression is even stronger in Asia.

Why in Asia? **JFT:** Probably because, right now, we live more in a one currency world rather than in the often mentioned "three currency world". As could be seen during the recent monetary turmoils in South East Asia, there is no real "Yen zone": one can go through all these Asian markets using only U.S. dollars. As for the DM zone, it is a relatively small one. By contrast, after 1999, we shall live in a world of two currencies and two very large, very liquid and, I hope, very attractive financial markets.

But does this not assume as a precondition that the euro will be a strong, stable currency? **JFT:** Let me suggest, rather, that these are two different issues. The big change for European markets will not have to do so much with "strength" of currencies as with the *liquidity* and *size* of the market. Providing market participants with such a huge pool of euro-denominated securities will change investment opportunities and perspectives.

Does this mean that there is less emphasis on the stability issue in France than, let's say, in Germany? **JFT:** I am really speaking as a market technician, which leads me to call attention to the overarching importance of liquidity. Maybe one could add, on that matter, that the markets in euro will be compact, enough, "domestic" enough, to be less affected by volatility and that the exchange rate between the euro and the U.S. dollar will be simpler to understand.

> ...and a big bang for the markets!

Well, here comes the morning of January 4, 1999: is the Paris Bourse ready to go with its chairman relaxed and confident? Will everything be ready on time? **JFT:** I don't know whether I'll be relaxed but, yes indeed, we will be ready! Ready to list in euros, ready to quote in euros, ready to disseminate in euros and ready to trade in euros!

And this will be true not only in the professional sphere but for every part of the system up to settlement. The customers will still be able to give orders in French Francs but, starting from the bank branch, all operations will be in euros. The euro will be used for all transactions and only the net payment to be debited or credited to the final customer will be in French Francs. Everything in the French markets will be in euros.

Is the French Bourse the only one to carry out this transition as one single Big Bang for its market organization, rather than spread it between 1999 and 2002 as the Treaty allows?

JFT: The French financial community has always favoured implementing the changes in the capital markets in one swift move rather than spreading them over time. This is usually referred to as the "*big bang*" *approach*, speaking, this time, not of the impact of the euro on the markets as we have just discussed but of the way in which markets are organized.

I can see that almost all our partners are now sharing the view that this "big bang" approach is the most appropriate. The difference may be that Paris has started about one year earlier than the others and has put in place a very comprehensive procedure. Also our more centralized system gives us a stronger capacity to organize the transition in a swift and efficient manner.

We have also been helped in meeting this challenge in France by the fact that we had dematerialized everything related to securities as far back as 1984, which means that our markets can adapt more straightforwardly. Other markets insist on preserving the possibility for small investors to still hold a paper security in their hands. Our Cartesian logic tells us that a clear cut choice is better, and in this case full dematerialisation really helped to keep this complex project manageable.

Is this transition to the euro absorbing a lot of your own time and attention? And what about the scarce resources of SBF - Bourse de Paris: management time, IT development, communication budget? **JFT:** The euro is a very important project for the financial markets and the economy as a whole. Now if we look at the specific tasks to be carried out, the paradox may be that a lot of the action is at the periphery rather than at the center.

For SBF - Bourse de Paris as such, strategic as it is, the euro is *not* a huge project. You could say that it boils down to folding operations in French francs on December 30th, 1998 and to resuming operations four days later in euros, after a big and busy week-end but with the same system. So it is not terribly demanding in terms of resources and manpower: we will be ready to "turn the key" and switch on the euro relatively smoothly.

There will be of course additional side aspects, such as converting our statistical records into euros so that market participants can use them easily

Dematerialization, computerization and international links: the French revolution.

Beginning with the Paris Big Bang of the mid 1980's, changes have swept the Paris Bourse which has capitalized on its fully computerized and fully dematerialized market, the first of its kind in Europe, to move into the top league of international financial markets.

The Paris equities markets have changed more in the past ten years than in two centuries before. Beginning in 1986, open outcry trading was phased out. Floors in Paris and the six regional stock exchanges of Bordeaux, Lille, Lyon, Marseille, Nancy and Nantes were replaced with the CAC computerized trading system. Completely revamped in 1995 under the name of SuperCAC or *Nouveau Système CAC* (NSC), the system handles transactions through workstations installed in member firms' own premises and linked to the central computers of the Paris Bourse.

SuperCAC has allowed the Paris Bourse, a centralized order driven market, to cope with increasingly growing volumes that totalled 1 000 billion French francs in 1994 for the first time and reached well over 2 400 billion in 1997. It can handle up to 100 orders per second in complete safety, providing full transparency to protect market integrity.

Its versatility has made SuperCAC a successful export item. It has been purchased by leading stock markets around the world: Brussels, Toronto, Sao Paolo, Lisbon, Warsaw, as well as MATIF and the Chicago Mercantile Exchange in a version adapted for futures and options. A version adapted for emerging markets operates in Beirut, Tunis, Casablanca and Amman.

While the Bourse was undergoing its revolution, back offices were also revamped under the auspices of SICOVAM SA. Market participants now use RELIT, a fully automated and user-friendly DVP system that will be upgraded in 1998 into RELIT Grande Vitesse, to offer high speed settlement in real time.

Ten years of computerized trading have given the Paris markets a depth of expertise that will be particularly useful in the transition to the single currency.

Bruno Rossignol
SBF Bourse de Paris

in connection with their trading activities. But I see the real challenge as being of a different nature: to me, the challenge is really about co-ordination and communication.

Co-ordination: the key is to have everybody fully ready for the euro on the morning of January 4, 1999, in a totally coherent manner across the whole market. The quality of the co-ordination matters just as much as the quality of each individual actor's preparedness.

Communication: the euro also involves a lot of communication, at least for the equity market: the euro is really a two stage affair. European citizens will have to wait until the year 2002 to really hold it in their hands. However the real change will happen in 1999 for financial markets, not only for professionals but also for the six or seven million small shareholders in this country who will thus be able to familiarize themselves by dealing in euros already.

Does this mean that the transition, narrowly speaking, is mostly an operational matter? **JFT:** At the center, we have a set of large systems: those of Banque de France, SBF itself and SICOVAM, of course, as well as a whole set of inter-bank systems. The key decision was to have all these systems ready to work in euros without having to change them. To me, a real understanding of the transformation underway here in Paris should not be restricted to the *transition* project per se but should also encompass the major *modernization efforts* that have been carried out by this financial center as we call it in the preceding years.

The operational constraint is how many IT/software operations can be carried out during that four day week end for which so many people are preparing.

Again, this is first and foremost a co-ordination job. It is our responsibility to make sure that all institutions have put in place the necessary converters and the back office changes. These have been identified in the blue print called the "*schéma de place*" which describes how every financial institution in Paris should prepare for the euro. The imperative is to insure that all participants in that chain are ready to interact among themselves in a coordinated way using these central systems. To that effect, we have put in place a very comprehensive review and counselling process.

In other words, the euro will be casting you in the role of a conductor rather than in that of a big project manager?
JFT: Yes, if you want to put it that way. Our responsibility is to make sure

everyone plays the same symphony, without any "fausse note". The human side is just as important as the technical side.

Clearly, the transition to the euro is not limited to adapting our computers systems. For us, at SBF - Bourse de Paris, it is part of a broader project that involves our role in the economy and in society at large.

> The coming wave of european financial integration

Do you think that the euro will foster an accelerating trend toward convergence and common practices in the various European capital markets, or will the present differences persist almost as before? **JFT:** One should distinguish very clearly between bonds and equities.

For the bond markets, the change will be immediate and complete: there will be one and only *one bond market* in Europe the minute the euro comes to life. And this will be true also of bond derivatives. Already, as you can see, all issuers are trying to position themselves for the euro "yield curve" still to come, if possible as one of the "benchmark issuers" which will set the tone for the euro zone as a whole.

For *equities*, things will be quite different because of all the national rules that will continue to affect the performances and behaviour of companies (rules for take-over, accounting standards, corporate law etc.) and also, quite simply, because a company has a "personality" and a history that are still grounded, most of the time, in a national culture: Siemens and Alcatel have a lot in common but they are not interchangeable or comparable like two government bonds!

But, even for equities, this will be only a starting point. The euro will unleash a new wave of expectations not just in Europe but in the global financial market. The "global investor" will be shopping for major new investment opportunities, and in doing so, sooner rather than later, she or he will ask for one, or rather for several "*pan-European systems*". Investors will move away from the country per country approach, swiftly and decisively. They will adopt sectoral approaches that will put tremendous pressure on market participants and on governments to do away with the remaining sources of fragmentation. Even if every European stock exchange remains independent, global investors will not put up with a whole set of different quote dissemination systems, accounting standards, take-over rules and the like.

Again, the euro of 1999 must be seen as the beginning of a new phase of convergence and integration rather than as the end of the transformation. The euro "big bang" will be followed by wave after wave of financial integration that will profoundly influence the relationship of European capital markets within global finance.

What will come first in this wave of further market integration that the euro will unleash? Will it be the development of pan-European market infrastructures or will it be deeper convergence in the rules and standards that we at PROMETHEE call "infostructure"? **JFT:** At first, I would say the emphasis will be on infrastructures. What is needed is an interconnected network of networks able to serve European finance as a whole. Actually, this is what we are already planning with Deutsche Börse and the Swiss Exchange creating a single unified panEuropean market, one single "log-in" for traders, and cross-membership agreements. Then, in a second stage, the differences in national rules and in market practices will come to the forefront.

So the emphasis should be on interconnecting market infrastructures? **JFT:** Yes, the more so as computer systems are neutral and have no mood. Asking countries or organizations to change their rules and habits is always more difficult than reprogramming computers! Considering that there is already some significant legal and regulatory harmonization, the priority will be *interconnection* of markets.

Let me stress, however, that there will be no monopoly as three or four systems, each of them offering access to the euro zone or to Europe as a whole, are likely to compete.

What makes Paris special in this context? And on what strength are you endeavouring to capitalize in this competition among pan-European networks? **JFT:** Well, for one thing, Paris is already geared for a world of fully computerised markets that know no border. Paris has made a major investment to offer the most efficient trading platform and support networks. These systems are working and are largely amortized. Other financial centers like Stockholm also have made such investments but, if one concentrates on the first wave of euro countries, then Paris is in the unique position of having been fully modernized at the end of the eighties, and to have installed a second generation of systems in 1995, which puts us at least a couple of years ahead of London or even Frankfurt.

Of course, other exchanges will do their very best to catch up. *London* is in the process of changing to an *order-driven trading system* operating under principles similar to the ones we have had in Paris since the mid-1980s. So, if everything works well, London will be technically ready just in time for the euro. But technology is only one aspect of such a change, and market participants will still need to adapt their culture to an order-driven environment quite different from the present London environment of market makers and quote-driven trading.

More generally, Paris has proven to be "*comme un poisson dans l'eau*", already swimming with these new currents and fully prepared for the waves of changes that will take us to new levels of competition.

The French are often described as mesmerized by high technology projects. How would you define the role of CAC, Super-CAC, Relit, TGV and other techno-achievements in the overall Paris momentum? In other words, are "networked markets" IT driven? And if not, where exactly do you see the Paris advantage? **JFT:** Yes, maybe we are sometimes mesmerized by high technology. But we are also fully aware that if technology is necessary it is not sufficient. So we have become increasingly "business driven" and we operate under the assumption that the Paris technology is only one of several major strategic assets.

Having the capacity to develop the software that we need rather than depending on suppliers is nevertheless a source of strength.

If I may speak for the techno-driven companies, having this capacity is, and will remain, an important competitive advantage. The trading platforms, clearing and settlement systems, central securities depositories, routing networks etc. These are our "means of production"! Having the best - or rather the most efficient - systems does matter especially when the previous monopolies based upon geography are disappearing like water in the sand!

As you know, *Institutional Investor*, a leading U.S. financial magazine, recently reported that, according to a study by Elkins/Mc Sherry, the Paris Bourse is the world's cheapest exchange for trade execution, cheaper than the NYSE, cheaper than London, cheaper than Frankfurt. But we must focus on the future and maintain this superior position in the interest of all market participants.

This being said, let me admit readily that our Bourse would benefit if the levels of French savings were higher and if our culture gave greater weight to what we call "*la culture financière*", namely the awareness of how financial

How the cost of executing trades varies in the world's key markets

Country	Average commissions (basis point)	Average fees (basis point)	Market impact (basis point)	1996 Total (basis point)
Austria	23.6	4.2	12.5	40.3
Belgium	23.8	3.2	10.7	37.1
Brazil	35.7	6.0	21.4	63.1
Canada	26.9	4.2	31.9	63.0
Czech Republic	66.0	4.6	64.0	134.6
Finland	25.6	1.8	14.5	41.9
France	21.6	1.5	6.8	29.9
Germany	21.4	2.8	15.1	39.3
Greece	52.7	8.8	2.9	64.4
Hong Kong	41.6	12.2	5.4	59.2
Hungary	70.9	5.6	68.7	145.2
India	7.0	0.0	78.8	85.8
Italy	23.7	3.1	9.3	36.1
Japan — Buys	24.9	0.5	5.2	30.6
Japan — Sells	26.1	18.1	11.8	56.0
Luxembourg	16.1	0.8	58.6	75.5
Malaysia	65.9	9.8	11.6	87.3
Mexico	33.2	1.7	34.4	69.3
Netherlands	21.2	2.3	18.5	42.0
Portugal	37.5	6.5	18.7	62.7
Singapore	57.4	57.4	11.1	71.9
South Africa	33.3	33.3	52.5	89.6
South Korea	46.6	46.6	159.1	228.9
Spain	28.6	28.6	14.0	47.1
Sweden	23.3	23.3	10.3	36.1
Switzerland	23.9	23.9	7.4	37.1
Taiwan	31.2	31.2	17.9	72.9
Turkey	38.5	38.5	28.5	77.2
U.K. — Buys	21.1	21.1	13.4	73.7
U.K. — Sells	15.9	15.9	16.3	32.8
U.S. — NYSE	13.3	13.3	20.8	34.1
U.S. — OTC	1.2	1.2	50.7	51.9
Average	**36.8**	**9.0**	**27.5**	**73.2**

Sources: Adapted from Elkins/McSherry Co. and Institutional Investor, November 1997.

markets work and of the contribution they can make to economic and social progress!

At the end of the day, we want technology to help the Paris financial center maintain or develop three sets of "best practice" regarding, respectively, flexibility, competitiveness, and cost effectiveness. This is an ambitious program, but we will work hard to achieve it!

> Co-operating to compete, competing to co-operate: the networked geography of finance in euros

If we may shift now to the Paris "big bang" to the new financial geography taking shape in Europe, let us ask you whether the euro is bringing you closer to your European counterparts or whether it is generating strong polarization of strategies that will push each of these centers further and further away from one another? **JFT:** No European exchange can run the risk of being simply a "regional" market. It would put it in the same situation as the local small stock exchange in national systems before they were consolidated into national stock exchange organizations as has happened in the UK, in France and, now, in Germany.

Meanwhile, no exchange can hope to become "the" European market.

Not even London? **JFT:** I would say "no", especially if the UK is not in the first group of euro participants as has now being decided by the government of Tony Blair. So, as a result of these two constraints we are likely to see a few "*super-regional*" *strategies* – as we can already see in Scandinavia – as well as a number of *specialization strategies.* A number of exchanges will probably be looking for niches and this will lead to a new wave of co-operative agreements built on complementarities and cost sharing.

Our choice is to build the Euro-strategic alliance of markets, interconnecting with the German and Swiss Exchanges. Together, we already are the leading European market for equity derivatives, we are due to be the one for fixed income derivatives and we represent 50% of continental Europe capitalization for equity cash markets.

It has often been remarked in PROMETHEE meetings that a hallmark of the "networked economy" is a tighter and tighter

combination of co-operation and competition (C&C). On what sort of alliances or co-operative agreements is the Paris Bourse counting to compete in this fierce environment? **JFT:** We have taken three major initiatives with quite different flavours. Let me give you the headlines in this trilogy of initiatives.

First, we have set up a cooperative venture in Europe called EURONEXT. Second, we have entered into a very significant technology sharing agreement across the Atlantic with the Chicago Mercantile Exchange (CME). Last but not least, we are engaged in far reaching and very open discussions with Deutsche Börse to give flesh to our common objective of cross-membership agreement, in cooperation with the Swiss market.

What about the cooperation with Sao Paulo? **JFT:** It is of a different nature. It's a very important and very friendly transfer of technology agreement to help our Brazilian friends of BOVESPA – already the largest stock market in Latin America – to take a further step in their modernization drive. But it will not lead – in the short term at least – to some kind of joint venture or common business. Our business plans for Europe and Latin America are still rather different.

In other words, globalization still has quite a few steps to go! But do you think that the next stage in financial globalization will be twenty-four hour trading and the fully fledged competition across continents that it would foster? **JFT:** Well, overall, I feel twenty-four hour trading is still mostly a gleam in the eye, as the notion of time zones is still very strong.

But over the years, this mix of co-operation and competition between time zones could evolve toward more direct competition. Clearly, the place to look at for such trends is New York. The New York Stock Exchange (NYSE) is a special, very powerful player. This year, its capitalization has overcome in size the whole U.S. GDP! They may be interested in pursuing the truly global opportunities associated with non American "super blue chips".

Right now, however, this level of competition has not really developed – or not yet. There are not very many European companies listed in New York, and these listings are bringing additional liquidity to European markets rather than taking liquidity away from European markets. Of course, we are talking about a very powerful player and the U.S. Securities and Exchange Commission (SEC) may rethink some of its standards and rules to facilitate the *global listing* strategy. So far the effort by the NYSE to list non U.S. companies seems to focus on emerging markets rather than on Europe.

Nevertheless, it looks as if the NYSE will be the only market where investors will be able to buy shares in all of the European countries in important sectors like telecommunications since companies in the process of privatization (Deutsche Telekom, STET, France Telecom) will be listed in two markets: their home market and New York. **JFT:** Telecom may be a special case in the sense that these companies are truly comparable from one country to the other, which is less true in other sectors. But, in any case, we will make sure that the NYSE is not the only game in the town of global listing!

The high visibility and the size of the NYSE do not imply, by far, that Europe is staying idle in this global competition for listing. Actually, this is one key reason behind our efforts to link and interconnect. The European Union is a net saver, a net exporter of capital. The euro will create an even more impressive pool of capital which will attract emerging markets experiences provided we develop the appropriate tools and the appropriate cooperation.

What sort of co-operation between European stock exchanges will it take for a non-European company to be able to tap several markets at the same time? Past efforts in that direction under flashy banners like "Euroquote" or "Eurolist" did not go very far... **JFT:** This is something we certainly want to think about. Our co-operation could take the form of a *joint subsidiary* or of enabling issuers to be listed with one stock exchange with an agreement with the other members of the networks for *simultaneous trading*. It can also take different forms such as the EURO NM network set up among a number of European exchanges for small, high growth companies to facilitate cross border trading in these less well known securities.

The only thing that I am sure of at this stage is that this will be a field where things are likely to change. At the moment, the focus is on getting the technology and the economics right, as a preparation for higher and higher levels of competition once the euro is in place.

In this respect, I would like to give you more details about EURONEXT and the second level I have mentioned in our present trilogy of initiatives. Let me observe, as background information, that the securities industry is not unlike the partners of Airbus twenty years ago. The stock exchanges taking part in EURONEXT realize that the costs of developments are now very large and they have to look for co-operative approaches.

EURONEXT brings together a number of stock exchanges around the state-of-the-art technology developed here for trading the NSC system. But it is not just about using the same system in the framework, for instance, of licensing agreements and temporary alliances. Rather, it is about being co-owners and co-developers of these systems.

Before you describe what is implied there, let us ask you how high are the costs of developing a new state of the art trading platform? In other words, how strong are the pressures for cooperation around the economies of scale made possible by sharing such platforms as you are doing through EURONEXT?
JFT: The NSC system carries a price tag of 50 million U.S. dollars, just for the software, and one should bear in mind that this is, so to speak, at a discount as we were able to take advantage of the well performing CAC system that already existed. A green field system would cost much more to develop from scratch. Remember when the London Stock Exchange had to abandon its TAURUS project for automated clearing and settlement.

So stock exchanges are confronted with a choice between a very expensive go-it-alone strategy and a set of co-operative strategies enabling them to share at least a part of the costs of large development and upgrade.

What is implied by "co-ownership"? **JFT:** Quite simply, one of these entities called a Groupement d'Intérêt Economique Européen (GIEE) in which we combine the "one country/one vote" approach with a sharing of costs in proportion to the use that each exchange makes of the common system. Being able to develop the necessary technical tools at an acceptable cost also allows to avoid becoming dependent on all outside suppliers of ready made systems.

Maybe we can look beyond these specific initiatives to adopt a global perspective. Let us reflect on the type of market structure, the type of geography that takes shape as a result of market globalization, technology and the euro. First of all, do you believe the very notion of "financial center" still has a meaning? Is it going to be Paris-Europlace vs. Frankfurt-Europlace etc. or rather a unified Europlace-Paris/Frankfurt/London.
JFT: The old geography of financial centers is giving way to what those of you at PROMETHEE, were among the first to call the network of networks. The monopolies based on geographic location will disappear and there will be a strong trend toward decentralisation. Looking at the U.S. for instance, one can see that the trend has not been toward concentration of trading in New York but rather that many traders can live and trade, actively and often more pleasantly out of California.

EURONEXT: a consortium to develop and upgrade technology.

EURONEXT is a consortium, jointly created in 1996 by the Paris and Brussels bourses, for the development of technical cooperation between European stock exchanges. This will involve in particular shared ownership of trading software and upgrades.

EURONEXT will promote and sell the software based on the Paris trading system. This includes NSC software for markets handling significant volumes, Unix packages designed for trading on smaller, emerging markets and the special version of NSC designed for derivatives trading.

It will also take responsibility for the future development of this software in the interest of its membership as a whole or on behalf of individual members. Finally, it will provide members with maintenance and other technical support.

EURONEXT is open to all operators of cash and derivative markets wishing to install an electronic trading system and maintain control of its development at lower cost.

There are three kinds of participants: members, associate members and others. Members subscribe to a portion of EURONEXT's capital, thereby acquiring joint ownership of the software. EURONEXT members will acquire an equal equity interest in the consortium, regardless of the relative size of the volumes that they handle through the trading system.

Associate members are those willing to acquire a licence to use the software but not an equity interest.

Members and associates have access to advanced trading software, internationally recognized for the quality of its performance, and thus avoid the need to develop their own system.

Other exchanges interested in the expertise of EURONEXT members can develop ad hoc links.

EURONEXT members are assured to own a «state of the art» trading system enabling them to remain competitive for the future by pursuing their own

enhancement policy and by building on the expertise and technology of other markets.
Each member will be represented on the Board of Directors, the latter being assisted by a technical committee in charge of development strategy and implementation. All EURONEXT members will be represented on this committee.
Currently, eleven exchanges are using or are planning to use NSC technology (list in insert above).

Bruno Rossignol,
SBF - Bourse de Paris

Financial centers therefore will not necessarily coincide with a large concentration of people. Instead, they will probably take one of the two possible forms:
– that of a *hub in the network of networks*, namely a place through which market participants find it in their interests to operate, in terms for instance of the costs that they save, of the liquidity that they gain or of the value that they can add to their own activity;
– or that of an entry point – *a gateway* as people are now fond of saying – into that network of networks.

Let me stress again that this new financial geography will not be centered on one single "mega network". Instead, it is clear that the new geography will be shaped by competing networks.

In the Europe of the euro, it is clear that one of these major networks will be the one that we are committed to develop around *French and German co-operation*. It is just as clear that *London* will also be at the center of one such network, thereby bringing to the whole market a buoyant and creative source of competition.

But it is very conceivable also that other players can develop *a third major network* at the core of this new European financial market. Such newcomers need not be restricted to the present world of stock exchanges but might come from the world of telecoms, multimedia or information technology.

The co-operation between the French and German markets that you have mentioned repeatedly seems to have experienced

EURO NM: A European networked market for high growth companies.

Many companies in Europe -particularly those that have been in operation for only a short time- need considerable amounts of capital to finance their growth but are unable to find them on existing markets or through the banking system. Listing requirements on traditional bourses are often unsuited to such companies since authorities as well as financial intermediaries tend to reserve listing to more mature businesses with proven track records.

Yet businesses must stake out market positions quickly if they are to succeed and need long-term capital to avoid losing momentum and continue expanding. In 1996, to answer this dilemma, SBF - Bourse de Paris has created le Nouveau Marché, a new market designed to fill the gap in this area by offering entrepreneurial companies with high growth potential the access they need to capital markets and by providing venture capitalists with a market in which to resell their investments in start up companies.

At the same time, SBF - Bourse de Paris has fostered the creation of Euro NM, establishing links with three other stock markets also dedicated to innovative high growth companies namely NMAX of Amsterdam, Euro NM Belgium and Neuer Markt in Frankfurt. All these markets are regulated and share common standards concerning listing requirements, membership and market rules.

This original cooperation scheme is a shared network aimed at the need of investors who want to combine easy access to cross-border trading opportunities with maintaining the comfort of dealing through domestic stockbrokers. The network should function effectively in 1998, Paris and Brussels being so far the only computerized markets operating around the same NSC system.

In terms of listing, Euro NM can already be said to bring together successful markets as more than 60 companies capitalizing over 6 billion dollars are listed in the participating markets. Its goal is to be the networked home of about 500 listed companies by the year 2000.

Bruno Rossignol
SBF - Bourse de Paris

serious difficulties a year ago when the project of a common trading platform had to be abandoned. What makes you think that it remains a central feature of the emerging financial geography in Europe? **JFT:** The common Franco-German platform was only a means toward an end. And the end has not varied.

The strategic idea was to create an integrated market on the continent based notably on close co-operation – and even on forms of integration – of the French and German markets. This strategic idea has not changed. It has not lost in importance, and it has not lost in energy and quality of support.

What has changed is our initial project to use the French NSC trading system as the common trading platform for the French and German cash markets and the DTB platform for the futures markets. We had believed that proposing an existing French platform could be an easy, natural answer to the needs of our German partners for a trading tool able to replace their ageing IBIS screens. Such a proposition, as logical as it may sound, can be at odds with the operating procedures or with the expectations of a given organization, at the technical or managerial level. But we have easily reconciled ourselves to the fact that the initial objective had to be pursued through a different set of means.

The tools on which we rely now are a combination of co-operative undertakings that have the potential, taken together, to bring our two markets to the same high level of integration that we had envisioned. These tools include, notably, *interconnection of the trading system*, a common *clearing solution* and a common *marketing* approach, all this converging around a *cross-membership agreement.*

It seems that the new global information economy is about "the taming of the co": co-regulation, co-sovereignty, co-production, etc. Could you explain what is implied by "co-membership" or "cross-membership"? How does it relate to what you have described as "co-ownership" within the EURONEXT network? **JFT:** The EURONEXT agreement that I discussed previously is about the co-ownership of a technical tool. It is, first and foremost, about *economies of scale* although it can only be the entry point into more in-depth relations.

The type of "strategic interconnection" that we are developing with the Deutsche Börse by contrast leads to a unified offer. It can only work if members of one exchange have access to the privileges of membership in the other exchange – what is called in the industry cross-membership.

Cross-membership is an ambitious objective as it implies developing a number of products in common and sharing costs as well as profits for the joint operations. This can lead to what you at PROMETHEE call "co-production" around, for instance, stock indexes like the one we are co-developing with the Swiss exchange and the Deutsche Börse.

The interlinking agreements that I just mentioned allow market participants to reap the fruits from this cross-membership status: they imply that the end user will have one "log-in", that he or she will be faced with only one entry point into several systems forming together a common network.

Could you elaborate on the other forms of alliances that you mentioned, notably EURONEXT, and elaborate on the map of European finance that will emerge from these various processes and strategies in the aftermath of the euro? **JFT:** Let me use again the analogy of other industries such as car manufacturing or air transportation where capital costs are so high that there is a constant search for economies of scale.

A first trend is for automobile manufacturers to supply components from one another so as to keep investment budgets down and to achieve lower unit costs. Similarly, in the world of exchanges, we can share or swap costly technical tools as we have just done with our friends at the Chicago Mercantile Exchange (CME). As you know, they have found our NSC trading system efficient and powerful enough to adopt it for their derivative products, which saved them several dozen million dollars. On our side, we were happy to save our members about 40 million U.S. dollars in development costs by swapping the licence for NSC against a similar licence to use "Clearing 21", the superb clearing system developed by CME.

The open architecture vision is now well mastered and this leads us to emphasise *such co-operative strategies to reduce our costs* and to better serve our members and the financial community at large.

This sort of ad hoc technical alliance is a first level of co-operation shaping the geography of financial markets. It tends to express itself through the back offices, but the impact is felt all the way into the front offices as cost savings are passed along to members.

A second level of co-operation is achieved when automobile manufacturers – or stock exchanges for that matter – set up a joint venture as a way to share the costs and the benefits of certain developments in a lasting manner.

In France, for instance, Renault and Peugeot have embarked upon an ambitious program to develop an automatic gear adapted to the driving habits of Europeans. I imagine that they will remain allies beyond the first generation of gears that they will co-produce as they will be led into a continuing stream of improvements and adaptations. Well, we and a number of European exchanges find ourselves in the same position through our EURONEXT joint venture.

As I stressed earlier, EURONEXT is not a licensing agreement but a framework for the joint ownership and the joint development of state-of-the-art trading systems. The exchanges involved in this co-operation belong in the same market, they often interact with the same member firms and they will soon end up trading the same products in euros or products that will complement one another in the integrated euro markets. Hence, one should expect that the co-operation set up around the present NSC platform will evolve into an ongoing process of co-operation for the long stream of improvements and adaptations that the integrated European market will call for. In turn, this will probably prepare and position these exchanges to take the next "big step" together when the time comes for a new trading system...

A *third level of cooperation* is the strategic interconnection that I have just described in the case of the French and German financial places. It goes well beyond the other forms of alliances that we encounter in our activity. To understand what I mean, you may say again that our co-operation with Deutsche Börse can be compared to the type of "strategic interconnection" that develops between some airlines. If you look at the links between Lufthansa and United Airlines, or at those between British Airways and American Airlines, you can see that an interconnection develops at many levels simultaneously as it involves joint reservation systems, shared "frequent flyer" programs, co-ordinated schedules, use of the same hubs, common maintenance of aircraft, joint marketing strategies... Indeed, a customer may end up buying a ticket that bears only one code and that appears to be produced by only one airline but that consists of several legs operated by the different partners.

The airline analogy is probably appropriate also in the sense that in both industries the identification with the home country is quite strong. Many airlines are "national flag carriers" and the same is also true, in a way, of the national exchanges. In such industries, outright mergers raise more sensitive issues, which explains that new forms of alliances tend to achieve many of the benefits of a merger without having to hurt these deeply held feelings or sensitivities.

So networks of all types, networks of strategic alliances and

interconnected networks, will continue to transform the geography of finance? **JFT:** Yes, and altogether, this new geography of competition and co-operation will be shaped by three types of rivers: by *ad hoc* cost-sharing alliances, by ad hoc cost-sharing alliances like the one we have with CME, and by ongoing co-operations around lasting joint ventures like EURONEXT which I have described in the case of the French and German small stock exchanges.

If you allow us to refer to the PROMETHEE model of "networked markets", we have discussed two of the three fundamental dimensions of networking: the infrastructures and the rules and standards that we call "infostructures". But there is a third dimension which may be less visible but which nevertheless shapes mutual expectations: "infoculture". From that perspective, the European continent today seems to be in a "bond culture" rather than in an Anglo-Saxon type of "equity culture". Will the euro trigger changes in this respect? **JFT:** A very large market, attractive to investors from the whole world and in which corporations from all over Europe will compete for investors' attention can be expected to take our countries quite a few steps closer to the "equity culture"!

One can already see it very clearly in Germany, and I would like to refer you to the book written by my German counterpart and friend Werner Seifert for telling illustrations. Keeping public deficits under the 3% of GDP limit mandated in the Maastricht Treaty and, beyond that, in the Growth and Stability Pact will foster an environment of low inflation and low interest rates. Investing in equities will then be far more attractive.

Investing in government bonds has traditionally been seen as the sound, *pater familias* investment *par excellence.* With the euro, government bonds will no longer keep the status of *de facto* benchmarks. As is the case in a federation like the U.S.A., they will operate under competitive market principles and will no longer necessary be at the center of national capital markets. In other words, they will become securities among many others.

Status is not just about psychology but it is also a legal matter. The Central European Bank will not be the lender of last resort under any circumstances. On the contrary, bond issuance will be subject to the disciplines and the control mechanisms established in the Growth and Stability Pact.

Imagine now that we are in 2012, ten years after citizens and entrepreneurs in Europe have received their first euro bank notes. What sort of place will the Paris Bourse be? **JFT:** It is the excitement and challenge of our job to be unable to predict what the business scene will be at such a distant horizon. Technology, regulation, monetary matters and market psychology evolve so fast that the future is wide open, at the global as well as at the European level. When I talk to new recruits or to job applicants, my first move is to stress that they know where we are now but that they cannot expect things to be still the same ten years from now. They have to expect the unexpected!

Just imagine we had had this conversation 15 years ago in 1982. At that time, our exchange enjoyed the rights of a national monopoly, brokers were public officers, trade was done on the open outcry mode with no computerized trading. The SBF - Bourse de Paris of 1997 would have been quite hard to imagine, not to mention the euro of 1999!

So my modest contribution to your effort to anticipating the European financial markets of the euro era will be to forecast that Paris and Europe will still be very challenging, very exciting places in the networked financial geography still to come! ■

France preparing for the euro.

The European Union is already one of the largest markets in the world, ranking alongside the U.S. and Japan in terms of population (370 million), GDP (8.5 trillion U.S. dollar), outstanding government debt (5.9 trillion U.S. dollar) and total savings (1.70 trillion U.S. dollar). The bond market in euros will rank second only to that of the United States, as will stock market capitalization.

Since 1996, the various participants in the Paris market place have been preparing actively to meet the challenge of the euro. Under the auspices of the Banque de France and of the French Association of Credit Institutions and Investment Firms (AFECF), they have been working together to produce the general framework for the transition to the euro, the "schéma de place".

To ensure an immediate and smooth transition to the euro, all French financial markets participants have committed themselves to making the switch simultaneously on the earliest possible date: January 1, 1999. The money market, the foreign exchange markets, the stock exchange, the derivatives markets will all operate in euros from that day onward. The French Treasury will convert its existing debt into euros and will proceed to issue euro-denominated debt. It is worth noting that the French Treasury is already the main and most active issuer in ECUs. Banks will be capable of handling all types of transactions in euros, whether wholesale or retail. The consensus was that this "big bang" scenario would minimize costs and maximize efficiency for all parties as well as for the general public.

In addition, an interministerial task force in charge of preparations in general governement agencies has started to define the methods and means for the changeover to the euro by these agencies. Various working groups have begun putting forward proposals, particularly for non-financial firms.

Over the next few months, a national "euro" Committee, reporting to the Minister for Economy, Finance and Industry, will review in details the overall framework in which to conduct changeover in France's economy, in French society in general and the relationships between all players.

An extensive communication plan has been launched by the Government, with 20 million brochures "l'euro et moi" ("The euro and me") being distributed, as well as series of meetings, TV and radio ads. In 1998, SBF - Bourse de Paris will launch an information campaign of its own in the national and regional press to help the public prepare for the euro and for the changeover.

Bruno Rossignol
SBF - Bourse de Paris

PROMETHEE INSERT

The Networked Markets Study Group: concepts and tools on the shift from I-tech to R-tech

Can there be something new about the market as the organizing principle for economic interactions? Since 1991, PROMETHEE, in co-operation with SBF-Bourse de Paris, Euroclear, Deutsche Börse AG (previously the Frankfurt Stock Exchange), the Kassenverein, MATIF, MEFF, the FIBV and regulators of the EU and U.S. has convened the *Networked Markets Study Group* to review the impact of electronic networks on markets[1].

The consensus has been that, indeed, some fundamental changes were happening[2].

These changes, admittedly, are not as spectacular as the fall of the Iron Curtain: the present competition between different ways to organize markets is less easily described than the previous competition between markets and central planning. Yet, markets are also witnessing changes of a far-reaching, even if subtle, nature. The meeting of networks and markets is more than a marriage of convenience. The "networked markets" now reshaping global finance are hybrid forms of organization calling for a new conceptual map.

Shaking hand with the Walras auctioneer

One traditional way to describe markets to economic students is to refer to the famous "Walras auctioneer", a virtual "person" operating at the intersection of the supply and demand curve to determine instantaneously the market clearing price. Actually, technology is now giving life to what was merely a

1. The group is indebted to notably Jean Saint-Geours and René de La Serre, its successive chairmen, to Carter Beese (Commissioner, SEC), Bénédicte Doumayrou (COB), Helen Dean (Thomson Financial Services), Martine Dinne (Euroclear), Paul-François Dubrœucq (SBF) and Didier Davidoff (COB and later SBF), Pierre Duminil (GIA), José Fombellida (DG-15), Randall Guynn (International Bar Association), Antony Kirby and Nadine Limbourg (S.W.I.F.T.), Philippe Loumeau (MATIF), Gerrit de Marez Oyens (FIBV), Jeremy Penn (Reuters), Gérard Pfauwadel (MATIF) and Jose Luis Oller (MEFF).

2. For presentation of these discussions see "Networks and markets: more than a marriage of convenience" and "Rock around the pit" issues n° 21, December 1992, and n° 22, February 1994, of *PROJECT PROMETHEE PERSPECTIVES*. See also Albert Bressand and Catherine Distler "Le 'village global' financier", Futuribles, Paris, Novembre 1994 and Albert Bressand "Réseaux bancaires et financiers : une coopération multiforme sur fond de concurrence exacerbée", *Revue d'Economie Financière*, n° 33, Paris, été 1995.

metaphor for Léon Walras, a famous 19th century's economist. It does so in the concrete form of software programs running virtual auctions or matching orders among market participants.

We are used to thinking of markets in terms of the pricing by the market participants; we must now think of markets in terms of the *"price discovery mechanisms"*, in which the economic process generates the price. In order to translate into a "price", orders need to be complemented with capacities internal —and specific— to each market . "Market making", automatized auctions or other rules and procedures must be explicitly chosen and written into the software, with major implications for intermediation and dis-intermediation patterns.

As a consequence, to quote FIBV's Gerrit de Marez Oyens, the notion of "best price" –as embodied for instance in different codes of business conduct and trading rules– probably needs to be replaced with that of *"fair price"*, a *relative* rather than an absolute notion as it also depends on the specific architecture chosen for the market. Recent controversies and decisions in major markets like NASDAQ have illustrated the growing importance of fairness in pricing in high-tech networked markets...

Liquid definitions of liquidity

This is not to say that technology determines what markets are. At heart, markets are still about *the meeting of supply and demand* in ways which technology can make easier as well as more complex without changing the underlying forces. Yet, networked markets generate such precise expectations, measures and regulations as to lead one to wonder at what point a difference in degree becomes a difference in nature.

Transparency, an overarching concern for all participants in all markets, can now be measured in terms of the time elapsed –accurate to seconds– between a deal and its disclosure. Hence the need for exchanges or for market participants themselves to choose between different options that may have quite significant implications in terms of the working of markets. Continental exchanges and the London Stock Exchange debated the possible relaxation of transparency rules that the latter deemed acceptable for *wholesale markets* among sophisticated professionals. A higher degree of consensus has now developed on the need to be fully transparent, and London is now taking steps toward continental-style order-driven markets. But other networks - notably the TARGET network for large payments in euros - generate new waves of discussions on the strategic and regulatory implications of seemingly technical choices.

As for *liquidity* - the bedrock of market quality - it begins to elude definition in a world in which the quality of a given market is assessed in terms of the greater or lesser "immediacy" of the response that a given participant can expect at any given time.

Macro, micro... and nano

Thus, the "macro" world, of which markets are the foundation, can no longer be discussed separately from the "micro" strategies of the intermediaries who concur to "produce" prices. And both these "macro" and "micro" worlds cannot be understood without explicit reference to the "nano" world, namely the C&C tools that allow to monitor and assess market opportunities, to trigger decisions, to transmit and match orders, to conduct virtual auctions, to settle deals, to store property in dematerialized registers...

The development of networks has a major impact on stock exchanges and financial markets. Operating a market, today, cannot be done successfully without a keen sense of strategic positioning within "the network of networks" (N^2).

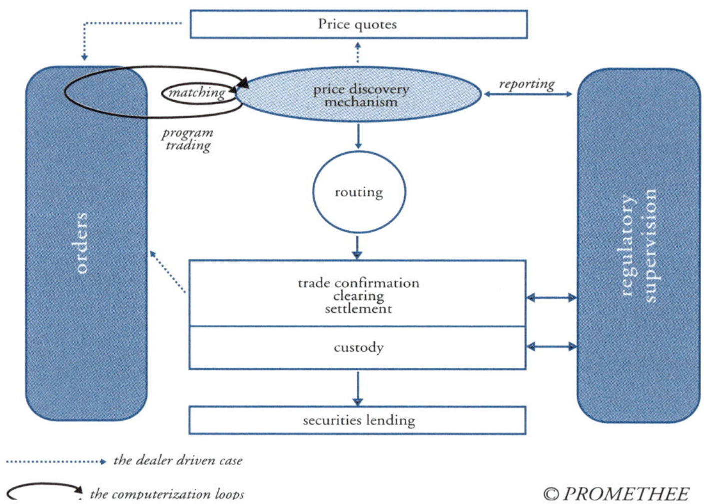

© PROMETHEE

Networks as relationship management machines

But what is a network? The word is used so often and in so many different contexts as to run the risk of meaning everything to everyone. One will hear about "old boy networks", "telecom networks" and "networks of strategic alliances". In an effort to identify the common elements behind these very different meanings, PROMETHEE has put forward the following definition:

"A network is a set of technical means (*"infrastructure"*) and of privately and/or publicly defined rules and norms (*"infostructure"*) that users with rights of access can take the initiative to mobilize in order to set up and to manage relationships coherent with a given set of expectations (*"infoculture"*) ".

This three-tier definition is complex, but it can be summarized by calling a network a "relationship management machine" or even, as explained in Chapter 12, a "linking machine". For actors to enter into a workable market relationship, networks must fulfil three different types of tasks related to what PROMETHEE sees as the three basic aspects of any relationship: contact, contract and commitment[3]. Networks are used to generate gains of *productivity* and *predictability* (hence the term "machine") with respect to the management of relationships. In particular, within markets, the role of the network can make possible the whole process, or parts of the process, whereby buyers enter into relationship with sellers and a price is formed.

In discussing this marriage between networks and markets, the Study Group agreed that a network must not be seen just as a channel (even if this channel is a very sophisticated infrastructure) but that an essential part of a network is its "infostructure". Sometimes the infostructure can be defined as the full discretion of network members ("club" rules), sometimes they can be borrowed from society at large (constitutional rights, laws, directives...) and, in many cases, they are a combination of public and private rules.

Automation, value adding and hubs: the network life cycle

Against this broader definition, an important question is whether the impact of networks will remain confined to the market functions for which they are

3. See the Wired Interviews: interview of Albert Bressand and Catherine Distler by Peter Schwartz, *WIRED MAGAZINE*, June 1996.

brought into the picture or whether they will trigger a set of deeper, open-ended changes in the relationships between market participants. An observation of "network life-cycles" suggests that networks tend to be deployed, first, to automatize what already exist and to cut costs. Once the network is in place, users become aware of new possibilities to *add value*. Some of them also see the network as a key tool in their effort to position at the center of one or several markets, in other words to be a *"hub"*.

The network life cycle: three types of strategies for network-based competitive advantages

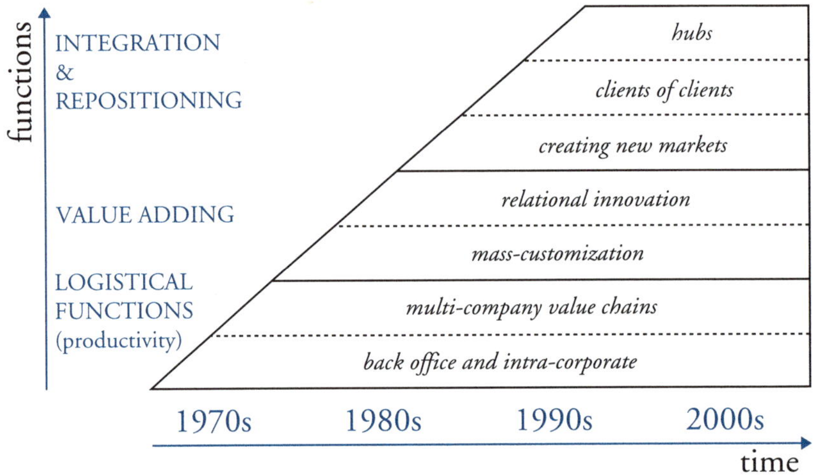

©PROMETHEE, 1991 and 1997

In this light, the group found it useful to look at electronic networks not just as a product of *I-tech* ("information technology") but as prime tools of *"relationship management technology"* —in short, *R-tech*.

Regulated exchanges, PTS and network governance

To understand the *governance* of networks and the division of labor to which they give rise, analysis should not be limited to the traders ("users") interacting through the networks but should also include the various network operators and supervisors:

• *Operators* put in place and manage the infrastructures, thereby allowing users to enter into *contact* with one another. Reuters, for instance, is the operator of the Globex network.

• *Supervisors* —whether in the network itself or in the society at large— design and/or enforce the *infostructures* thereby allowing users to *contract* and transact with one another. Supervision is the function most critical to, and most specific of, exchanges as opposed to over the counter (OTC) networks.

• *Users* must take infrastructures and infostructures as givens (at least in the short term), yet they are not taking orders from operators or supervisors. On the contrary, they are the ones who have to take the *initiative* to establish a relationship among two or several of them. The type of *commitment* into which they can enter is a critical aspect of networks and, even more so, of networked markets.

The Networked Market Study Group has discussed various ways in which these three functions (operator, supervisor and user) can be discharged, and notably the ways in which the same entity can fulfill several of these functions. The governance and evolution of networked markets has also been studied in connection with the *"Market 2000"* report of the SEC (around Commissioner Carter Beese[4]) and the *"Marché 2001"* report by COB (around COB Chairman Jean Saint-Geours).

The competition between regulated exchanges and Private Trading Systems (PTS) is a central aspect of this fruitful marriage between networks and markets.

Catherine Distler **Albert Bressand**

4. See Carter Beese "Patterns of Integration in and among International Financial Markets" *PROJECT PROMETHEE PERSPECTIVES*, "Rock Around the Pit", n° 22, February 1994.

Chapter II

The strategic issues *behind the conversation*

German attitudes toward the euro may be the most critical political ingredient in the delicate balance of national, European and global influences on which European integration now depends. Hence the importance of the perspective put forward by the German stock market and the Finanzplatz.
The importance of the deadline, the exact interpretation of the Maastricht criteria and the consequences of not creating the euro are short term issues that tend to receive special attention in Germany. Beyond the still controversial transition, however, the post-euro agenda is already in place, with notably the search for new financial benchmarks and different types of strategic agreements with the Swiss and French markets.
The conversation did not limit itself to the euro and its strategic implications. In the global perspective well in place at Deutsche Börse, prominent issues also include the lag in the productivity of capital between Europe and the U.S., the ways to preserve a sense of community among traders in the electronic age and the likelihood that Germany itself will become a more friendly place for those who take risk.
The euro can then be seen as part of a deeper transformation that will manifest itself through the rise of an "equity culture" in which private initiatives enjoy the type of respectability presently reserved to government decisions and to social consensus. Hence, maybe, the attention given here to financial deregulation as an engine for job creation in the highly regulated societies of the core euro countries... On this subject, actually, Werner Seifert when we met him was putting the final touch to a book of his own that could be the subject of many more "strategic conversations"... *A.B.*

conversation with

WERNER SEIFERT,
DEUTSCHE BÖRSE AG

This conversation with Werner Seifert, CEO of Deutsche Börse AG, was conducted in Frankfurt by Albert Bressand and Catherine Distler (PROMETHEE) and Joachim Epperlein (Schitag Ernst & Young).

The euro and beyond: financial markets and the search for renewed economic dynamism in Europe

In just a few months now, after a lot of hard work, a number of countries will give up their national currencies and take their monetary marching orders from the new European Central Bank here in Frankfurt. To most of them, this is tantamount to adopting German economic principles. And yet, Germans themselves appear worried and reluctant. What is on their mind? **Werner Seifert:** The questions on the mind of the German public are not of a philosophical nature: the support for Europe and European integration is very strong at the level of principles and of political philosophy. Rather, the questions behind the worries that you have mentioned are focused on the impact that the euro can have on people's daily lives, on their savings, on their standard of living…So the answer to your question is protecting the value of their assets! Germany has gone through two currency reforms already. Hence, people here are keenly aware that economic and political forces can be a source of fundamental change for currencies and for their value. They have no blind faith in the decisions that governments take in such matters.

With the coming of the euro, their question tends to be "how can I protect myself from a weak euro?". So, protecting the value of their assets over a long period of time is what Germans care about. This is what's really on their mind.

Does that mean that the value of German assets is threatened by European integration? **WS:** To answer your question and that of German public opinion, one needs an objective test of what happens to the value of assets as a result of currency decisions. Such an objective test could be to compare the way in which the value of European currencies has developed during preceding phases of monetary integration with the development of a trustworthy benchmark.

May I suggest that we use the Swiss franc as benchmark? As you know Switzerland is more immune than any other European country to the effects of political and economic integration as it is not a member of the European Union and not even a member of the European Economic Area through which Norway, Iceland and tiny Lichtenstein share in the process of integration of a common European market. In addition, as we all know, Switzerland is a highly respected financial center, where money is treated in a serious and disciplined manner. So many people would accept the Swiss franc as a benchmark.

And indeed there is a study that carried out this "objective test" by comparing changes in the value of the Swiss franc to the value of a weighted basket of the currencies that have participated in the European Monetary System (EMS) for the period 1983-1993. These currencies include the Deutsche mark but also the French franc, the lira and other currencies of future participants in the euro. The currencies in the EMS basket used in this study are weighted according to population size and GDP to get a robust measure of their relative importance. The weakness or strength of currencies is expressed in terms of inflation which is the most straightforward measure of asset depreciation. Now, which of these two assets that I have just described would have provided savers and investors with the best protection? A one hundred Swiss franc bank note or its equivalent in the basket of EMS currencies?

We have not seen the study, but we have the feeling that we should prepare for a surprise! **WS:** Indeed! On average the Swiss bank note lost 2.7% of its value per year in this ten year period as a result of inflation when the EMS basket lost only 2.3%. Now, admittedly, this is a close call: one could easily come up with other relative weights among the currencies in the EMS basket or with different periods of time and give the trophy to the Swiss (being Swiss myself, I would read such alternative views with sympathy). But the point is that protecting the value of assets, the objective to which the German public is rightly attached, is compatible with monetary integration. And, what was true of the EMS, can be true also of the euro: European monetary integration *per se* will not depreciate the value of assets.

This being said, hard facts will not suffice to dispel people's anxieties... I am puzzled to see that there are countries where people are almost exuberant about the euro while, in other countries, they are deeply mistrustful. In both cases people would have a hard time giving rational explanations for their exuberance or for their anxieties.

To come back to Germany, the situation is further complicated by the important role played by the länder in matters of taxes and of monetary policy. The Bundesrat represents all German state governments. Due to the German constitution most of the decisions concerning taxes have to be accepted by the Bundesrat. Also at the Bundesbank, decisions are made by the Bundesbank Central Council. Among the members of this body are the presidents of the state central banks.

Can Deutsche Börse AG play a role in helping people deal with these issues that preoccupy them so much? In other words, is your role a technical one limited to the smooth operation of markets - whether in marks or in euros - or do you feel that Deutsche Börse has something to contribute to these millions of people worried about their savings and about the possibility to find or to keep a job? **WS:** We do not see ourselves as playing such an important role. Let us take a conceptual perspective of the type that think-tanks are familiar with. So let me stress that there are three sorts of markets on which an economy depends, three sorts of markets that set the tune for growth, wealth creation and jobs: they are the *labour* market, the markets for *products and services* and the *financial* markets.

Understandably, people tend to associate jobs, first and foremost, with the labour market. So the most straightforward approach to job creation is the one followed by Margaret Thatcher in the UK: deregulate the labour market, remove the bottlenecks, the rigidities and monopolies that put a lid on job creation... Though it sounds natural, this approach can be highly controversial in countries like Germany, to the point that it can be extremely difficult to build the consensus needed for such policies.

The U.S. reforms have emphasised deregulating markets for goods and services by pioneering deregulation in sectors like energy, telecommunications, airlines and more generally by fostering competition through policies favouring new entrants. The "internal market" is giving us some of that dynamism in Europe. Unfortunately, however, we do not seem to have achieved yet the "critical mass" that it would take to generate enough activity to put millions of unemployed at work over a short period of time.

To use a mountaineering metaphor, public opinion in all continental European countries wants to conquer the great *Peak of Full Employment* out there in the economy. But the most direct route – the Thatcherite one – is difficult to carry out politically: so many expeditions have been launched already, from the left as well as from the right, that have had to stop well before the summit is reached or even that have been sent back to base camp by the electorate! So, it is worth our while to reflect on the nature of the terrain that separates us from that Peak, because, after all, full employment is not some isolated goal but is an integral part of a whole chain of mountains in which policy makers have to find their way. This is where I want to come back to the strong links between the three types of markets – for labour, for products and for capital. If we move swiftly toward *financial deregulation,* we can get closer to the Peak of Full Employment in less time, and with less social and political disruptions, than through the other routes!

Thus, indeed, my answer to your question is that we in the financial markets have a special responsibility in facilitating growth, in fostering job creation and in unleashing the forces of economic and social progress. And in my view, this more indirect approach of job creation is in good synergy with deeper changes in the nature of wealth-creation in the contemporary world.

A problem in this strategy of "growth through financial deregulation" could be that 19 German households out of 20 do not own stocks. In France, financial markets are more often associated, in people's mind, with *"la bulle financière"* – a financial bubble hanging over the "real" economy – than with job creation. So we are fascinated to learn more about the role that you think German stock exchanges can play in job creation! **WS:** Except for their own very small number of employees, stock exchanges are not influential enough to create jobs. So let us return to the interdependence between job creation and capital markets. Actually, by the time this set of "strategic conversations" organised by PROMETHEE and Ernst & Young comes out, Frank Mattern, Clara Streit, Jürgen Voth and I will have published a book in German that you may find relevant. This book will attempt to explain this role of financial markets and to derive recommendations from it[1].

We are not alone and I have great respect for scholars who have investigated the various ways in which a country can go about creating jobs. For example, I found Horace Brock's analysis[2] of the links between the three types of markets very illuminating when it comes to understanding the various national economic strategies in Europe and their results or lack thereof. I hope our own book, written from the viewpoint of a practitioner, can foster greater awareness of these links and of these policy options.

What type of "policy options" or strategy do you have in mind to transform financial markets into the new engine for job creation? **WS:** What is at stake is both subtle and fundamental: it implies becoming *a more risk-friendly nation.*

Such a change would have pervasive effect. By accepting risk as a more normal part of economic activity, we will be able to channel resources toward the more productive uses. And in so doing, we will be fostering job creation and social progress.

To achieve that objective, I see five driving forces that financial markets can set in motion: the *force of deregulation*, the *force of tax-reform*, the force of *pension reform*, from pay-as-you-go to fully funded systems, the *force of corporate governance* and a fifth one that is less immediate to comprehend a functioning market for takeovers.

Harnessing these five forces, Germany can become a country that creates capitalism for everybody. In doing so, it would change behaviours regarding risk and return, thereby unleashing a dynamics of growth and employment.

My first answer when you asked me about Germany and the euro was to highlight the importance of value *protection* in shaping people and values. But *creation* of value is the other side of the coin with which growth and jobs can be acquired.

Drawing on these five forces, the reforms that the book just mentioned proposes would make individuals more willing to create, they would make them better prepared to take risks – the seed of all creation.

---

1. *Aktie, Arbeit, Aufschwung: Wie der Finanzplatz Wirtschaft und Gesellschaft wieder in Schwung bringt;* Frankfurt am Main, Campus, October 1997.
2. Horace W. Brock "The nation that fired the most hired the most", *Profile Forecast Report*, Summer 1996, Strategic Economic Decision Inc., Menlo Park, California.

So, next time we visit, we expect to see the hi-tech building that headquarters Deutsche Börse AG decorated with a new logo: "conserve and create!". What role will the euro play in this strategy for a more creative, a more risk-friendly Germany? **WS:** The euro is helping not just Germany, but all participating countries in managing risk differently. And it does so in several ways.

First, most obviously the euro removes one of the sources of fragmentation in European markets – not just in currency markets but also, thanks to the links that I mentioned, in the market for products and to some extent in the labour market. Prices will become far more predictable across borders and also far more transparent as people will no longer have to play chess in their head with several currencies.

The same will be true of the market for corporate control, as investors will be able to acquire shares in companies in what will be, at least *de facto*, a unified equity market in euros.

So, to put it simply, the euro will help accept the risks of Schumpeter's creative destruction because such risks will no longer be compounded by currency instability and its macroeconomic implications.

A second set of reasons why the euro will make Germany and Europe more risk-friendly has to do with *the policy path* that governments have to follow to make the euro happen. The Maastricht criteria are not terribly popular these days, yet they are forcing participant countries to accelerate the type of reform of public finance which they would need in any case to create a pro-growth, pro-job environment.

It is not simply that government deficits do not create lasting jobs – a truth now recognized all over the world. Sooner or later, keeping *deficits* under control also implies keeping government *expenditures* under control. And this, in turn, frees resources for risk taking.

Looking at the Maastricht Treaty as a hotbed of entrepreneurship may sound slighly paradoxical. In French debates for instance, Maastricht tends to be associated more commonly with some technocratic "pensée unique" than with the exuberance and creativity of entrepreneurship. Could you explain why you think that the effort by European governments to meet the Maastricht criteria will foster more risk taking? **WS:** Well, one could think that all Deutsche marks are interchangeable. Yet, in reality, all marks (or all francs or dollars) are not spent in the same fashion. As each one of us allocates his or her available resources, expenditures range from the most compulsory – food, lodging etc. – to the most discretionary. And, if we have some resources to save and invest, we usually begin with the safer investments, the less risky ones. In the "conserve and create" as you phrased it, the first thousand marks of most investors are tilted toward the conservative side, and it is only as more resources become available that the risk implied in more creative ventures begins to appear more attractive.

In other words, when governments absorb higher shares of national resources and national savings, they deprive us of our most "risk-friendly" marks or francs! And vice versa, the sums that they could free by better controlling their spending habits would be spent by private individuals and companies in ways more open to risk than is the case in present spending patterns.

In that sense, the euro and the reduction in government spending that it encourages is helping reduce the crowding-out of risk-friendly money. It is fostering resource allocation patterns more in tune with a better balance between conservation and creation.

Do your positive feelings about the Maastricht process imply that Maastricht criteria, like the 3.0% of GDP ("three point zero") limit, is like some magic number, from which no country should deviate in its efforts to reduce public deficits if it wants to achieve the positive effects that you describe?

WS: The numbers are not sacred, and the diplomats who drafted the Maastricht treaty could probably have come up with different ones. Beyond numbers as such, what may have the most lasting impact is the set of policies and attitudes that are triggered by the efforts to meet these targets.

In that sense, setting quantitative criteria does help to produce the right attitudes and to set the right dynamics in motion.

And what about the deadline itself? Time has always been a critical dimension of European integration. Deadlines such as "a common market by July 1968", "Europe 1992", "full competition in telecoms by January 1, 1998" have played a great role in mobilizing political and business energies in Europe. The same appears to hold for the latest and most spectacular deadline of all: "the euro on January 1, 1999". But what you just said suggests that the policy path followed on the way to such a deadline is more important than the deadline itself. So would it not be thinkable to "stop the clock"

for a few months in the case that circumstances were not favourable for the launch of the euro in early 1999? **WS:** By setting a deadline, one commits oneself to reaching a target at a precise moment. Then arises a dilemma like the one companies have always confronted regarding punctuality and budget. The old management attitude used to be "stick to the budget" even if this delayed the project. Today, companies tend to find that punctuality is more important, that time is becoming a more critical variable. This sets a context that we must bear in mind when discussing the euro.

In addition, as human beings, we all have an intuition that if something is postponed once, then it is quite likely to be postponed again. Governments are even more open to that intuition: people know that, and they are likely to bear in mind this readiness to postpone when assessing the implications (probability) of delays.

So respecting the agreed deadline is of critical importance. Without the euro, European governments would not be pursuing the policies of deficit reduction that we can see today, at least not with the same dedication. Take away the deadline and the magic will be gone.

Nevertheless, what would you do if something wrong happened and the euro project crumbled at the last minute? And what would happen to the value of traded companies in this "postponement scenario"? **WS:** First things first, the stock exchange would continue to run smoothly, irrespective of whether the euro is created or not. Of course, turbulences would develop, but turbulences would be followed by a new balance.

Now, let us assume again that the euro will happen, as most or all our guests in these conversations seem to believe. How do you see the effect of the euro on the European stock exchanges? **WS:** Taking away the currency fragmentation will remove one of the barriers that market participants encounter in Europe today, and it will free a certain amount of capital that is presently invested to hedge against currency risks. But Europe will still have other major barriers to reckon with such as the absence of a European *company law,* the existence of different *accounting standards* and the *fragmentation* of various aspects of market operations like share-trading and settlement.

The euro will create momentum for eliminating these other barriers. The euro will also put competitive pressure on players. We should remember that what happened in the 1980s was not only pension funds looking for investment opportunities: those were also the days when the Wall Street firms were actively modernizing. Accordingly, Europeans should prepare for massive structural adaptation in financial firms and in banks themselves, a process which has already begun but which will be fuelled by the euro.

How are German firms preparing for the euro? Do they believe in it? Are they ready, so to speak, to "fight for it" or are they simply fearing to be left behind if it happens? **WS:** Investors have already built the euro into their strategies. Deutsche Bank, to take the largest bank in this country, has invested 400 million Deutsche marks to prepare for the euro. If one multiplies this by all the banks, the figure is much higher and if one also considers the money invested by the industry, it is clear that the players have already put their chips on the table!

This being said, I am sometimes surprised that representatives of the industry and banks do not speak more openly and more frequently in favour of this major change that they are greatly contributing to make happen. Sometimes I see these people listening for a whole morning to lectures by famous economists on the dangers of having a common currency and I wonder why so few of them take it upon themselves to reply. Most of them could talk about the huge investment they have already made in the euro and about the reasons they have done it.

If the German economy invested that much money, and if one can still deplore such a lack of communication who should do the big teaching job needed for the German public and for German companies? And what is Deutsche Börse doing to contribute to the public debate about the transition to the euro and its implications for companies and for individuals here in Germany? **WS:** One might think this is a role for governments, but it is a big task. By contrast, if you look at what our friends and partners in Paris are doing with their Paris-Europlace-Association, you can see that they have found a good way to proceed. Changing mind-sets is the real challenge...

We are all learning by doing. Hence in Germany a similar association, the *Aktionskreis Finanzplatz e.v.*, was founded in the winter of 1996 by prominent members of German politics, industry, banks and other institutions. The Aktionskreis's board of directors represents a wide variety of individuals who contribute to the prosperity of Germany as a financial center. Their goal is to make the financial center even more international. This includes information about the importance of the euro.

Companies in some sectors, such as real estate, have used the euro and the economic climate generated by the Maastricht criteria as an excuse for their negative performances. Is this the sign of a deeper anxiety? What would be the dark side of the euro? Do you believe that the budgetary stringency associated with the Maastricht criteria will have negative effects, as a number of economists are arguing, on job creation, or do you believe on the contrary that better control over public finance will lead to higher growth? **WS:** In light of what we have just discussed, it is clear that the preparation of the euro is good for jobs, good for welfare. A few companies may find it convenient to blame the restructuring process itself, but on the whole this process is an engine for growth and for job creation.

So why don't politicians just say that to the electorate? Is it because we are still prisoners of the old view and, even indirectly, of the Marxist intellectual perspective according to which finance is either just a "shadow of the real economy" or a "speculative bubble" from which nothing good can come? **WS:** Rather than settling old accounts with Karl Marx, let me go back a mere 30 years in time and suggest that we are still thinking in Bretton Woods terms, namely as a world in which the national systems were neatly separated from one another and in which the U.S. Federal Reserve played a role close to that of a global central bank.

In this period, the "equity culture" flourished in the Anglo-Saxon countries and we on the European continent, developed a "bond-centered culture". The latter was very dependent on the world of Bretton Woods. We must now go beyond that perspective.

The law of one global price is taking hold for bonds, for derivatives and for equities where the volume of trading is expected to double again in just a few years. So the post-Bretton-Woods economy is continuing toward much higher levels of financial integration.

Some observers might suggest an alternative explanation for the relative lack of outspoken advocates for the euro by printing out that the volatility of currency has been already largely eliminated by the EMS and that the euro boils down to just a nominal change. Or do we understand you correctly by saying that the euro is the *catalyst* for a major change in policy that goes well beyond monetary convergence? **WS:** True,

Europe has already achieved a high level of currency stability. But the EMS did not include the efforts I have described to meet the Maastricht criteria.

The policy drive that the euro is producing is very impressive in terms of the convergence of macroeconomic fundamentals and fiscal policies. May I show you a diagram, which vividly shows the tremendous efforts behind the convergence?

In the run-up to the euro, European bond trading becomes more aligned

Average yield-difference between European * and German government bonds

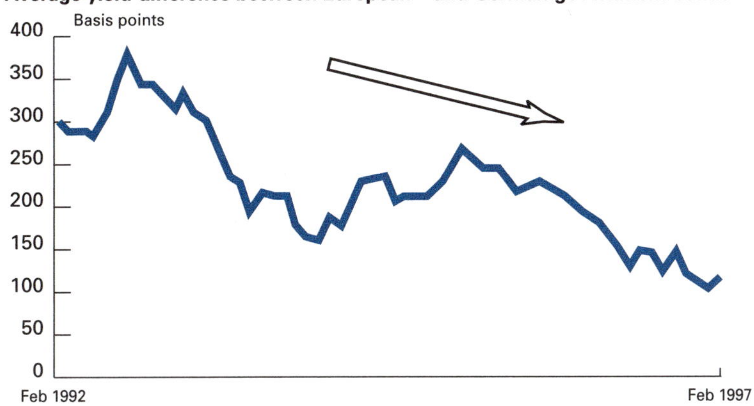

** Basket of long-term government bonds from potential euro member states (F, B, NL, L, A, IRL, P, I, SP, GE)*
Source Datastream

The fact that the euro will have an impact first on capital markets should not limit our vision and our ambitions to the technicalities of finance. On the contrary, the time has come to think of finance in terms of the leverage it gives to our countries for making their economies as a whole more dynamic, more creative.

The same strategy that we propose for Germany could apply to Europe as a whole. The investment revolution will carry into the labour and product markets.

Speaking of "investment revolution", do you think that the euro will be an accelerator of a broader move toward an equity culture in Germany? **WS:** The age of the bond is already coming to an end!

Yes, a lasting change is under way from one type of financial culture to another. That change is rooted in a combination of developments regarding consumption and savings as well as in the search for ways to reconcile progress on the two fronts.

One of the most important things for people now is their old age pension. They are now looking for higher yields in order to be able to consume more while saving enough for their old age. They understand the power of compounded interest and they demand financial products that can help them make both ends meet, that can allow to prepare for retirement while living well now. Actually, we have a little table on that which you may want to insert in the transcript of our conversation.

This will also drive up the Price Earnings Ratio (PER) of companies and will bring more companies to the stock exchange. Indeed, this is already happening. So, yes, the age of bond culture is over, and the age of equity culture has arrived, in Germany as well as in the rest of Europe.

My feeling is that we are headed toward an equity culture because there is no other way that will enable us to meet the pension challenge.

What is the driving force behind the strategy you recommend? And how does it relate to this change in financial culture that you see as taking hold in Germany and on the continent?

W.S.: The starting point is *capital productivity* and its major contribution to the welfare of a country. In this respect, Germany is still far behind: a recent McKinsey study, looking at a 20-year period, found that capital productivity in Germany was only 65% of what it is in the U.S., the figure being 70% for Japan.

Roughly speaking, this large difference in capital productivity has two origins of equal importance. Half of it comes from the fact that, in Germany, the number of hours during which a company can utilize its machinery is about 20% less than what it is in the U.S. which is a rather traditional explanation. But the other half can be attributed to the efficiency of the capital markets in the countries surveyed.

What is at stake is very large. More than 0.5 billion Deutsche marks per day, which means an additional 5% of GDP, would be generated if Germany could achieve the same level of capital productivity as the U.S.

Dealing with the first source of lower productivity would involve thorough reforms of the labour market and would, probably, be very controversial. Hence, again, the importance of focusing on *financial deregulation* as an engine for higher capital productivity and for overall competitiveness.

The problem is to attract capital toward the most productive uses. To do so, we must overcome the risk aversion that is characteristic of our financial culture.

The pension challenge, the need for higher yield and the coming equity culture in continental Europe *

There was a time when the capacity of Europeans to prepare for retirement depended on little more than the willingness of generations at work to pay for the pensions of retirees. Fundamental demographic changes however are at work: they include major gains in life expectancy, major reductions in fertility rates and high levels of unemployment. The baby-boom euphoria in which this sharing could be spread over a large number of employed people is turning into a more sober mood: the number of people at work is becoming only marginally superior to the number of people expecting decent retirement benefits. In this context, financial markets assume an increasingly important role in the intermediation process needed to fund old-age pensions. The yields that can be expected from the markets put a major limit on what can be done. Meanwhile, the ambitions of future retirees can be expressed in terms of the value of the pensions that they want to receive as a proportion of their present working revenues [3].

The following table combines these two parameters and identifies which type of return is needed to provide a given level of work income replacement.

A sufficiently high yield for the financing of old-age pension provision is only achievable with equities

Reserve-financing of own pension — MODEL CALCULATION

Pension as percent of average net income	Real return (before taxes), percent: 2	4	6	7
80	26	14	7	5
70	23	12	6	4
60	20	10	5	4
50	16	9	4	3

Necessary savings ratio

Monthly savings rate average household -200 DM

Assumptions: starting age 25 years
pensions indexed to net wage

* *We are grateful to Dr. Albert Geiger for this insert as well as for his help in preparing for this "strategic conversation".*

3. For detailed analysis, see "Social systems, markets and democracy: the Networked Markets Study Group's Barcelona meeting" PROMETHEE Perspective n° 26-27, November 1995 as well as *Europe 2012, globalisation et cohésion sociale: les scénarios luxembourgeois*, Albert Bressand, Bruce Scott, Manuel Baldauff, Léon Helbach, Gérard Hoffmann, Thierry Wolter, Paris, Economica, 1997, chap. 3, 7 and 12.

Risk aversion is embedded in national standards and in reward systems rather than just in individual mind-sets. For the same risk, a German investor receives today 400 basic points less than his or her American counterpart in the U.S. market. The difference between return on equity and return on bonds is higher in the U.S. (around 490 basic points today, or 4,9 percentage points) than in Germany (320 basic points or 3,2 percentage points). In any case, investors stand to win quite dramatically if they invest more in equity, even if they don't reach the much higher return levels of the U.S.

Low return on equities in Germany

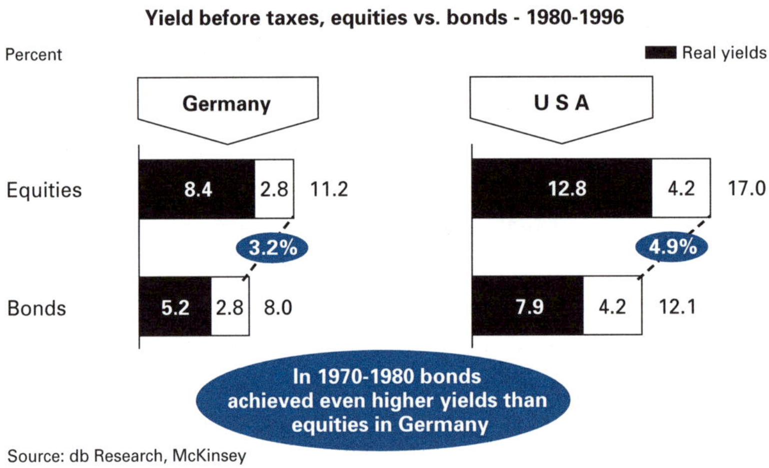

Source: db Research, McKinsey

> European stock exchanges and the euro watershed

You have described how important the financial sector was for economic dynamism and job creation and the positive effects of the euro in this respect. But what is being done to adapt Gruppe Deutsche Börse and the German financial markets to the challenge of the euro? **WS:** We are only one of the components of a financial center. My answer, therefore, should not be narrowly confined to Gruppe Deutsche Börse as one specific institution but should refer to the whole picture. Here again, let me start with a brief description of what we can see in the "big picture", as a framework for this part of our conversation.

The financial center can be described with a three layer model:

• at the center, any financial center needs an infrastructure which may or may not be a stock exchange but which must include a whole gamut of systems and networks for trading, routing, clearing and settlement as well as an appropriated oversight.

• around this infrastructure is a second layer consisting of the market as usually described in its human and financial dimensions, namely:
– a community of professional market participants,
– a set of products which should be as attractive as possible to these professionals.

• then comes a third layer which consists of the economic environment and of the regulatory framework in which market interactions are conducted.

The modernization of the financial center and its adaptation to the euro involve actions in all of these three layers.

It sounds natural enough to begin with the first layer in this three layer model. Could you say what the euro is changing in terms of market infrastructure? **WS:** Not much! Most modern systems are able to handle many currencies, and so, from a pure technological perspective, the euro is not a major operational challenge. You could even say that the euro is almost a "non-issue" in trading, a little less so in settlement.

The infrastructure must be *secure, reliable* and *cheap*. And when one looks at the exchange in its role of provider of infrastructures, achieving this triple objective is the end of the story.

Actually, we have internalized this and we make it clear to our members that we do understand that they are purchasing a service from us which is indispensable to them, which must be completely safe and secure, and which they could procure from several competing sources if we failed to meet their very high expectations.

If the infrastructure for the market is becoming almost a utility, as you suggest, does that mean that all European exchanges will coalesce around one single infrastructure, one single European market "pipe"? What is the link between technology and consolidation of stock exchanges? **WS:** In Europe as a whole, only London can claim to be a financial center of time-zone proportions and then there are two emerging centers sharing the same

Five factors for success of a top-notch financial center

Profile of Germany as a financial center

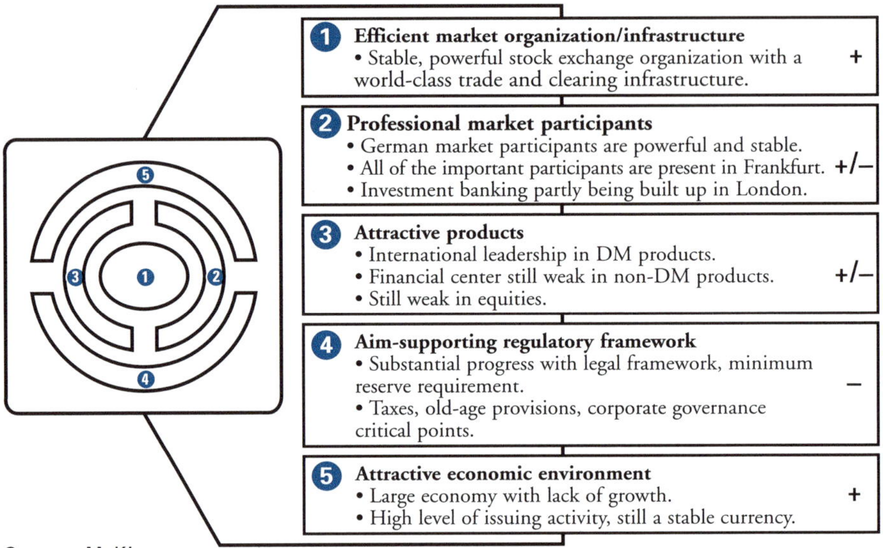

Source: McKinsey

ambition to be the second financial center in the European time zone – Frankfurt and Paris.

London is ahead in terms of internationalisation but there are major opportunities on which Frankfurt can capitalize. So infrastructure remains a competitive tool for these exchanges as they compete for the cross-border business.

The competitive threshold between exchanges is being raised rather than lowered by the technical sophistication and the price tag of the new generation of infrastructures. Few can afford the investment for a real-time settlement system for instance.

What will the impact of the euro be on financial institutions in Germany and Europe? **WS:** Most people would agree that Europe is overbanked in every sense of the term. Europe is also "overinsured" and it is home to a much greater number of financial markets than the post Bretton Woods world would probably call for.

Hence, it is clear that Europe is already embarking toward a big consolidation process, a process in which German and Swiss banks and insurance companies are very well positioned. In that respect, what has just happened in Bavaria (the merger of Bayerische Vereinsbank and Bayerische

Hypotheken und Wechselbank) or between Crédit Suisse and Winterthur as well as UBS and Swiss Banking Corporation must be seen as only a beginning...

Let's look at it from the perspective of corporate clients. With the coming of the euro, the demand of such corporate clients for cross-border consolidation among financial institutions will be very strong. Not many banks or many insurance companies will be able to play in the top league, although it would seem that quite a large number of them will be German or Swiss…

In assessing the impact of the euro on the banking and financial sector, one should bear in mind that it is rapidly becoming a two-tier financial community in which fifteen or so very large banks stand apart from all others. The euro is beneficial for both groups. But while the institutions in the top league are able to approach the transition to the euro with "strategies of strength", the others are more likely to approach it in terms of niches. Sectoral and industrial niches will be important. The questions asked will be "where should I specialize?" and "for whom should I specialize?".

Will the big players in your "top league" be strong enough to dis-intermediate organisations like Deutsche Börse AG? In other words, will the consolidation process triggered by the euro take place within the present market structure, or will it also pit exchanges against some of their largest members?

WS: Well, it is a pleasure to acknowledge that a number of these big players have settlement systems that are as good as ours and that they have routing systems that are probably better than ours as they have built these systems to integrate their trading activities across borders. So, let me venture to say that such big players could create and operate a stock exchange of their own if they wanted.

However, we do not see this as a threat because exchanges are not used simply for their technical capacities: *liquidity* is the real driver. As long as we can provide the liquidity for blue-chip companies, we are unlikely to be dis-intermediated. For instance, it is clear that Deutsche Börse Clearing AG, our settlement organization, is able to achieve higher economies of scale regarding settlement than any European bank using the most advanced systems.

What about the competition beginning to take shape between the various financial centers in Europe? Which of them will be

the hubs for products of the euro age? WS: In all segments of the markets, participants have begun to gear up for the euro. One way to describe this competition is to talk about the search for "benchmarks" namely of products that will be a central reference in light of the volumes, growth rates, global distribution and also of the efficiency of the market as measured for instance by the spread between bids and offers to which their trading gives rise.

Regarding government bonds, it is quite unthinkable that the unified market in euro would work around several benchmarks. Looking at present figures and notably at the spreads on government bonds, it seems that Germany has a head start to provide the market with this "government debt-benchmark".

DM bonds will enter the competition as benchmark bonds

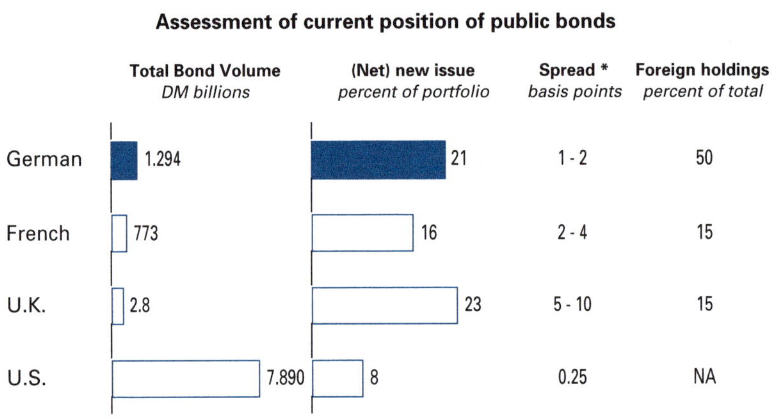

** Survey of large German banks for liquid issues*
Source: Bundesbank, Bank of England, Banque de France, US Treasury Bulletin

Volume and spreads, as well as other market elements such as issuing methods, regulatory framework for central bank actions and standing of the issuer have to be considered. The French government, very early on, has been making major efforts to improve the competitiveness of the French bond market. Standardization of the issued bonds, supply of the whole range of maturities and the possibility of bond stripping are some of the initiatives they have taken. The Bundesbank and the German government are now reacting and catching up, but there is still a time lag. In this spirit, the German government decided to redenominate its outstanding debt in euros as of January 1, 1999.

This being said, Government bonds as a whole will play a less important role than other financial instruments in the capital markets of the euro era. This is largely due to the reduction in deficits and to the limits on government debt embodied in the Maastricht criteria and in the Stability and Growth Pact. It is also due to the growing importance of equities for reasons that have to do with privatisation, globalization and cultural changes. This means again that the euro will foster *an equity culture in Europe*, thereby leading to more intense competition between European equity exchanges.

Altogether, what will be the essential impact of the euro, for you, in terms not just of markets but of the type of economy and society around us? **WS:** For me, the euro will be a tremendous step toward freer capital markets in which resources are allocated not on the basis of administrative guidance or of old habits but of real-life opportunities. Talking about returns and about the impact of the euro on yields and resources allocation is *not* a technical observation, on the contrary. What I mean is that the euro will present our European democracies with a tremendous opportunity to use our resources more effectively for the good of society at a time when this will be most needed. ■

Chapter III

The strategic issues *behind the conversation*

A stimulating insight from the conversation with Jörg Fischer is that Europe can learn from the approach first designed when the Swiss Confederation still had seven different regional stock exchanges. Indeed, the Swiss experience offers previews of the capital markets of the euro era, in Europe and beyond.
It illustrates a momentum for deeper and deeper integration extending to an "out-out" country, out not just of the euro - like Sweden or the U.K. - but of the EU and of its associate EEA.
It also illustrates the role of technology in bringing about radically different types of strategic interconnections and market structures, across and above political borders. Technology can foster straightforward mergers, as between the Swiss and German derivatives markets in the newly created Eurex. It can also lead to using the same screen as a gateway into different markets like MATIF and Eurex. And it can support the "international exchange" that Jörg Fischer sees as the exchange of the future.
Strategic issues addressed here have to do with market structures, with the pace at which they can evolve and with the complementary roles of technology, law and patient execution...

A.B.

conversation with

Jörg Fischer,

SWX Swiss Exchange, Eurex

This conversation with Jörg Fischer, President of the SWX Swiss Exchange, President of Eurex and Chairman of the Executive Board of Bank J. Vontobel & Company, was conducted in Zurich by Albert Bressand (PROMETHEE) and Ivan Wagner (Atag Ernst & Young) on two occasions in the fall of 1997.

Close to the euro and close to the world: a swiss perspective on the global networks of exchanges of the future

A special reason we have to thank you for the time you are contributing to this project is the screen quietly blipping on your desk right now, or rather the information about markets that it is conveying: Wall Street has just registered its largest ever fall. We are not sure whether it is right to engage you in a conversation, even a "strategic conversation", about the years 1999, 2002 and beyond when immediate developments in the market are so intense! **Jörg Fischer:** This moment is special indeed but what happens in the markets today is not foreign to one central theme of our conversation, I mean electronic trading and how it can contribute to making markets more efficient.

On days like this, traders have precious little time to take the right decision and to do so in an informed manner. Actually, "circuit breakers" have interrupted trading on the New York Stock Exchange twice over the last twenty four hours. This is a procedure designed after the crash of 1987 to give traders a chance to collect their thoughts, call clients and inform themselves as fully as possible about the factors behind the selling frenzy! Now, for many years, my personal opinion has been that electronic trading gives traders a superior environment in which to gather the relevant information, consult with in house analysts and to take the decisions they need to take at the speed called for by today's markets...

Actually, the Swiss Exchange did not wait for the market crash of 1987 to embrace electronic trading! So, before we ask you about implications for the continent-wide market in euro, could you tell us how the Swiss Exchange was led into adopting electronic trading in the first place? **JF:** This is a story that began two decades ago. In those days, we had seven markets in Switzerland (Zurich, Geneva, Basle, St. Gallen, Bern, Lausanne and Neuchâtel). These seven exchanges were redundant. On top of that, the members were basically the same. Trading places were many, innovation was scarce: taken together, these seven markets did not offer one single derivative product and they had generally quite poor know-how in technology and in organizing an efficient state-of-the-art market.

Not everybody was unhappy about the slow pace of change: Americans sometimes refer to that happy period in banking and finance as the "three times three" era by which they mean "borrow at 3%, lend 3% points above, and be on the golf course at 3:00 PM!" In the seven Swiss exchanges of the time we could speak of the "ten to twelve" market: be on the floor around ten or ten thirty, expedite your business and leave the floor at twelve...

Something must have happened for people like yourself to succeed in challenging this comfortable, cosy world. What were the key events that took Switzerland from the "10 to 12.00 am market" of the early 1980s toward the present world of full computerisation, global networking and Eurex?
JF: To put it in a nutshell, the driving factor was *technology*, and the catalyst were *derivatives.*

The information systems we had in the 1980s were not particularly sophisticated and this had translated into a growing concern, quite perceptible in the early 1980s, about the tools that would be needed to make Swiss markets more efficient. Working actively in the eurobond markets as they did, Swiss banks were becoming more skilful, faster and more tuned to global competition. They were therefore looking for technology and, more precisely, for the higher and higher levels of efficiency it can bring.

This is where derivatives entered the picture as they could not be accommodated within the *status quo* or simply by acquiring a few additional tools.

It was clear, indeed, that we could not replicate the situation we had in bonds and equities in the fields of derivatives by creating seven derivatives markets! No one could seriously contemplate creating twice as many futures and options markets in tiny Switzerland alone than there were for the whole U.S. market! And yet, none of the seven Swiss financial centers would accept to be left out.

In other words, we had to find a way to trade derivatives in which all members of the Swiss financial community could take part, without having to locate trading in one of the centers at the expense of the others. So, in 1985, the decision was taken to create one delocalized derivatives market that would spare us the agony of deciding which of the seven centers would be the location of this new and important activity. This is how *electronic* trading entered the picture.

Having made the decision to connect the different financial centers in Switzerland, we launched SOFFEX, the Swiss Options and Financial Futures Exchange. Not only did we cut the Gordian knot of competition among the Swiss cantons, but we ended up on what this book calls "the global integration frontier" with the first electronic derivatives market in the world.

And it worked. It was successful to the point that no none really liked it because this very attractive alternative was beginning to appear as an across-the-board challenge to the traditional way of running a market.

You are now bringing the whole cash market to an electronic platform. This suggests that the signals first sent by SOFFEX in the derivatives markets have created a momentum that now extends to financial centers as a whole. Do you feel that this Swiss approach holds lessons for the markets of Europe at a time when the euro pushes toward radical rethinking?

JF: Exactly. The success of SOFFEX supported the recognition that there exists a genuine *electronic* alternative to the strongly segmented *open outcry* trading. However, even before SOFFEX began trading, we had developed such a plan for products other than derivatives.

In proceeding along that road, we recognized that the reorganization of the existing cash market would be much more difficult than the launching of a new derivatives market. This assessment proved right: on the route to *electronic trade* and *electronic market operations*, major difficulties have to be overcome. Not just regarding the development of the technical platforms but also with respect to the design of a new organisation for the stock exchange as a whole. Indeed, this even implied a new market within a new *regulatory* and *legislative* framework!

This is how we created the Swiss Exchange, which emerged from the merger of the Geneva, Basle and Zurich cash markets with SOFFEX. The remaining regional cash markets ceased operations in 1991. After over ten years of implementation, we could see that our initial idea had really caught on: between December 1995 and August 1996, gradually, equities, bonds and warrants switched to electronic trade.

1997 was the first full year of electronic trading in all these markets together. *Efficiency* of the market is clearly on the rise: we can see, for instance, that the spread between the buying and selling prices in the equity market has been reduced by about a quarter, down to 0.15%. Meanwhile, *liquidity* developed more than proportionally than it did in other international financial centers.

Technically, the central system behind the stock exchange had an availability record of 100%. More importantly the *high acceptance* of the Swiss Exchange by traders was shown in the fact that 90% of transactions and 70% of the volume were carried out on the stock exchange itself. The attractiveness of the Swiss Exchange for issuers is also shown in the increasing number of *new listings*: since 1995 we have had twenty successful domestic and foreign Initial Public Offerings.

Our conversation is not about advertising this organisation, but even if we limit our discussion to "the global integration frontier", I think it can be said that the Swiss Exchange is at the cutting edge of technology worldwide, in terms of the degree of integration that we have achieved between all compartments of the market on the same platform. From this strong position, we are looking at new opportunities to actively take part in the structural changes now about to reshape the financial markets of continental Europe. After all, the Swiss Exchange is the third largest stock exchange in Europe and the seventh largest in the world, and the changes we have discussed make us feel quite confident about the future.

Technology is a very powerful driving force as electronic *infrastructures* become "global information highways". But regulations and contractual rules - what PROMETHEE calls

"infostructures" - as well as the culture characteristic of a given market also have a strong influence over the process of dis-intermediation and re-intermediation that develops around electronic networks. How did these legal and cultural factors affect the developments that you had described as being mostly "technology led"? **JF:** I always thought that modern communication technology would produce major improvements, which in turn would change fundamental aspects of market operations. Nevertheless, you are right: when we presented our first ideas, it was really too early. People had not really broken away from the national monopoly culture and, in our case here, from the protected regional markets.

But at that time we were in the lucky situation of operating within a liberal legal framework. Actually, in early 1990, we did not even have a national law in Switzerland. So, at the same time as we worked on the introduction of electronic trading, a completely new *legal and regulatory environment* was created. While other countries tend to find themselves with too many laws and rules and are then led to deregulate their financial markets, Switzerland was in the opposite situation of having to *introduce* regulation and legislation, which it did step-by-step.

If you combine these twin trends of deregulation and new legislation, you can see that over the last years, we have seen a tremendous re-regulation of financial markets, all over the world, in order to meet the demands of the international investor.

But to bring it to the point, what really made our approach work was a combination of different things:

– First, we were open-minded to *technology* by which I mean that we started from the question of what technology was going to make possible rather than trying to fit technology in a procrustean bed of inherited habits, products and procedures.

– Second, we profited from a *regulatory environment* that didn't block our moves and from close collaboration and support of all parties involved in such a complex project.

– And, last but not least, we have been very *business-minded* when looking for new ways of trading and clearing in Switzerland.

These are the ingredients behind the success story in establishing electronic trading and clearing in, both, the derivatives and cash market. As you suggested, these ingredients are not limited to technology itself but also include regulation and market culture as well as a lot of attention to the practical details. Indeed, important as technology can be, anyone working on this type of projects quickly realizes that *execution* is ninety percent of the challenge and *technology* only ten percent!

Your said that electronic networks open up new opportunities for the Swiss Exchange. The process you have described does not strike as being "European" by nature. So what happened between the creation of SOFFEX for the Swiss derivatives markets of the 1980s and the present co-operation taking shape with Frankfurt and Paris? **JF:** A key factor was that our SOFFEX system drew the attention of the German financial community as they faced a very similar situation of having many redundant exchanges and no derivatives market at all. This is how Rolf-E. Breuer decided to license SOFFEX for what was at the time the Frankfurt stock exchange. In 1990, the Deutsche Termin Börse took up its operations.

It became obvious very early that the type of integration that had led to a central electronic market for cash products and derivatives under the roof of the Swiss Exchange needed not stop at national borders. Already we could see that the same concept, the same type of network-driven integration could be replicated in Germany, and there was no reason why these processes of integration could not converge as well as extend to other financial centers. It was clear that the tools which had now become common to the Frankfurt market and to ourselves could also develop as a European platform.

The business concept has been clear for many years even though, at first, we were not really able to convince our German colleagues of the merits of moving from simply *using* similar platforms to the much more ambitious stage of *sharing* the same platform. The reason for such reluctance is, of course, that sharing a system creates a "level playing field", as Americans are fond to say, in which the two exchanges are in direct competition.

An electronic platform for trading and clearing opens up new opportunities in the sense that you can connect markets. This is particularly important with regard to the outdated national segmentation that can be found in continental European stock exchanges. In this respect, the electronisation of markets opens a new era of cross-border network connections. This works to the general advantage by improving the efficiency of markets. Eurex is a first important step in this direction.

Can you say more about Eurex and about the driving forces behind this Swiss-German undertaking? **JF:** Eurex expresses co-operation between the Swiss Exchange and the Deutsche Börse and implies the *merger* of the Swiss and German derivatives markets SOFFEX and DTB. This merger will be effective during the second half of 1998. From a Swiss perspective, it is a way to capitalize on our efficient electronic approach to trading, but this time in a borderless manner.

On the Eurex platform, all existing SOFFEX and DTB products will be available for trade. Furthermore there will be a range of new products that we will launch in connection with the introduction of the euro. In addition to supporting trade in this wide range of products, Eurex also has the advantage of combining clearing and settlement on one platform. This enables to carry out margining in a cross-border integrated fashion, thereby allowing market participants to meet their financial reserve obligations *("Margenhinterlagen")* in several countries with the same pool of money. By eliminating overlaps, they are able to reduce the amount of capital needed to meet their obligations.

In describing our objectives, you may have noticed that I used the term "borderless": our objective is not limited to Switzerland and Germany, it is to create *an international exchange* in which all those who want to belong and to contribute will be welcome.

Indeed, our perspective gives weight to the expectations and needs of international market *participants.* Many of today's asset managers are very eager to manage portfolios in a global perspective without having to use a whole set of different, incompatible systems as they combine securities from different markets. Their desire for common systems is made stronger by the fact that market fragmentation implies that they commit capital for clearing purposes in a redundant and therefore costly manner.

How does your co-operation with the French MATIF futures market fit into that vision of an international exchange? And what does this mean for the role of London? **JF:** What you have in mind is an undertaking between Eurex and MATIF in the field of fixed-income products (interest-rate products).

Whereas SOFFEX and DTB are *merging* into Eurex, thereby creating a new market, we are *connecting* the markets of Eurex and MATIF through an electronic interface. A trader will have access to all interest-rate products of both markets through *one* single screen. But formally, behind the screen, there are still *two* markets and *two* exchanges. Hence a big difference between the merger of SOFFEX and DTB and the *network* we are establishing between Eurex and MATIF.

But these differences also shed light on the large opportunities offered by technology when it comes to integrating financial markets: technology does not impose solutions, on the contrary, there are different types of integration and co-operation that it makes possible and this is a matter for strategic decisions. Technology is the basis for tailor made decision, it allows co-operation *and* integration.

Within the next few months, we will establish a close collaboration between the largest continental European derivatives exchanges. By unifying our forces we are creating an efficient market that knows no borders. By this we serve the needs of our clients, market participants as well as investors. Together with our French partners, right before the introduction of the euro, we are laying the foundation for *a genuine European-wide market for interest-rate products.*

By combining the strengths of previously separated markets, we are promoting stronger competition. *London* will continue to play an important role in Europe, but with our approach (an electronic trading and a fully integrated clearing network), we offer a very attractive *alternative* for the international investor.

Events have moved very fast. To the point that Switzerland, which is not a member of the European Union finds itself very close to the center of a continental "networked market", to use the PROMETHEE phrase, and is getting ready to quote and trade in euro on the same day as France and Germany. Has speed become a national characteristic of the Swiss people? Is Switzerland giving up its borders to integrate in a larger Europe? **JF:** As you know, competition means more and more *competing in time.* The euro does inject an element of urgency into anything related to capital markets in Europe.

Monday, January 4, 1999 will be the day when the system has to handle trades, those who will not be ready on time will loose everything and be out of the market altogether. Actually, this kind of deadline does concentrate the mind. One has to reach decisions quickly.

Switzerland is not a member of the European Union but, as far as supra-national stock markets are concerned, this does not really matter. Being an *"out-out-country"*, which is out of the euro and does not belong in the EU, she will nevertheless participate in the developments to come. Markets are flexible, and they move where the overall framework is best. Present technology puts us in the position to overcome political or regulatory obstacles. The task of an exchange is to operate an *efficient* and hence *international market.*

The time of national markets in continental Europe has gone.

The question of *where* an exchange is located is not really important any more. More relevant is the question of how the supervision is organized. In this respect, it is obvious that Europe's national regulatory authorities face huge challenges.

Toward which sort of regulatory structure do you see Europe evolving? Do we need a "European SEC"? As an "out-out" country, to use your word, is Switzerland enjoying and granting to other the benefits and freedoms created by the Investment Services Directive? **JF:** Authorities will have to work together. I do not believe this will evolve toward one single exchange governed from Brussels but regulators are now able to discharge their responsibilities with the benefit of networks. It can be the case that choosing a *lead regulator* for various types of situations that can arise will make this networking easier and more efficient.

Networking is not at all about avoiding regulations, on the contrary, regulations are essential. The challenge is about achieving the benefits of good regulations in a global market *without* a global regulator. Networking is an important part of the answer.

As for the benefits and reciprocity of cross-exchange membership, we are a member of the German DTB, here, out of Zurich. Meanwhile, SOFFEX has German members and the Swiss law was drafted with the Investment Services Directive in mind. So, you see, the network has changed many things already!

Are risks increasing as a result of market globalization? And how important are systemic risks considerations in your strategy? **JF:** One benefit of Eurex that we try to point to regulators is the reduction in systemic risk that comes with real-time technology and with cross-border consolidation.

We recognise that it is very complicated to interconnect many different systems! From that perspective also, the future, as we see here, is *one system.*

In practice, however, one can only move step by step. Everybody needs to be given the time to understand new concepts.

Derivatives markets are at the forefront, in part because they are less politically sensitive than equity markets. Another difference between cash and derivatives markets is, precisely, the type of *risks* involved. In derivatives markets, clearing and settlement revolve around margining, with substantial risks to take into account. Sharing the same system is then a great benefit for *better risk management.* In the equity markets, by contrast, risk is more limited and real-time technology allows to eliminate a large part of it.

How comes, then, that *derivatives* markets and *cash* markets are coming closer and closer together in developing their international strategies when derivatives markets are more open to global forces and could probably proceed much faster?
JF: Cash markets are also subject to strong pressures for cross-border integration, but this comes more from the *trading* side, rather than from the risk-management side that I mentioned in the case of clearing and settlement. Traders want to manage their positions from one single "log-in". All these forces are converging, even though, in practice, one still needs to move step by step.

What is the demand from participants that you anticipate in connection with the euro? And how are you preparing to meet that demand? **JF:** With respect to the introduction of the euro, it is obvious that the Swiss Exchange has to be ready to match the demands of the market. We will be ready to trade derivatives and cash products in euros from the beginning. But when to switch from Swiss Francs to euros for a specific security will be decided by the market.

Do you think the strategic networking under Eurex can extend to the whole of Europe, including London, or is it the basis of a continental market that will develop as the key competitor to London? **JF:** I think that London will always have the critical mass of skills in asset management, investment banking, legal and accounting services and many of the complex set of inter-related services that it takes to form a fully-fledged financial center. Hence, London does not need an elaborate strategy of alliances to survive and develop.

On the continent, by contrast, most of the exchanges still lack the critical mass to be a natural hub for finance in euro. One might even say that no exchange could be certain to survive the type of intense competition that is likely to develop once the monetary barriers are removed. Investors will begin to think in terms of "sectoral allocation" among assets rather than in terms of allocation among countries and this will be quite a shockwave for many!

This is what attracted me to the concept of a trading network. A *trading network,* as I saw it, would be structured around remote trading as the avenue to gathering critical mass.

Does this mean that you see a bipolar financial Europe around London on one side and one continental financial center on the other side, Switzerland being an important part of the second center? What sort of market structure do you see developing in the securities market in Europe after the euro? **JF:** The euro will move our markets away from the national structure of the past, that was built on the co-existence of national monopolies, toward a fully open "European time zone". But it would be probably an oversimplification to see market structure simply in terms of competition between London and the continent.

Competition takes place *between different types of intermediation.* In this respect, I find it useful to look at the American capital markets for insights about this more complex form of competition at work in today's capital markets.

In the U.S, they have two major competing structures: the New-York Stock Exchange based on *open outcry* and the role of "specialists", and the NASDAQ structure built on *market makers* and a *quote driven trading system* that operate at the level of the U.S. as a whole.

A first lesson is that there is room for *several* types of intermediation to co-exist and to compete. A second lesson is that such a competition is a great source of strength and dynamism for the market as a whole.

A key variable is *speed of adaptation.* Markets are fast, capital markets move extremely rapidly and the last thing we need in Europe is a structure in which regulation and innovation would be hostage to intergovernmental politics and to committees and commissions of all types!

Being a fast-moving organisation was an essential asset on which we were able to create completely new structures for the Swiss financial market. Other continental European countries go in their own way in the same direction. The structure of the European market of the future is likely to be more complex than the American one – but it will still be much simpler than today.

On the eve of the creation of the euro, and as this "simpler" yet complex structure begins to take shape, what is the message that you would draw from your experience in Swiss capital markets for the European financial community as a whole? **JF:** We have talked about technology, about market integration, about step by step alliances, and you are now asking me, if I understand you well, for my "vision"! Actually, as we discussed already, my lesson could be a minimalist one, namely that the vision is only ten percent of the problem and that implementing one's vision is the challenge that will really call for one's energy and commitment.

Here in Switzerland, we have been able to use *technology* to change the market structure in a quite radical manner. In so doing, we have seen that the law also needed to be adapted. Putting in place *one* law for the whole country, rather than one for each of its financial centers, has clearly been a major strategic move which is not so easily replicated at the European level. But there are many other ways in which one can detect the importance of *good regulation* and *appropriate laws* in reshaping markets, together with technology. A *network of cooperation among regulators* is just as important as electronic networks for traders in the good working of markets across borders.

Globalization will keep breaking new grounds, but a stock exchange will always have to think of its members, of investors and of issuers. What are the economic needs of these members, investors and issuers? And how can we organise the services that they will need in a secured, state-of-the-art technological environment? What can be the role of networks of cooperation among stock exchanges that have the potential to develop way beyond the Europe of the euro?

With these questions in mind, one can see that more *revolutions* are coming. But, again, *execution* will be the key. Moving *toward* the goal, such will be the challenge in the future. This is what it has been during these many years that have revolutionized the structure of Swiss capital markets and positioned us on the frontier of technology. ■

Chapter IV

The strategic issues *behind the conversation*

Differences between equity markets and bond markets are the first that come to mind when trying to map the impact of the euro. But looking at these dynamics from the perspective of Amsterdam Exchanges allows to identify more subtle patterns.

Financial centers need to "walk on their two feet": cash and derivatives markets. Money markets and derivatives are where the unifying impact of the euro will be most spectacular. But innovation, research, centers of excellence, "critical mass" and liquidity interact in diverse ways. The euro will bring new types of issuers and investors to the markets. Pension funds and high growth companies will play a greater role...

Strategic issues addressed here have to do with the combination between these various forces, with the links between euro and global momentum, with benefits and limits of technology, all as assessed with the rich and global experience of the city where the term "bourse" was first coined. ***A.B.***

conversation with

GEORGE MÖLLER,

AMSTERDAM EXCHANGES

This conversation with George Möller, Chairman and President of Amsterdam Exchanges, was conducted in Amsterdam by Albert Bressand and Catherine Distler (PROMETHEE) and Hans de Haan (Moret Ernst & Young).

The "European big board" of the euro era and its implications for the Amsterdam Financial Center

Financial markets will consolidate now that the national borders will no longer protect the 45 domestic exchanges and the 16 future markets in Europe. How is this viewed from Amsterdam? What do you think are the changes that the euro will introduce in European capital markets? **George Möller:** Although we are proud that the Netherlands has hosted recent key landmark European meetings in places like Maastricht or Amsterdam, we should remember that European integration did not begin with the treaties bearing these Dutch names and with the creation of the euro. The common currency is the latest development in a much longer process in which we have already seen major developments such as the 1968 common market for goods, its extension to many services – notably financial services – as part of "Europe 1992" and the 1996 Investment Services Directive (ISD).

The impact of the euro will be felt most vividly in the capital markets, mainly on the *money market* and *bond market* where it will remove one type of barrier that had remained untouched in the European integration process until now, namely the barriers stemming from the existence of different national currencies.

As a result, we will be very close to having one common bond market. Fixed income instruments (government and non government bonds) will only differ in terms of *credit risk* as is the case within one national market today.

What is true of bonds however is not true of stocks because we already have the Investment Services Directive (ISD). Equity markets will continue to come closer together but equities themselves will still have a bit of national flavour, even if less pronounced.

Does that mean that equities and equities trading will retain enough national flavour for stock exchanges to be sheltered from the concentration process? **GM:** In addition to the differences I briefly mentioned, one should bear in mind the synergies between these different compartments of capital markets. The impact of the euro on one given exchange can be indirect as well as direct and the future of a given exchange will depend on more complex interactions, spill over and dynamics that mere consideration of how "national" a given set of instruments is likely to remain.

Today, *money markets* and *derivatives markets on fixed income products* are where the battle is being fought. Liffe, DTB, MATIF can now take for granted that they will soon end up trading the same products as their clients turn to them to hedge or take positions along the same "yield curve" in the same currency. German and French government debts are going to be almost interchangeable and liquidity will tend to concentrate in one market.

The people at MATIF understood very early on that the time for go-it-alone future contracts on strategies in fixed income derivatives market had passed and that they had to make up their mind and choose. And they chose to increase co-operation with their German and Swiss counterparts. This need for close co-operation or even for merger in this segment of the derivatives markets was the strong, inescapable reason we now have Eurex, a company bringing together the Swiss and German exchanges and, soon, the French one, a subject that Jörg Fischer addresses at greater length in this same volume.

But synergies are not simply to be sought across country lines; they also reflect growing interdependence between the various markets at national level.

A financial center needs to "walk on its two feet" and to develop both the *cash* and *derivatives markets*. We cannot afford fights or even sour relations between these two markets within a given financial center, because clients use both in the same trade. So we need to bring them together within *the same legal entity*, as we have done here by creating Amsterdam Exchanges.

In other words, you are saying that while exchanges can still prosper at the national level, thanks to the equity business, they cannot hope to retain that equity business if they do not manage, somehow, to also retain significant derivatives business? **GM:** In general, market organisations have been under strong pressure to get their act together in Switzerland, in Germany, in Belgium and in France just like here in the Netherlands. In all these countries, one has seen cash markets (the traditional "stock exchange" best known by the general public) and derivatives markets brought together under one roof.

This trend toward convergence between the two types of markets is very pronounced in the pre-euro Europe. You could see it at work in Germany where Deutsche Terminbörse (DTB), the German futures market merged with the Frankfurt Stock Exchange to become Deutsche Börse. You could see it also in France very recently when SBF Bourse de Paris raised its stake in MATIF, the fixed income derivatives market, from 30% to 100%, thereby creating one single entity.

You have mentioned the difference between what happens in London and the continental trend toward integration of cash and derivative markets. How do you see competition shaping for a long time between London and the continent? How many financial centers can co-exist in our common European time zone? **GM:** To give you a complete answer regarding "London and the continent", I feel I should begin with a more general picture of financial geography after the euro, with due attention to the technological side.

If you look at government bonds, then it is clear that these financial products will be completely commoditized. In such markets, what economists call "price discovery" and "price formation" – the processes whereby supply and demand interact in a market to determine prices – already take place in a global perspective, above and beyond the confines of a given exchange. In addition, participants in these markets can settle through the two global networks, Euroclear or Cedel.

In this type of environment, the very notion of "geographic location" is hard to reconcile with the ways markets work. Of course, looking at where the trade is announced, one can always claim that it has taken place in that specific financial center. Yet, trade said to be in London can actually be anywhere. The market still will be in London in the sense that this is where it materialises in the form of dots on a screen or of physical presence of decision makers and intermediaries, but the London Stock exchange cannot have the privilege to own this market. The processes behind the market are not grounded in a given territory, even though at the end they need to materialise in one particular place.

But not everything can be commoditized. London is a center of excellence for important activities like M & As, and this capacity is grounded in processes which take place physically quite largely in the London financial center. The capacities it has built over centuries are hard to copy. This is where the delocalized networks of financial geography combine with clearly localized communities and cities.

The same is true of many other types of activities which cannot be easily replicated or that no one else has had the time yet to copy. Financial innovation tends to happen within a given human community rather than on line. Providing this human melting pot for innovation involves a depth and variety of interactions that are far more likely within a city like London than on even the best electronic net work.

What are the most important types of innovation that could change the face of European or global finance over the next few years? **GM:** Partly as a result of the growing integrations of the European capital market, trade in up-market products tends to be siphoned off to the over-the-counter (OTC) market. Despite this trend, and despite the integration of the various capital markets, it is still too early to conclude that this presents a threat to the existence of the 45 cash exchanges and the 16 futures markets in Europe.

Moreover, such trends as securitisation, unbundling and disintermediation tend to have a positive effect on the development of national stock exchanges. One result of these trends is that more independent research organisations and rating organisations are being established to analyse credit risks and make it possible for more down-market debt titles to become suitable for trading and listing. As a result, provincial and local authorities, hospitals as well as public service corporations will begin to come to the exchange, to list and trade debt instruments, probably in the form of corporate bonds. Also, more and more medium sized businesses will have risk bearing capital (i.e. shares) listed and traded on the exchange. Even young, high growth and relatively high risk enterprises are welcome on most exchanges. In the Netherlands these businesses can apply for a listing on the New Market of Amsterdam Exchanges (NMAX), a unit of the Euro-NM collaboration.

As a result, the exchange will gradually complement the old fashioned financing function of investment companies and venture capital with a product of its own. Of course, this will apply first to mature, market-tested financing products, but the trend seems irreversible.

Turning to those aspects of financial geography, new innovations are not the central issue; what then about the competition between regulated exchanges and "off-exchange" trading? Rather than competition among existing regulated exchanges, is not the key competition among that of private trading systems (PTS)? **GM:** For quite a number of years now, trading of the up-market products has been moving off exchanges. The remaining link is that off-exchange trades must be *reported* to an exchange, and the latter counts it as a part of its turnover as if the trade had taken place on its floor. Besides, the producers of lots of "off-exchange" products, with the "click funds" as a shining example, often use the exchange to hedge their risks.

Are we moving toward one single European money market? **GM:** Regarding money market and markets on government debt, as I said, we have, or we are on the verge of having one single market in Europe.

For equities, things are different and one can see a number of European countries developing their own listing and trading platforms. So what we may see could be the continental equivalent of London's SEAQ International, namely a two-tier architecture in which price discovery is still centred on national exchanges but with a wholesale market developing, at least for large European "blue chip" companies.

Potentially, things can go further and we may see the development of one trading platform, a European Big Board. For middle-sized and small companies however, a listing on their national exchanges will always be favourable, because these companies are less known outside their national borders. Besides, next to a hypothetical European Big Board, there will be niche-markets in Europe. For example, Amsterdam Exchanges, possessing within Europe the exclusive right to trade options and futures on the FTSE

Eurotop 100 index, will be for a long time the centre of trade in these contracts on the FTSE Eurotop 100 index.

What do you think will be the patterns of specialisation among exchanges in the euro era? **GM:** The broad picture is relatively clear, but the fine prints on which each market will depend are still not fully identified.

Regarding the broad picture, one can one look at countries like Canada to see that capital markets organise around three compartments:
– the fixed income products market;
– the large caps market, namely the market for companies with a large capitalization such as those represented in CAC 40 in France or AEX in Amsterdam;
– and the small caps market which has received much attention recently.

In particular, a strong exchange needs a highly developed research capacity, and this is difficult to build from scratch. Suppose, for instance, that the Brussels exchange attempts to develop as the real estate center of Europe. This will be a very difficult undertaking if they cannot rely on a strong community of professionals active in various aspects of the real estate industry and if they cannot position themselves as the center of excellence for research on the companies operating in that sector.

In that perspective, what are the building blocks that you see as most appropriate for the development of the Amsterdam Exchanges after the euro requires this second level of specialisation in a much sharper fashion than in today's protected markets? **GM:** In general terms, the Netherlands is a trading nation, with an ancient trading culture. We have a strong research capacity- although London clearly has major competitive advantages in this respect – and we have the benefit of operating within a very dynamic and open economic environment which creates many opportunities for companies and for financiers.

This is a position on which we can build. Look at electricity and at the whole web of future contracts that needs to be developed. The electric utility industry here is fully deregulated. Yet, this is not enough creating a continent-wide center of excellence without a strong commitment from other European exchanges.

It is important to create and sustain a win-win perspective. Otherwise the initiatives taken by one market tend to be blocked by counter initiatives from other markets.

In the case of the future contracts for electricity that I just mentioned, we need to go for a Europe-wide approach. We need co-operation in that specific industry segment as a prerequisite for successful initiatives in that field.

To what extent has co-operation already begun between Amsterdam Exchanges and other European exchanges in preparation for the brave new world about to take shape around the euro? **GM:** We are already active participants in European networks like EURO NM. This helps us very much in the development of a capital market for high growth and high risk companies.

For the time being, we are not in the Eurex project. We may take part in the future and we are keeping our options open but, anyway, we were under the impression that the French, Germans and Swiss wanted to go ahead and to establish a tripartite foundation before asking other markets for co-operation.

There are areas of co-operation. I cannot think all markets will co-operate and live happily ever after rather that but several co-operation blocks are likely to emerge in Europe.

It is possible, for instance, that the Benelux countries will get together and create one such co-operation platform on the side of the British and Franco-German-Swiss ones.

Together with the U.K., The Netherlands are unique in Europe for the care they have taken to address the pension liability issue through pension funds which greatly reduce the burden on pay-as-you-go pension systems. Where does this come from? **GM:** This could be another reflection of the fact that we have a mentality of savers! People in this country are very concerned about saving for their children and grand-children. This may be because, here in Holland, we have more rainy days than you have in France! Germans also save, but usually within the company which means, so to speak, that, for them, the company is the pension fund.

In any case, the existence of this very active pension fund industry is one of the specific building blocks from which the Dutch capital markets can benefit for their further development and which will help position us for the competition in the capital markets in euro. Like the U.K., being home to a set of very large pension funds is a key asset for the development of this financial center.

Also, this has spillover effects beyond the pension fund industry itself as it contributes greatly to creating a vibrant equity culture.

We can use the fact that we have this large pension fund industry in The Netherlands and the technology needed to leverage our skills globally as the basis of some of the building blocks for a strong positioning of Amsterdam on the financial map of the euro era. This would be all the more important as government deficit should now be kept under tighter control, thereby reducing the business opportunities associated with the issuance and managements of government debt which is still such an important part of continental finance.

The (true) public debt:
What unfunded *pensions* do to Maastricht!

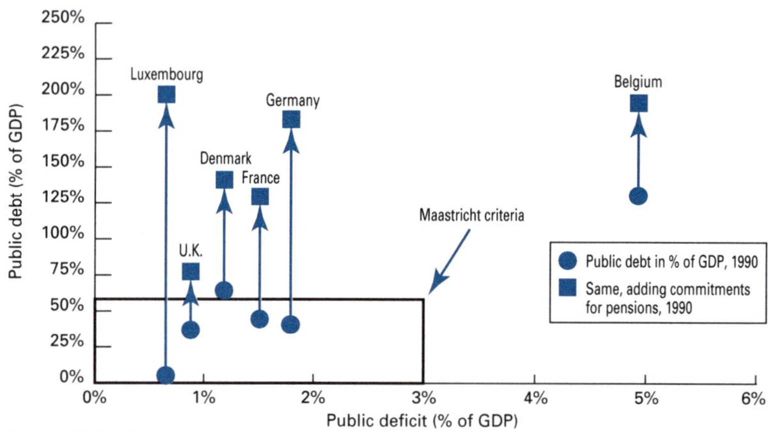

Source: CS First Boston

In this perspective, how do you see Dutch pension funds developing? What are the chances that they can assume a European role? **GM:** I can imagine that Dutch pension funds would be more than happy to leverage their skills across borders and to see their standards more widely adopted!

However, we must keep globalization in its proper historic and geographic perspective.

We can also see a lot of dis-intermediation that is already changing the face of this important industry. The manager of the Philips pension fund, in effect, is becoming, quite simply, "a fund manager".

What such funds develop and bring to market are fund management skills. This can be packaged in different ways by unbundling services that used to go together and by identifying special knowledge and skills to be leveraged through the creation of new companies, new activities and new market niches.

Do you believe that the euro will have strong repercussions not just for Europe but for global financial markets?
GM: The answer is yes. Actually, one reason why I never doubted that the United Kingdom would end up adopting the euro is that we will soon live and operate in a two currency world. In that type of world, a Japanese car manufacturer, for instance, will not be thrilled at the prospect of taking the risk of 15% appreciation in a currency that will be neither the euro nor the dollar. The euro can become an invoicing currency at a level much more comparable to the dollar.

As for the role of a *reserve currency*, there is already a small trend in favour of the Deutsche mark but this is very limited compared to what can be expected in the case of the euro.

A driving factor behind all these developments is that multinational corporations will live in a two currency world, operate in a two currency world and think in terms of a two-currency world. This will trigger a new set of business and financial practices that intermediaries, including stock exchanges, will have in mind in developing their own products and services. In other words, the story will not end with the replacement of the present national currencies by the euro. This will be a beginning rather than an end.

What about relationships with U.S. exchanges? We can see that all the major European exchanges are entering into some sort of transatlantic relationship. Paris with the CME, Zurich and Frankfurt with CBoE, the London Stock Exchange with the CBoT. What are the reasons for these link ups, and what do they add up to? **GM:** We too have developed friendly relations in the U.S., partly as a consequence of the fact that a lot of Dutch corporations (i.e. Shell, Unilever, KLM, Akzo Nobel, Philips) have been listed in the U.S. for a long time. Also, we authorised the AMEX and Comex to trade options and futures on our FTSE Eurotop 100 index in the U.S..

In a sense, across the ocean, everybody has become a good friend of everybody else as these relations do not develop in ways that would tend toward exclusiveness.

It is often a matter of buying technology or trading a few products from one another. On the whole, these sorts of links tend to develop in a very pragmatic, *ad hoc* fashion.

LIFFE, the London futures market and the Chicago Board of Trade (CBoT) did their best to develop a more ambitious relationship in which U.S. products were listed and traded in London and vice versa. But as far as I can tell, this has developed relatively modestly and does not amount to an integrated exchange spanning two time zones.

The only real exception to this general rule of ad hoc relations is the link developed between the Singaporian futures market (Simex) and the Chicago Mercantile Exchange. In that case, one can really see contracts traded in the U.S. and then, later in the day, the same contracts actively traded in Asia. But in all other cases, Trans-Atlantic or Trans-Pacific relations have not developed in such a convincing manner. They boil down to product-by-product or technology-by-technology agreements

A few years ago, one could not read an article or a book about global finance without encountering description of global financial institutions that would soon be "passing the book" seamlessly from one continent to the next in a never ending game of "round the globe, round the world" trading. For these institutions, the sun would never set. What do you see coming in terms of a 24 hour trading day? **GM:** Only government debt may some day be traded in this continuous, seamless fashion. But you have to realize that, today, not even U.S. government debt is traded 24 hours per day!

There are exceptions however to this more sober view on the resilience of the traditional time and space structure that has governed markets in the past. Oil is traded around the clock, and this can lead to the equities of oil companies being traded also around the clock.

This being said, I would not want you to believe that Amsterdam Exchanges are born sceptics regarding the globalization of trading and of exchanges. On the contrary, at the time you were alluding to when "24 hour a day trading" seemed to be just around the corner. We did our best to give global trading a chance. We set up a detailed, ambitious arrangement with two distant exchanges of a size and culture that fitted well with ours, namely the Montreal exchange and the Sidney exchange.

At the time, a dozen years ago, our traders were provided with the tools to pass the book from one time zone to the next, from Europe to the Americas and then across the Pacific. Technically, things worked well, but the demand for these tools was quite modest and, after we had given the idea a good try, we all agreed that the arrangement could be discontinued without putting global finance in general and our members in particular in any type of disarray.

Passing the book around the globe, around the clock may have been a too ambitious image, at least for the near future. What seems to be more successful is for one exchange to place a number of its screens in other places, like Deutsche Börse is now doing with its workstations. This allows traders from other time zones to enter orders that are routed toward the exchange itself before trading begins.

If trading around the clock does not really capture the reality of the present stage in the globalization of markets, what are the more nuanced, more subtle visions that could help us understand what is really going on? **GM:** I agree with you that terms like global or globalization may hide as much as they reveal. Actually, in Europe, we are used to talking about integration in terms of depth as well as of width of the market. Similarly, when looking at financial integration, I feel that we should focus not simply on the widening of the horizon associated with globalization but also on the depth of whatever integration is achieved. A good way to do it is probably to focus on liquidity.

Take the case of a U.S. investor interested in European securities. He or she is likely to want to trade in those securities *at the time* when the market is *the most liquid*, the most alive. Which means that even if people could be awake 24 hours a day, that investor will want to be in the market when it is the most liquid. The priority is to get the best price, to benefit from the full power of an efficient price discovery mechanism, and, in most cases, this is better achieved by being in the market at times of high liquidity than by coming to the market at any time if any time happens to be the low tide of liquidity

Let me add also from the investors perspective, that most companies do not trade. They manage their positions, which is something different. They need a presence in the market.

So, on the one hand, there are forces of globalization which open new possibilities – such as passing the book "Around the globe, around the clock". This is the technically possible. But, on the other hand, there are natural clusters, natural ways for investors to gather at certain points in time, around certain markets.

As our experience with our Canadian and Australian partners should, products tend to stay in certain time zones. True believers in globalization may call it inertia but it has also to do with the search for liquidity, for quality of information and quality of attention, for *best prices*.

Against the background of this more nuanced view of globalization, you are nevertheless also identifying a number of important exceptions. Trading equities of very large companies – Shell, Unilever and the like – as the Amsterdam Exchanges does, you must be keeping an eye on the rise of global blue chips and on the risk that trading could move away from your floor. **GM:** There will be global blue chips, companies known and active all around the world that will be traded anytime from almost anywhere.

The competitive pressure on an exchange like ours should not be assessed – and answered – in terms of volume. What we must follow with great attention is the creation, or further developments of "*centers of excellence*".

It is conceivable for instance that New York could become a center of excellence for oil products and oil related activities so important that investors here, on our side of the Atlantic, would wait for New York to be open before seriously trading in Royal Dutch Shell on our exchange.

Exchanges will do their best to be at the forefront of these developments. As a result, I think that we will see the gradual emergence of something which one might call, by reference to the New York Stock Exchanges Big Board, the *European Big Board.*

In addition to the synergies that you have mentioned earlier between equity and bond markets as well as between cash and derivatives markets, what are the factors that will help a stock exchange or a financial center preserve its role in this global network of networks? **GM:** Well, I would like to conclude by drawing attention to an aspect of financial markets that tend to be underestimated by many observers, although I was impressed to see that it was the subject of the second part of this book. This important aspect is the role of clearing, settlement and custody in the working of capital markets.

This is often seen as merely a back-office issue. Yet if one looks at it from the perspective of financial centers and of the new "financial geography", one needs to go beyond this old distinction between the more glamorous world of trading and the less eye-catching world of clearing, settlement and custody.

If you ask a trader whether he wants to trade in one place or another, he may well tell you that he does not really care. But if you own stocks from many markets and you ask a custodian where to locate, the answer will be far less indifferent to geography...

In that sense, indeed, clearing, settlement and custody is going to be quite critical in shaping the financial architectures of the post euro geography. This is why I would suggest that co-operation in this field is strategically as important as the type of co-operation for trading that is developing around initiatives like Eurex. ■

Chapter V

The strategic issues *behind the conversation*

Gérard Pfauwadel accepted to take part in these conversations at a critical time in MATIF existence as the German futures market gains large market shares in anticipation of the benchmark role of key German financial instruments and as all derivative products based on national currencies are about to disappear.

The full integration of MATIF in the SBF-Bourse de Paris group is discussed in relation with these changes and with broader synergies between cash and derivatives, and between fixed-income and equity markets.

"Open architecture" is a key word to describe the network of alliances developing among derivatives market on the continent. Such alliances shed new light on the decade old debate between "open outcry" and "electronic" markets, a debate that Gérard Pfauwadel approaches in terms of the search for higher liquidity rather than for lower costs.

Derivatives markets are tools to manage risk. But are they not also a source of risk? The discussion concludes with the vision of "a IATA for futures markets" that would preserve the spirit of global competition and yet insure the highest levels of co-operation and harmonization regarding safety and integrity of markets.

A.B.

conversation with

GÉRARD PFAUWADEL,

MATIF SA

This conversation with Gérard Pfauwadel, Chairman & CEO of MATIF SA was conducted by Albert Bressand, Catherine Distler (PROMETHEE) and Patrick Gounelle (Ernst & Young) in Paris.

Beyond country risks: derivatives markets and risk taking in the euro era

The anticipation of the advent of the euro is already a factor of radical change of financial European markets. Will its impact be limited to Europe? **Gérard Pfauwadel:** The euro already has an impact on fixed income markets where we are experiencing a consolidation and a "Europeanization of perspective". But this cannot be separated from what's taking place in the rest of the world.

The euro will not only substitute for *national* currencies, it will also play *global* functions and enter into direct competition with the U.S. dollar at the global level. We are experimenting an acceleration of history and the landscape is going to be very different in just a short period of time.

Is this unique to derivative markets? **GP:** No, I feel we are simply at the forefront, at the "vanguard", as you say in this book.

A first major difference between our markets and equity markets is that a dozen markets will completely disappear, and will do so overnight on December 31, 1998 when the national currencies behind the futures contracts disappear. Add to that the fact that there are 23 European futures exchanges behind the 15 national "yield curves" of today... Then you begin to see that high level competition and bulldozer consolidation are going to be difficult to avoid!

Can you tell us more about financial markets in euros? What will be the role of London in this new landscape?
GP: There are four major financial markets:
– currency markets;
– commodity markets;
– fixed income markets (cash and derivatives);
– equity markets (cash and derivatives).

The *currency* market is already largely in London. What exists on the continent is bound to disappear as it centers on national currencies. Furthermore, there is a non-organised market in currencies which operates as an "over the counter" (OTC) market out of London and a few off-shore places. Hence it will be very difficult for continental centers to repatriate them.

Almost the same applies to *commodity* markets. Petroleum, sugar and the like are clearly centered in London. Only some markets for agricultural products, like wheat notably, are on the continent. MATIF has introduced new contracts for some agricultural products, but their role remains marginal as the European Commission is setting most of the prices in the framework of the Common Agricultural Policy. Oil seed is no longer regulated from Brussels, so it begins to make sense to set up markets that are part of global trading networks. This is, in any case, a very small part of our activity which we take seriously but which we don't hope to develop beyond the role of useful complement to our core business.

So the two markets in which the continent can have a future, including a "future in futures" are: *fixed income products* and *equity products.* In both cases, cash markets and derivatives markets are intimately intertwined as a critical mass in futures and derivatives is necessary to serve the needs of market participants related to the cash products.

But wouldn't you say that equity exchanges will be the more important as the euro eliminates or consolidates so many fixed income products as to render many derivatives markets redundant? **GP:** The situation is not as simple as you seem to suggest to test my reactions! True, for a while, equity markets will keep a more pronounced national character as a result of the absence of European company law, of the language barriers and of what economists call "implicit knowledge" needed to assess and trade the shares of the less well known companies. Yet, even in equities, it is clear that Europe will be moving away from a *country* approach toward a *sectoral* approach. I believe Philippe Collas of Société Générale Asset Management will not contradict me in his "conversation" with you. Let us assume therefore that, after a transition phase, consolidation among exchanges is likely to develop in equities as well as in fixed income products.

Fixed income products will not live a life of their own. On the contrary, they will be critical to the existence of a financial center and to its "staying power" after the introduction of the euro. This is why so many domestic exchanges are merging their cash and derivatives components. The idea may still sound "extraordinary" in London, to quote my friend and counterpart from Liffe, but, in every national financial center on the continent, there is a growing awareness of the strategic necessity to integrate bond, equities and futures markets.

Meanwhile, cross-border links are multiplying. Altogether, the process of integration among markets develops at two levels, within and among financial centers.

Hence the recent strategic move between SBF - Bourse de Paris and MATIF. It is costing SBF - Bourse de Paris 500 million francs to fully integrate MATIF, and this is a high stake game. But SBF realizes that if fixed income products begin to leave a financial center for another one in another place, then the capacity to preserve a strong equity and equity derivatives market is greatly reduced.

What about the timing? Why did not this merger happen earlier? And how does it relate to the integration process that we have discussed with Jean François Théodore, Werner Seiffert and Jörg Fischer? **GP:** Whether this is the "right moment" for this merger, I cannot say. But I am sure that it is the last opportunity! It is also one way to facilitate discussions with the German financial centers. The first agreement between MATIF and DTB took place in 1991 but things did not move as fast as they could have. One of the factors that slowed the process was that Germans had integrated their cash and futures markets while we had not; in that sense, it would have been better for Paris to move two years earlier. But, anyway, now is the time to catch the last train before the euro modifies everything quite radically.

What is special to derivative markets as far as the euro is concerned? **GP:** First, let me say that the real difference is not between "derivatives" and "non-derivatives" ("cash" as we say). The real distinction is between the four families of products that I mentioned: currency products, commodities, fixed income products and equities, each of them with their derivatives.

Fixed income products account for 85% of our activities and the same is true for Liffe in London and for CBOT in Chicago. Let's talk about the impact of euro on those products. There are many different markets accessible to financial firms, but many markets are not institutionalised. The most visible compartments are the institutionalised ones, which explains that attention tends to focus on MATIF, Liffe and DTB rather than on the very large volume of activity also taking place "over the counter" in the other market compartments.

The key factor in this competition is *liquidity*. And liquidity is not something that can be shared among a set of contenders: it is clearly a "winner-take-all" game, so don't be surprised to see the various exchanges fighting hard to win.

How has MATIF fared so far in this tough competition?
GP: We have been losing market share. This has not been as a reflection of inferior quality of products but because of a fundamental trend, the strong convergence between the French franc and the Deutsche mark. Market participants want to position *vis-à-vis* the benchmark, and now the Deutsche mark is the benchmark.

Until 1994, the year when we broke the level of 100 million contracts for the year, the proportion of *international* investors holding the public debt was 40% in Paris and 10% in Germany. Now, as business moves toward the mark, the situation has been reversed and we have international investors account for only 8% of market capitalization here against 45% in Germany.

We are selling tools to protect against volatility. But volatility has been seriously reduced by the monetary policy carried out very successfully by Banque de France. Meanwhile, the underlying market was moving to Franckfurt and international investors were looking at Germany as the natural home for the benchmark in euros. We used to be twice as large as DTB, today we are about the same size.

So this must be a time of radical questioning of the strategy at MATIF? **GP:** It is because so far I have only been giving you the "old" part of the story, the defensive part. But, this is not a time of competition "other things being equal". Other things are *not* staying equal as a major wave of change has already begun to unfold, with the French and German markets at the center. These markets are the moving forces behind finance in the euro, and we have begun to create an integrated Franco-German platform that will give us all a major competitive advantage.

Could you say more about this common platform and the process that led to this agreement? **GP:** There were really three steps in that process:

The first phase was the agreement of 1991 between MATIF and DTB that provided for a migration of MATIF products toward the German electronic trading platform as part of a cross-market trading agreement and of a thorough integration of these two markets. That first phase was brought to a halt by the purchase of DTB by Deutsche Börse AG.

The second phase was the proposal to our German friends made by the whole financial center here to use the French NSC platform for cash markets while we would have used the German one for derivatives. This proposal did not meet the approval of our German counterparts who decided to develop their own technology.

So, in a third stage, we have kept national trading platforms for cash and futures products (in our case the NSC platform) and we have agreed to connect the French and the electronic system now common to Germans and Swiss. We will have mutual access as part of an agreement with Eurex that should be a solid foundation for co-operation even if nothing is irreversible.

You could compare this process to the Airbus story: first came a period when the MATIF "notional" contract was a very successful but purely national product, like the plane named "Caravelle". Then came a period when key manufacturers – key exchanges in our case – need to co-produce rather than to produce separately.

Unlike the more ambitious attempts described in your first two phases, the solution now chosen in order to co-produce with other European exchanges will remain reversible. Is this a satisfactory outcome? **GP:** True, this is a reversible agreement in which each financial center preserves its identity and autonomy. But, on the other hand, one of its strategic interest for us is its *open architecture.* This agreement can be expended to other European financial centers and this can be done very easily.

The technology we use for interlinking, known as GL, can also support links with other electronic platforms. If Eurex succeeds, it will exert a very strong attraction on other *electronic* exchanges, but not on London which intends to remain an *open outcry* exchange.

Also this agreement does not stop at interlinking as we have added two additional elements of integration. This will mean for instance that we will co-operate in the development of euro products.

One one side, you say that the two markets remain separate, on the other you say they are integrated. So what exactly is involved by this interconnection which you call the GL link and what are these "additional elements of integration"? **GP:** For traders, there will be *one single interface* as the GL screen will give them access to all products without even having to know on which of the participating platform that specific product is being traded.

But this connection is not simply a matter of providing some sort of invisible "switchboard" for traders to call whichever exchange they need to use for trading a certain contract. The present agreement involves in depth co-operation and even integration as it combines three mutually reinforcing elements that go beyond the single interface for traders. These three elements are:
– a *technological* integration in the working of our markets;
– a *commercial* agreement to develop a common line of products and to allocate trading of each of these products to only one of the two platforms, thereby creating strong momentum toward common marketing. You can see that logic at work in our case as well as in the development of common equity indices;
– a *financial* agreement to share the revenues from this co-operation in a fair manner.

Turning to the competition with London, what are the assets and liabilities of Paris? **GP:** The assets are many: the quality of people, good regulatory framework, state of the art technology... In the world of services, people are absolutely essential and France is a great place for its quality of education and people. Actually, I can visit quite a few places in the City of London without having to stop speaking French, places where bright young people are using their advanced mathematical skills to put prices on the most exotic options or financial products.

But the quality of individual persons is not enough and if I can meet so many French professionals in London it is probably in part because our tax system tends to forget that, to be distributed and shared, wealth must, first, be produced. People – notably bright and well paid people – are even more mobile than before. Pushing them to expatriate is a source of other job losses too.

If we move beyond specific exchanges to look at the markets in euros, how will rates be set? And, first of all, what will be "the" rate for the money market in euro? **GP:** One difficulty has to do with identifying the rate that can be used in short term contracts to allow money market participants to speak of "the" rate in euros. This involves finding an appropriate reference against which to define future changes in rates. Right now, in France, the French Banking Association (AFB) calls a group of banks everyday to know their rates, it then disregards the extremes and defines the average of the remaining rates as the Paris Interbank Offered Rate (PIBOR). But what will replace the present rates as a common reference for the euro zone as a whole, and who is going to do this work?

In London, they think of course that *their* money market will be the most relevant and that a panel of international banks in London can provide the individual bank rates needed to establish the euro-LIBOR as the central market reference for the euro. On the continent, we tend to be of a different opinion and we are in the process of putting together the procedures necessary to compute and disseminate EURIBOR.

It is quite likely therefore that LIBOR and EURIBOR will coexist. True, they may be very similar. Yet, if one remembers the dollar and the eurodollar, one realises that they can also evolve differently.

But what will happen when these two central references for money markets in euro will differ? **GP:** Oh, in that case, we will be more than happy to develop a contract allowing market participants to deal efficiently with this element of volatility!

And what about long-term rates? **GP:** Here in Paris, we had created a highly successful "notional" contract *(le notionnel)* on the basis of a highly liquid pool of French government bonds (OAT, Obligations Assimilables du Trésor) whose maturities range between 8.5 to 10.5 year. The issue now is which set of "underlying" issues will provide the best foundation for long-term future contracts in euros.

One way to go would be to restrict the underlying to high grade paper from, maybe, only one or two countries (in practice, probably French and German paper). This was the successful strategy we followed with our contract in ECUs.

Are there concrete implications of the present debates on EURIBOR and other references, or is this a theological, "sex of angels" type of question of interest only to statisticians and exchange officials? **GP:** Having a *liquid* secondary market and a *liquid* derivatives market makes it cheaper for governments to issue debt. So the governments of France, Italy or Spain cannot be indifferent to how the future contracts in euro will be built and to the underlying that will be used for its definition.

To be very practical, let me suggest that the difference for the issuer can be on the order of ten basic points. For a country like France, with issues of 300 billion French francs per year, the difference can be on the order of several billion French francs. Is this "sex of angels" money? Taxpayers probably will not think so!

So you are saying that what is at stake is not so much which *market* will be used but rather where *liquidity* will develop. How do you see future competition develop? **GP:** Let us assume we have two big markets in Europe, one in London, one on the continent. Europe will then begin to look a little like Chicago where two large markets coexist to the satisfaction of large firms. If liquidity is satisfactory in these two markets, cost will then be the critical factor in the competition between them.

We launched a five-year contract in euros on September 10, 1997. Liffe, the British futures market, did the same and so did the German DTB the next week. The latter then announced that it would not charge any fee, hoping to position itself as *the* financial center where liquidity in euros would develop. Liffe had to follow suite, and so did we! In the long-term, computer trading is a means to reduce the costs of doing business through one exchange.

Back in 1986 when it was created, MATIF made the choice to be an open outcry market in which real life traders look one another in the eyes and trade in the pit. Since then, electronic price discovery mechanisms have been the preferred choice of all new markets. Would the same choice be as natural today for MATIF? **GP:** Today, if you look not just at Europe but also at the rest of the world including the largest markets in Chicago, you can see that 85% of the business is still carried out on the open outcry mode. But MEFF in Barcelona, DTB in Frankfurt and Soffex in Switzerland have shown that technology now makes it possible to trade on screen as efficiently as in the pit.

We had also begun to follow the same route, as you well know, with the GLOBEX system. But, as André Villeneuve can confirm in his own "strategic conversation" with you, MATIF was, by far, the single largest user of that trading network, and there was not enough activity for Reuters to continue developing this system. We are now confident that the NSC system developed by SBF - Bourse de Paris will provide a powerful, – low cost platform. Its open architecture will be a great asset in the next stage of market globalization – I would say the best of the world if you had not asked that these conversations depart from anything resembling self congratulation! In any case, MATIF is looking forward to being totally integrated in the NSC network in May 1998.

Computers can now provide trading capacity at one-seventh of the cost of open outcry. But this is dependent on achieving liquidity: once you have large order-books, all the good things follows... So we based our decision on the fact that, for a very long time, open outcry has been conducive to superior liquidity, leading therefore to much smaller "spreads" between offer and bid prices. The price charged by brokers and exchanges was small compared to spread. So, everything considered together, open outcry remained the least costly price-discovery mechanism.

When the general public hears about futures markets, it is usually because of some type of hazardous trade that has turned sour, as happened for Barings. Do you feel that you are living dangerously -and making us all live more dangerously?

GP: When I arrived here ten years ago, it was in the wake of the large loss incurred by Cogema and of the 700 million French francs loss of no less than the Chambre Syndicale des Agents de Change. Our activity was seen as a high risk one, or even as so speculative as to be on the border of what is legitimate. A Nobel Prize winner, economist Maurice Allais, spoke strongly at the time against the financial bubble and the esoteric instruments that he saw feeding it. The failure of Barings could be seen as a major illustration of such risks.

The overall perception, however, has changed.

First, unlike stock exchanges, we refrain from anything that would attract *small individual investors.* They are accepted, but certainly not more than that and we have abstained from any publicity or marketing that would encourage them to participate. When they do participate, it is through mutual funds (SICAVs as we call them in France) that are in the hands of professionals.

Second, we have experienced no defaults over the last ten years, in spite of the high-risk nature of this activity. Some professionals may loose money on the MATIF but they are not keen on advertising it... More importantly, risks are monitored and kept in check with the utmost attention. As you know, *margining* is in place in all regulated futures-market to make sure that money is deposited and available in proportion to the losses that develop on any given position. On top of that, being a regulated exchange, we would substitute for the defaulting party and would bear the cost. There is no specific *"fond de garantie"* but our role is to make sure that risks are identified and held in check.

Another change is that today one cannot imagine any financial operation that would not involve "options". Take a commercial paper program. It will be issued by the bank on the market for a given company. Now, even if the company raising that money does not do it directly, the issuing bank will turn to derivatives to hedge the risk that it is assuming.

The risk associated with derivatives remind me of fire: when man first domesticated fire, it was a source of great progress, but also great risks. One should keep it out of the hands of children for example. All inventions – whether fire or derivatives – call for new levels of prudence, new disciplines and also new levels of education if the opportunities have to be harnessed while keeping risks in check! From time to time however, a house will burn, or a Barings will happen. But risks can be limited by collective discipline and oversight that are compatible with higher levels of competition. The difference is that it has taken twenty years to go through that learning (ten years in France) in derivatives markets rather than 4000 years for fire.

Have you changed your approach to market oversight since the Barings collapse? You have been reported to have asked for the creation of "a IATA for derivative markets". What is the link between futures markets and airlines? **GP:** Actually, we have not changed our way of doing because we have always followed large risks very closely. I never hesitated to consult other markets when I thought some major risk might be present but, previously, there were "lois de blocage" that could be invoked in several countries to block such exchanges of information. The difference now is that I feel in complete agreement with what regulators expect from us when I engage my counterparts in the exchange of information that I think is warranted by the size and nature of risk...

There were two real big problems behind Barings.

First, one trader had a big part of the market. Obviously, they were a lack of appropriate control *inside* Barings itself and the acquisition of that old British bank by ING has been the market response to that internal failure.

The second problem was of a systemic rather than individual nature as two exchanges, Osaka and Singapore, were fighting for liquidity in the same Nikkei 225 contract, a product critical commercially even for Singapore which has no domestic contract of the same importance. This intense competition led each exchange to reduce its apparent costs by requiring only small deposits from market participants: margining was down to 1% instead of the 10% and 9% levels with which the Singapore and Osaka exchanges had started before competition heated up between them! Such a trend can erode the very basis of safety in futures trading.

My conclusion is that competition must be about liquidity, about products, about technology but *not* about the reduction of the costs associated with keeping the market safe. To me, this is analogous to what you see in the airline industry: as passengers, we want airlines to compete fiercely to provide the best service at the best price but certainly not by flying poorly maintained planes! This is why, indeed, I invited my counterparts in one of our annual get together to develop a sort of IATA for derivatives markets.

So, altogether, what would you say about derivatives to people worried about the financial bubble and what they see as its negative impact on employment? And what will the euro change in this respect? **GP:** What matters is the spirit and the process of co-operation between markets to manage risks efficiently. In that sense, I feel the derivatives community – traders, exchanges and regulators – has done a good job. I believe that risk taking is at the heart of wealth creation, and I know that this industry will provide some of the essential tools needed for people working in our countries to take risk, to create wealth and to create jobs.

Schumpeter talked about "creative destruction", and derivatives markets such as MATIF provide some of what PROMETHEE calls "linking machines" that enable professional communities to cooperate in identifying and in controlling the risks that "creative destruction" always entail!

The euro, here at MATIF, has already happened. We have issued contracts in euros for 2002. By eliminating currency risks within the Union, the euro will make some of our products unnecessary, but it will also make our *core expertise* even more central and more relevant to growth and employment creation. So I look forward to the euro and to derivatives products in euros. And, also, to risk taking and risk control in the deeper and wider markets that the euro will bring to life. ■

Part II

European hubs **for** *global finance.*

Chapter VI

The strategic issues *behind the conversation*

Looking at the European capital markets from the EUROCLEAR standpoint implies to look at them as part of global markets. Settling 37 trillion dollars of securities in 30 countries every year and keeping 2.3 trillion dollars under custody, EUROCLEAR is a global hub for world finance.

The conversation with Luc Bomans illustrates the various levels of "quality" that are central to risk management. Beginning with quality of information and continuing toward the PROMETHEE trilogy of "best contact", "best contract" and "best commitment".

As a global hub, EUROCLEAR is involved, first and foremost, in the management of risk. This can be management by elimination – hence the strategic importance of the "best contact" now made possible by real-time settlement. Or this can be through appropriate legal frameworks tuned to the needs of moving the same security through many borders to pledge it as collateral for risk assumed elsewhere in the world (Belgium law and EUROCLEAR rules being geared toward "best contract").

As for "best commitment", EUROCLEAR is one of those commercial entities that also devote energy, talent and resources to understanding and enhancing the overall market framework. In cooperation with the Group of Thirty, it has commissioned major reports on various aspects of system risk and of risk management such as the "pipeline risk" associated with delays in settlement, interconnection of CSDs and cross-border pledging of collaterals. In the Morgan Guaranty Trust tradition, Luc Bomans discusses how capital markets can be made safer for global operations. Clearly, this involves setting new standards, as well as sticking adamantly to those standards that have been set.

A.B.

conversation with

LUC BOMANS,

EUROCLEAR

This strategic conversation with Luc Bomans, Managing Director and General Manager of Euroclear Operations Centre, was conducted by Albert Bressand and Marie-France Boudet (PROMETHEE) in Brussels.

Euroclear in the age of euro clearing: quality of information and risk management

Someone who would be about to create a clearing organization in Europe today would probably call it "euro-clear". How important is the "euro" prefix in "Euroclear"?

Luc Bomans: From the Euroclear System's inception in 1968, when our original aim was to provide risk-controlled delivery-versus-payment securities settlement services for the growing Eurobond market, the relative importance of the "euro" prefix was apparent. The *Euro*clear System was indeed conceived as the primary settlement system for *Euro*bonds.

In the mid-1980s, with the acceleration of cross-border trading in Continental European government bonds, the Euroclear System became the leader in settlement and custody services for these instruments, thereby redefining the importance of the "euro" prefix.

After nearly 30 years of leadership in cross-border securities services, we have built enormous equity in the Euroclear brand. Even though we see ourselves as a European institution offering global services to international clients within and beyond Europe, the prefix remains.

With the advent of the euro, maintaining the "euro" prefix in our name

is a unique opportunity to reinforce our position as the premier hub for cross-border services in the new EMU environment. There will be more and more cross-border flows within and into the euro zone, at least in the private sector, as the Stability Pact will place much higher limits on government deficits and debts. Once the euro is launched, this will probably lead to:
– a decline in the rate of growth in European government debt issues, although the proportion of debt that is held by foreign investors may increase;
– the disappearance of foreign exchange (FX) risk associated with the convergence of interest rates, thereby reducing volatility, and presenting the market with fewer arbitrage opportunities;
– less borrowing by European governments as privatization of state-owned enterprises continues to accelerate. Financing will move to the private sector, which means we will see an increase in both corporate bond and equity issuance activity, and more cross-border trading;
– and a shift in focus from FX risk to credit risk, thereby increasing the emphasis to invest by sector.

In addition, the pivotal role for institutions such as the Euroclear System will be to facilitate European access for investors located outside the euro zone. The inflow of capital is likely to increase, especially if the euro becomes a strong reserve currency. There will be a rebalancing of reserves and an overall rebalancing of portfolios.

So Euroclear can play the role of a magnet toward the euro – if the euro works, but will the euro really work?

LB: The penalties for not being ready for active and rapid use of the euro would be incalculable, so we operate under the assumption that the euro will happen. The euro zone would not be as "strong" if there were only six or seven countries that met all the EMU criteria, as was initially envisioned. It is now quite obvious that the Germans and French are more open to a larger euro zone than had been the case in mid-1997.

The role of Euroclear System is to serve as the hub to, from, and within Europe for international securities settlement and safekeeping activities. We see this function as three sides to the same triangle, namely acting as a gateway for non-European investment into the euro zone, paving the way for European investors to diversify their trading activity by providing access to the rest of the world, and facilitating intra-European cross-border transaction settlement.

Let me elaborate on the second element as it is the less intuitive aspect. It will be the capital flows from the euro zone toward the rest of the world that can be expected to rise in reaction to pension fund management reforms intensifying the "search for yield". The private sector increasingly will be financed by the savings traditionally invested in public debt. The increase in corporate bond and equity issuance will also give rise to more cross-border investment in order to take advantage of the benefits of portfolio diversification. The shift to bond and equity financing by corporate issuers will correspond to increasing demands from privatized retirement schemes for an ageing population, resulting in lower financing costs to those issuers. Furthermore, investors will begin to look at investing against risk on a given sector (e.g. pharmaceuticals, banks, technology) and increasingly will be investing against credit risk rather than currency movements.

It sounds like the euro will mean growth for Euroclear?
LB: Indeed, it does mean growth. The value of transactions to process will be enormous. Already, more than 150 billion U.S. dollars of securities transactions are settled in the Euroclear System everyday. This will greatly increase as a result of the three trends I have just mentioned. But the story does not stop at growth. This is where "quality" comes in, or I should say, where "risk control" comes in because we see them as being the same.

Why do you view the words "risk control" and "quality" as inseparable? **LB:** The financial industry has confronted risks in many ways. To monitor and mitigate risk is a universal challenge. There are mechanical ways to reduce risk, but many forms of risk will never disappear. In fact, the business of finance remains focused on taking and managing risk. Nevertheless, we must explore all ways to reduce risk through better design and better operation of these mechanisms. In other words, through improvements in "quality".

A high quality mechanism to reduce risk is real-time DVP settlement. We are working on a real-time settlement system which will contribute substantially to this phenomena.

Real-time settlement will go a long way towards eventually reducing the time element of risk. Of course, it is the market's usage of real-time settlement which will determine the actual level of reduced risk. The European Monetary Institute (EMI) is also offering guidance in the direction of risk reduction. By promoting the construction and use of the TARGET system for real-time cash transfers, it too will help reduce the duration of exposure to risk and will enable quick settlement of cross-system cash transactions. At the same time, it is promoting collateralization of exposures, something we have long advocated in the Euroclear System. Collateralization reduces associated systemic risk as large intraday exposures are created and then extinguished. More and more market participants will insist upon having their bilateral exposures collateralized so as to bring the risk into a manageable scope. Reputation will no longer suffice to fulfill this function in the future. So, the quality of mechanism achieved through the move to real-time settlement will be complemented by the quality of risk control through appropriate and efficient collateralization of exposures.

Nevertheless, Euroclear went on record in mid-August 1997 to warn of the risks of "serious markets disruptions" because of inadequate harmonization for euro standards. **LB:** As anyone involved in the conversion to the euro can testify, there is no single institution which has been mandated to provide a single set of guidelines for conversion to the single currency. If the transition process is not managed properly, the havoc that could reign in the international capital markets could be substantial. We went on record in August to recommend minimum parameters to the market for the communication of securities redenomination standards. But this is just the tip of the euro-conversion iceberg. We are working with several industry working groups to put forward uniform proposals, but it remains to be seen if these ideas will be accepted across all markets by all the various jurisdictions. The risk to which you refer in your question is specific to general market risk.

So where does risk reside now? In particular, what are the remaining systemic and technical risks? **LB:** Technology allows for the transmission of transactions as the French poetically put it "au fil de l'eau". In doing so, we can reduce a set of technical risks and we can greatly reduce systemic risk. Hence, we see a shift from bulk risk exposure, arising from large batch processes, to a combination of smaller, albeit continuous, systemic and technical risks as settlement and payment systems ultimately run for 24 hours a day.

With real-time settlement of both securities and cash transactions, systemic risk will not be eliminated, but the magnitude and duration of exposure to systemic risk will be substantially reduced. With the constant evolution of technological solutions, we see a gradual shift from systemic to systems risk. Hence, the reliability of the systems themselves becomes increasingly critical. Solid back-up and contingency measures, and ardent software testing, are imperative.

Moreover, with the complexity of financial instruments increasing, there is a growing risk associated with the ability to serve the custody-related needs of these instruments. Therefore, there is an exposure to market risk. No standardized solutions exist to address custody-related issues, as the economics of systems investments are not based on volume levels, as they are in the context of settlement.

You have talked about "quality" in terms of the various processes involved in supporting the market. But can we organize our thinking about the "quality" of these networks in terms of the contact, contract and commitment in which they allow participants to enter, if you agree with us that this is a useful trilogy to analyze relationships? **LB:** When I talk of systems, I am acutely aware that systems do not exist in and by themselves but, rather, that they cannot be separated from capital and human resources. You need money and people behind the best systems.

There will always be exposure to counterparty risk. The best guarantee is collateralization. Hence, quality information is essential information about the instruments and about your counterparties. Beyond this, it must also be crystal clear that if you have access to collaterals you can exercise your rights over them.

In the end, a part of quality is indeed both the *contact* with the client (both on a commercial and technical level) as well as the *contractual* and legal framework within which we operate.

Is this not where we move from quality of contact (best information etc.) to quality of contract? Randall Guynn has done interesting work [1] on these subjects. What can you say about "quality of contracts"? **LB:** Mr. Guynn has indeed done some excellent analysis and writing for the benefit of the market as a whole regarding multi-tier holdings of securities and international settlement. He suggests solutions for situations whereby the legal systems do not take a multi-tier holding structure into account, a result of which is a gap that has been created in many jurisdictions between law and practice.

I believe a key point in Mr. Guynn's findings is that there should be no confusion as to the law applicable. We all know where securities will end up, namely in the national CSDs, but with whom does the beneficiary have a relationship?

---

1. Modernizing Securities Ownership, Transfer and Pledging Laws, by Randall Guynn; Capital Market Forum, International Bar Association, London, 1996.

A clear legal framework is part of what we provide for intermediaries, sub-depositories, and others. I also believe we can help clients achieve higher quality in structuring these types of *cross-border contractual* links because of the time and effort we have invested over the years in providing and improving this legal framework.

In the study to which we have been referring, the Belgian and Luxembourg legal frameworks are considered the most advanced. In which sense is this Belgian regulatory framework so appropriate? And have other countries like the U.S. learnt from Belgium? **LB:** An important development within the Belgian legal system is that it has redefined the rights of depositors as a new category of property, that includes rights that are superior to those of the intermediary's creditors in the event of the intermediary's bankruptcy.

Indeed, the Belgian legal system is one of the most advanced in terms of settlement in the sense that securities can be physically held in other countries while investors can actually own part of a pool of assets that are held in custody in the Euroclear System. It is on the basis of that ownership that Belgian law allows clients to exercise their rights, irrespective of geographic locations.

How is Euroclear transforming itself these days, and how much of this transformation is specifically related to the euro?
LB: As mentioned earlier, our business has evolved over the past 30 years from providing services exclusively for Eurobonds to our current role as the premier hub for cross-border services in the new EMU environment. Rather than a transformation, I would say that we have undergone an evolution, which continues to evolve.

We are in the process of building the most advanced, real-time, cross-border transaction processing system, not simply for clearing and settlement, but to enhance all the basic operations involved in reducing and managing risk. We have been and continue to be very active in EMU and euro-related forums to ensure as smooth a transition as possible to the euro.

We will be ready for the euro by 1998. As the premier hub for cross-border services and the launch of our real-time settlement capability in mid-1998, we view the introduction of the euro as an opportunity more than a constraint. We will encourage rapid and active use of the euro for settlement activity and cash management from the start of EMU, although we will comply with the "no compulsion, no prohibition" principle. Above all, we aim for a smooth transition process.

Well, it seems we are now moving from the "quality of contract "to the quality of commitment"! Can you provide an example of this sustainability? **LB:** What people look for when entrusting you with the safekeeping of trillions of dollars of securities is stability in terms of cost-effectiveness, service quality, and risk awareness. Our commitment symbolizes that sustainability. Our market share has remained stable at about 70-75%, even though we have accepted a very open door with our main competitor through "the Bridge". I would say our quality of commitment is that we have and will never compromise on our principles.

As "linking machines", as we call them at PROMETHEE, networks produce trust. Is trust your fundamental product? **LB:** Trust is not abstract. Trust is measured by what you provide, by the quality of your brand, and in the people behind it. Each of the 55 000 instructions we handle every day and each dollar of depot under custody is a vote of trust.

Because the Euroclear System is operated by Morgan Guaranty Trust Company of New York, trust is certainly not a foreign concept to us.

In 1993, Euroclear took the initiative to present long-term visions and scenarios of the market structure that could emerge in clearing and settlement globally. One aspect of the disappearance of monetary borders between euro countries will be to reduce the difference between what were called "ICSD" (International Central Securities Depository) and "national" CSDs like Sicovam in France or Kassenverein in Germany. Will the division of labor change? Are your 1993 scenarios still relevant? **LB:** I believe you are referring to the study and publication called "Beyond the G30 Recommendations" which we view as the sequel to the G30 Recommendations issued in 1989 by the Group of Thirty. The G30 recommendations continue to be used today around the world as the benchmark to understand how different securities clearing and settlement systems compare. In fact, there are publishers who sell the results of their studies that compare different CSDs and ICSDs against these recommendations.

The models described in the Beyond G30 Recommendations study are still very relevant today. However, as the markets change and technology progresses, some of the models described in the Beyond G30 Recommendations are evolving. The *need for critical mass* to sustain the necessary investments in the business will continue to push for rationalization at all levels. We've seen this fairly recently at the CSD level in France. Germany, and Sweden, for example, and in the mergers and buy-outs among the global and local custodians. In fact, due to the launch of the single currency in Europe, some alternative, but known models are being explored by the CSDs and ICSDs to accommodate the euro in cross-border securities settlement.

What about the governance of Euroclear itself? Would you describe Euroclear as a "cooperative" or as a "company"?
LB: The Euroclear System structure is not very complicated. In 1968, the Brussels office of Morgan Guaranty Trust Company of New York created the Euroclear System to facilitate settlement of Eurobonds. In 1972, Morgan Guaranty sold the Euroclear System to more than 120 users of the System, thereby creating Euroclear Clearance System PLC. None of the shareholders, even today, own more than 4.9% of the shares in this entity. In 1986, to encourage further market ownership of the Euroclear System, the Euroclear Clearance System Société Coopérative, a Belgian cooperative, was formed. Today, about 2 000 of 2 400 Euroclear Participants own shares in the Cooperative. The Board of Directors of the Cooperative consists of 25 Board members, all senior executives in the international securities markets. Directors are nominated from highly prestigious firms using the Euroclear System representing various financial sectors as well as geographic regions.

The Euroclear System is governed by this Board of Directors. They are responsible for establishing matters of policy, including the determination of Euroclear fees and rebates, the categories of securities accepted in the System, and the approval of depositaries and sub-depositaries such as local clearing systems. In addition, the Board reviews and defines Euroclear Participant admission criteria, as well as the terms and conditions for participation.

The Cooperative has appointed Morgan Guaranty Trust Company of New York as operator of the Euroclear System. A dedicated team from the Morgan Guaranty Brussels office runs the Euroclear System through the Euroclear Operations Centre.

As a European in charge of one of the most elaborate "global financial networks", what are the changes that you would like to see happen over the next 10 years? And, when talking to young people today, what lessons and what hopes come to your mind? **LB:** I would like to keep my comment within the scope of the global financial network of which the Euroclear System is a part.

The trends I see over the next 10 years include:
– a greater *convergence of cash and securities* settlement systems, meaning that both systems will work more closely together;
– an increase in *outsourcing* of back office functions by small to mid-size firms, which will focus on asset management rather than asset servicing, in sync with the commoditization of the operational services business;
– a dilemma among financial institutions that continue to provide asset servicing functions in resolving the question of whether they are *financial* institutions or *software* houses;
– and *cost controls* will be even more important than today.

In parallel with these trends, I would also hope that the ethics in our industry do not suffer in the name of progress.

When talking with young people, I would say that the financial industry is like many other global industries in that mobility, language skills, and openness to other cultures will be the drivers for success. They can not ignore those trends, particularly in Europe. As the next 10-15 years will be transition years in Europe with the advent of the euro, the young adults of today will work and live in a very different environment than their parents.

I would also hope that *trust* remains an integral part of our society, which will indeed undergo rapid change. Be willing to participate in change by having the flexibility to question and improve upon the standards that were applicable in earlier generations. ■

Chapter VII

The strategic issues *behind the conversation*

Reducing risk and taking risk, such are the twin challenges behind this conversation with André Lussi.
Three conditions for reducing risk are: quality of intermediation, technology like real time settlement, and regulatory frameworks like the Luxembourg one that minimizes uncertainties and conflicts of law in cross-border operations. Concrete examples like Cedel's Global Credit Support Service illustrate this first challenge.
Taking risk is what André Lussi holds essential for Europe once the technical risks have been reduced. Hence, the various aspects of an entrepreneurial culture discussed here, with the beacon of a people-centered economy.
The time has come to realize that too much "security" breeds insecurity. By accelerating the shift of power away from the State, and by making it more difficult to constrain people, the euro can really become "the project of the century".
The issue for André Lussi is not strong or weak euro, but a strong or weak European economy able to mobilize Europe's intellectual capital. The true fundamentals are corporate competitiveness and collective governance. ***A.B.***

conversation with

ANDRÉ LUSSI,

CEDEL BANK

This strategic conversation with André Lussi, CEO of Cedel Bank, was conducted in Luxembourg by Albert Bressand (PROMETHEE) and Kenneth Hay (Ernst & Young S.A., Luxembourg).

The euro: the catalyst for entrepreneurial change in Europe?

Cedel Bank is an International Central Securities Depositary "ICSD", in other words a bank that keeps in custody assets from all over the world and that helps thousands of institutions transact, clear and settle so as to participate in global markets. So could you explain how Cedel Bank sees the "global integration frontier"? **André Lussi:** There are two major trends in the "broad picture" that explain why Cedel Bank and the Cedel Group have developed as they have: these are increased freedom of trade and capital movements *and* the decisive role that information technology now plays to manage efficiently the huge flows of capital across national borders.

Economic integration is frequently put on a par with globalization – understood as the elimination of natural barriers of time and space. In my view this definition is too narrow. Globalization is brought about and supported firstly by the *removal of restrictions* in trade in goods and services, in the free movement of persons and in the free flow of capital movements and secondly by information and communication technology and the *falling costs of communication.* Information and communication technology have made quantum leaps over the last years and increasingly determine our way of life. For banks and other providers of financial services, globalization means that their services are available "around the globe" and "around the clock". By this I mean not only world-wide *communication* and information available within seconds but also the simultaneous *evaluation* of financial data, electronic *access* to financial markets around the world and real-time *settlement* of the transactions carried out in these markets.

Cedel Bank as a global "hub" could be located almost anywhere in the world. How important is the "global" part of your activity, and how important is European integration in shaping the future of this company? **AL:** First of all, it is true that Cedel Bank is what you would call a "global player". The Bank was founded in September, 1970 by 66 of the world's major financial institutions, as a clearing organisation whose objective was (and still is) to minimise risk in the settlement of cross-border securities trading, particularly in the growing Eurobond market.

Settlement turnover is currently running at the annualised rate of 15 trillion U.S. dollars per annum and 1.4 trillion U.S. dollars of customer's securities are held in safekeeping against an already large 500 billion U.S. dollars in 1991. Trade worth up to 100 billion U.S. dollars can be settled in a business day. Our financial position is strong and is assigned with the highest possible short-term credit rating, A1+ by IBCA and Standard and Poors and a long-term credit rating of AA1+ by Standard and Poors and an AA rating from IBCA.

But we are a global player *based in Europe*, and this is extremely important to us. Let me also add that the European regulatory framework has been transferred to Luxembourg law in ways that have been very efficient and very supportive of the functions of a state-of-the-art financial center.

Let me explain the reasons. Firstly, the Luxembourg government has created optimal conditions for our business. By this I mean the quality of the regulatory framework, which is one of the most modern in the world and access to state of the art communication technology. We also benefit from being located in the region of the world where barriers have fallen most rapidly and most completely. As you know, the removal of barriers to trade in goods services, the free flow of capital and the movement of persons had both economic and political reasons.

So, we benefit also from being located in the region of the world where barriers have fallen the most rapidly and the most completely for a set of reasons that reflect not just economic forces but also the history of Europe.

ABC of Clearing and Settlement

Clearance/Clearings: Generally, the process by which a Central Securities Depository (CSD) or specialised clearing agency calculates the mutual obligations of market participants for the exchange of securities and money. In the context of Cedel Bank, clearing means the entire *settlement* cycle of a transaction, from receipt of the instruction, through matching and the various status levels in suspense, to final settlement and accounting. The final *clearance* of the transaction is the process of determining accountability for the exchange of cash and securities between the counterparties to a trade, clearance leads to new *book-entry* balances and positions in securities and/or funds.

Settlement: The final transfer of both the securities and money components of a transaction. In Cedel Bank, this refers to completion of the settlement cycle of a transaction resulting in an increase or decrease in an asset balance on a customer account.

Cross-border transaction: A transaction in an international or foreign security, or a transaction in a domestic security where at least one of the counterparties is located outside the home country of the domestic security.

Delivery against payment/Delivery versus payment (DVP): The irrevocable exchange of securities (the delivery) and cash value (the payment) to *settle* a transaction. True delivery against payment involves the simultaneous exchange of securities and cash, as in the case of internal transactions between Cedel Bank counterparties.

Dematerialisation/Book-entry: The elimination of physical certificates or documents of title to represent the ownership of securities so that securities exist only as accounting records on the book of the issuer or appropriate intermediaries. Securities that have been dematerialised are also referred to as *book-entry* or *uncertificated* securities.

Global Credit Support Service (GCSS): A 24 hours a day, real-time service for the movement of assets between counterparties to bilateral credit support agreements, most commonly entered for OTC derivatives transactions. Based on bilateral entry of credit exposure data and selected bilaterally customised information, GCSS will move assets to provide cover both automatically (during optimisation cycles) and manually (on-line) throughout a nineteen-hour day that bridges all time zones.

Global custodian: A custodian bank or trust company that provides custody services with respect to securities traded and settled in any of the major or other markets of the world. Services may be provided by the custodian bank *or trust company* or through a network of local *sub-custodians*.

International Central Securities Depository (ICSD): A Central Securities Depository that clears and settles international securities or cross-border transactions in domestic securities.

Matching: The process that compares settlement and trade details given by the counterparties to check accuracy and consistency.

Netting: The process of pooling transactions either on a bilateral or multi-lateral basis, offsetting buys and sells with each other resulting in one in a long or short position for each participant in the asset traded.

Real-time settlement: Real-time settlement is the instantaneous exchange of cash and securities upon receipt of matching instruction for same day settlement. If the securities are available and the buyer has sufficient cash or credit to purchase them, the transaction is settled.

Repurchase Agreement (Repo): A contract to execute simultaneous transactions for the sale of securities against payment and their repurchase at a future date.

Tripartite Repo Service: A repo transaction in which all the post-execution events in the life cycle of a repo transaction are handled by Cedel Bank as a third-party agent.

Liberty: Liberty is a fully owned subsidiary of Cedel International. Its order routing system, Inter Trade Direct, allows buyers and sellers of a variety of securities anywhere in the world to trade in a number of markets from their desktops. The orders are entered via the screen and sent to the Liberty system centre in London. Inter Trade Direct then routes the order to the chosen broker/dealer at the market execution venue. The broker/dealer executes the order and returns a notice of execution and a confirmation. The entire transaction takes place in seconds.

Thomas Rabe
Cedel Bank

This "Europe without borders" in which capital can flow freely as well as the internal market in financial services are critical elements behind our success.

After all, it was the foundation of the European Community in 1957, which – together with other developments – has paved the way for the global era. The foundation of what is now the European Union was based on three main factors:
– the awareness that the individual European countries were weak as power was concentrated in the hands of two super-powers, the United States and the Soviet Union;
– the tragic experience of the two world wars in this century, with the unnecessary loss of millions of human lives and the self-destruction of Europe;
– and the desire for a better world, with more freedom and equity.

The founding treaties of the European Union defined as their main objective maintaining peace and increasing economic wealth through the establishment of a common market. The plan of Robert Schuman and Jean Monnet, which led to the creation of the European Community for Coal and Steel had the express goal making armed conflicts in Europe impossible. This plan has been successful; the integration of the national economies has made significant progress. World-wide trade increased more than thirty-fold between 1958 and 1992 and trade between member states of the European Union has increased more than the forty-fold since its creation.

So it is perfectly appropriate – and very significant for us – to have our main office in the heart of Europe. I do not see being global and being based in Europe as antagonistic, quite the contrary. We are, so to speak, a "global European" and we feel in full sympathy with the objective of your project regarding the "European vanguard" in the global economy.

Yet, as you know, not all global companies choose to operate out of Europe, and the lack of European competitiveness vis-à-vis North America and Asia is often mentioned as a reason to localise (or even de-localise) elsewhere in the world. Is it your feeling that this "gap in competitiveness" can be solved, and how? **AL:** How competitive is Europe? According to a study conducted by the World Economic Forum, Europe is not very competitive. Asia, the United States, Canada and New Zealand rank highest. There are a number of research studies on this subject as there are a number of criteria and benchmarks to measure competitiveness. Nonetheless, you are right, whichever criteria and benchmarks you use, it is generally accepted that the competitiveness of Europe needs to be improved.

This is, first of all, a matter of *entrepreneurship*. Entrepreneurship means: taking the initiative and assuming responsibility, taking risks and being rewarded by profits for good decisions and being penalised for bad decisions by less profits or even losses. Entrepreneurs are not only the top managers or the owners of a company. *All employees* of a company should be entrepreneurs. The way to achieve economic and result-oriented thinking and acting among employees is to make them capitalists, meaning shareholders of the company for which they work and to increase the share of performance oriented pay.

Meanwhile, the task of governments is to set the right framework, one which allows and promotes entrepreneurship for the good of society as a whole notably through the right division of labour and synergies between markets and governments. Setting the framework implies limiting State intervention in the economy to those areas where the markets fail: In this regard the principle of "in favour of the market" should be applied. Meanwhile, all "stakeholders" need to co-operate to transform economic opportunities into opportunities for *social progress* and *personal fulfilment.*

From an entrepreneurial perspective, I think Europeans should be particularly concerned by the wide-spread unwillingness for reforms as well as by over-regulation of the labour market, not only by the State by also by the unions and the employees representatives. Deregulation and incentives for new employment are not only required, they are also desired by the people. Without increased flexibility, new work forms such as tele-working are not possible; accordingly entrepreneurs often invest and create employment in other parts of the world or content themselves with lower growth and lower job creation.

Is the euro going to help address this "entrepreneurial agenda", or does it take place in an entirely different sphere than the labour market you have just mentioned? **AL:** The competitiveness of Europe and the continuation of economic integration are closely linked. The European countries must work together to master the challenges and, in my mind, an economically integrated Europe also needs a single currency, the euro. The euro has numerous well known advantages but, in my view, the most fundamental benefit will be to accelerate the *shift in culture and in organization* away from the State-centered model *toward a people-centered model.*

In the markets of the euro, the capacity of governments to determine what people and companies do will be greatly reduced. As a result, people will have greater control over their lives. The cosy arrangements between business and government will be exposed to the full wind of competition.

This will work in favour of the more entrepreneurial companies that will be able to seize new opportunities without undue interference from cartels of all types. And more entrepreneurial companies are good for people: competition creates an incentive to do things better, with more highly trained people and for a broader market. Europe needs this sort of incentives if its citizens are to take part fully in the new economic opportunities.

But what if the process of convergence triggered by the euro has not gone far enough in the Spring of 1998? What if Germany itself experiences difficulties in reaching the targets set in the Maastricht's Treaty? Do you think the euro should be postponed?
AL: The introduction of the euro should not be delayed. I am convinced we cannot afford to – neither politically nor economically. A delay would lead to a confidence crisis and undermine this "project of the century". The discussions on the use of decimal points and on any delay in introducing the euro create uncertainty among market participants who are making significant efforts to be prepared for January 1st, 1999.

Economic convergence in the European Union is vast. The bases for a *stable euro* are good: in most European countries inflation has almost become an out-of-date term, public budgets are in a consolidation phase, interest rate levels are low and the exchange mechanism of the European Monetary System (EMS) is working.

The interest rate difference ("spreads") among loans to, or issues of, the different European governments has decreased significantly over the last two years. Financial markets expect EMU to start on time and are acting accordingly.

As the introduction of the euro appears increasingly likely, the critical question has become "will this be a strong euro or a weak euro?", referring to the external value of the euro and not simply to its value in terms of domestic prices. How strong do you think that the euro will be vis-à-vis the U.S. dollar?
AL: Over the medium and long term, I do not think that there will be "strong" or "weak" currencies. Instead, I believe there will be "strong" and "weak" economies. To me, therefore, the real issue is whether the euro will push Europe in the direction of *a stronger economy.*

Creating a common currency in Europe does not mean that the European economy will acquire the strength of the US economy overnight. In that sense, the euro is the beginning rather than the end of the process as the European economy still has a long way to go before it can compare to the American one. The euro will be there, the currency barriers will disappear but much will remain to be done to streamline and restructure the European economy. And this process will not be driven by politicians but by market forces.

Let me take the example of the Central Banks. Their role in the economy has changed substantially in the last years. National central banks can no longer conduct monetary policy with the level of discretion of the past. Instead they have to take market reactions as a fundamental reference.
To me, this is a sign of a deeper *shift of power* from the political establishment to the market logic, from the State (or politics) to market forces. The same shift of power can be detected in other areas. The most prominent example is the Internet which has developed rapidly outside of the traditional channels controlled (or at least supervised) by government. The Internet is empowering people to communicate and to interact in more flexible, more creative ways. Hence, in communication also, we witness the emergence of a people-centered paradigm which is more satisfactory than the traditional highly regulated paradigm of national communication monopolies.

The EU countries have become increasingly reliant on other members with over 60% of trade being intra-EU. This trade is conducted in fifteen currencies with organisations engaged in complex forex and hedging strategies to safeguard their profit line. The euro as a single currency would form approximately 40% of the world's export markets. Euro-currency government debt would be 42% of the world's total outstanding government debt whereas the U.S. dollar debt would be only 31%. Hence the market in euros represents a powerful market for the raising of finance, for trade and for investment.

The combined GDP of the EU is about 8.6 trillion U.S. dollars with 10% or 860 billion U.S. dollars of revenue relating to intra-EU imports and exports. The cost of multi-currency administration, forex and hedging is estimated at 1%; the savings associated with moving to a single currency would therefore be 8.6 billion U.S. dollars. A single currency will make Europe more efficient, more competitive.

So, altogether, the "strength" or "weakness" of the euro will depend on such fundamentals of *corporate competitiveness* and *collective governance* of society, rather than on narrow monetary considerations.

In this broad sense, clearly the euro will not solve all European problems in and by itself. In your view, what are the other

priorities for this continent to have an economy as "strong" as that of North America? **AL:** There are many dimensions in this search for a more competitive European economy. To me the central factor in all of them is *people*, I mean the women and men of Europe and their capacity to live and work very successfully in the fast changing global environment of today.

This importance of people expresses itself in many forms. One of the most fundamental aspect of the present transformation is demography, a very broad and complex subject. We all know how important the issue of ageing for savings and pensions is and that our situation is clearly less favourable than that of the United States and of Asia. In most European countries birth rates are decreasing. People are living longer and retiring earlier. Therefore, the ratio between contributors and recipients today is about 0.6. By the year 2015 this will increase to 1.1. This will increase labour costs unless state pensions are reduced and supplemented with different types of private savings.

Turning away from this outdated form of retirement provision – at least to put a stronger emphasis on private pensions and savings – is unavoidable.

Pension systems are still constrained by national borders and barriers. In the world of the euro I expect a certain degree of convergence of pension systems, including the more widespread use of pension funds. Many of the regulatory restrictions which are presently limiting pension funds (and their investments) to a national horizon will have no justification when the euro is introduced and currency risk in the euro zone disappears. Hence we should prepare for the development of a much stronger group of international investors in the European financial markets of the euro.

This is clearly a development that Cedel Bank will position itself in by providing the type of services that facilitate cross-border investment, make them less costly and more rewarding thereby contributing to a more efficient allocation of resources within the European Union.

Beyond pension funds and the policy agenda associated with the ageing of the European society, what are the other elements of this "people-centered approach" to economic development that you see as necessary for a stronger European economy?
AL: The key resource for European economic development is brain power or, in the language of economists, "intellectual capital". Intellectual capital is the new wealth. It is widely recognised that more than 50 per cent of companies' investments go into developing knowledge, key competencies, customer

relationships and information technology. But large parts of these investments do not show up in the balance sheets. A large Swedish insurance company estimates that only 1/7 of its total value is book value and 6/7 are hidden value.

The European countries, both governments and the private sector, will have to devise policies to maintain and develop this resource, i.e. policies on education and training at all levels. A key success factor for companies is and will be to ensure that their employees share knowledge and experience. To achieve this, it is essential to leverage the knowledge and experience generated by each and every member of a company through some sort of "information or knowledge exchange" to which all employees have access. At Cedel Bank we refer to this process as *knowledge engineering*. It is a combination of knowledge management and knowledge exchange that creates lateral thinking and innovation.

European companies are unable to compete with the developing countries which have much lower labour costs (despite lower productivity) in labour intensive low-technology products and services. They have to focus on information-based products or, at least, knowledge-intensive products. To maintain and improve our position in this field, we have to ensure first class education and *continuous training*. I purposely mention continuous training. Without the willingness to learn during our entire life, to continuously strive for new knowledge and learn about new developments – particularly in the domain of technology, the risk is to be *"dépassé"* sooner or later. The following formula applies: fifty per cent of our current knowledge will be outdated in three years.

But putting people at the center and recognizing intellectual capital is not simply a matter of developing new and better products and services. It is also a matter of enabling people to fully exploit their creative power. People must feel that they are the masters of their own destiny.

I do not hesitate to say that putting people at the center also calls for a revised concept of *economic security*. It is time that we ask ourselves about the relationship between high unemployment and the level of security and safety and the widespread reluctance to take risks.

The different attitude of the governments towards people explains to a large extent the economic success of the United States and Britain, in particular in creating new jobs. Providing safety and security and taking care of many of the people's needs at first sight appears highly desirable for the State to be doing. The problem is that the safety net becomes illusory when the governments are lacking the resources to finance it. Similarly, a number of countries have a negative attitude towards private pension funds because they fear that they will threaten the present pay-as-you go social security systems. The reality is that when the generation which is today 30 to 40 years old retires, the governments will be unable to pay adequate pensions.

Too much security is a source of insecurity. On the other hand, in order to develop and address the need of people for health, pensions and jobs we need to accept that the present world is highly unsecure, highly uncertain. Those who have failed in business in Europe are often crucified and they have a hard time finding resources for a new venture or even finding a new job. But we should look at them positively as people who have accepted a high level of uncertainty and who have learnt from their failure.

True security will come from *less* protection. It will come from creation, from initiatives, from risk taking.

How far reaching are the implications of the euro for Cedel Bank? Is it just an additional currency or a change of era? Is it mostly a matter of adapting systems or does it involve an active role, a "pro active" attitude as people like to say?
AL: We are of course preparing intensively for the introduction of the euro on January 1st, 1999 as well as for the year 2000. In regards to the euro, we have taken the leadership in the discussions and resolution of "open issues" and in the definition of market standards. There is still uncertainty on some critical areas including the timing and method by which securities are re-denominated and the design and operation of the payment systems that are needed to support the euro. Many of the changes we are planning cannot be finalised until the securities industry, in conjunction with the financial and monetary authorities of the various countries, has provided definitive answers and workable solutions to the outstanding problems.

But we see the introduction of the euro as much more than a technical matter. we see it as ushering in a new era with fundamental changes. This is particularly true in our business environment.

A new type of financial market will develop in Europe, and we want to identify and bring to market the new types of services to help our customers to be more competitive and successful in the very different environment of the euro. Enlargement toward the East is also very important to us.

What concrete measures are you taking at Cedel Bank, beyond adapting to the euro, to prepare for this more integrated "Europe of 21"? **AL:** The environment for our business has changed dramatically over the last years. The Cedel Group has always been a global player with a world-wide presence. Globalization, the technological revolution, the deregulation and liberalisation of markets, creation of the European Economic and Monetary Union and the appearance of new competitors; all these trends together will lead to consolidation of the financial markets, mergers of banks, insurance companies, exits of market participants, "commoditization" of services, pressure on margins and the requirement for rigorous cost management.

How do we, as the Cedel Group, react to these challenges? How do we position ourselves in this new environment?

We act through a large scale investment programme. The objectives are: the creation of a new technological platform for the real-time settlement of cross-border securities transactions, and a significant improvement in the quality of our custody services and customer communications through information transfers to and from our customers via various media. It is in this long term perspective that we are preparing very actively for the euro.

The most important point is not the size of the investment but the spirit in which we are making it. We want to prepare for a new type of financial markets in which cross-border activities will be the rule rather than the exception.

Could you be more specific as to the type of services that you think will be needed in this new financial and monetary environment? **AL:** To make the investment project described above attractive for our shareholders we have decided to enter new markets. We have set up a new subsidiary which will address the market demand for real-time settlement and straight-through processing. This new entity will provide three services: securities operations processing for other banks and financial institutions, a global highway and software development and sales. The global highway will create a seamless link between transactions, settlement of securities and custody services. Order processing, trade execution and confirmation of cross-border securities transactions as well as their settlement will be carried out within seconds and this at significantly lower cost and risk than is the case today.

Customers will benefit from these new services in different ways: they will gain from cost reductions as a result of economics of scale. They will have reduced investment in information technology. Perhaps more importantly they will be able to focus on their core activities and competencies.

I am convinced that banks and other financial institutions will need massive economies of scale to remain competitive. This will push them towards merging or outsourcing their back office. Processing will be done in *regional centres* as all functions that can be combined will be integrated while keeping separate front offices.

What sort of competition is likely to develop between Cedel Bank and the national CSDs which fulfil the same role as Cedel Bank but within national financial markets? As the euro leads to financial unification and market integration, will an "International" CSD still be needed? **AL:** We do not compete with CSDs. It is true that many CSDs are modelling themselves on the ICSDs – but we have operated that concept for over twenty years. The move to real time technology (RTGS and RTS) takes the market forward – indeed the market is undergoing a metamorphosis.

The term ICSD is an outdated concept and we are repositioning into *global risk management* by providing credit support, cash position and collateral management via a real-time, on-line global highway; the term ICSD is dead in the new millennium of virtual markets. In future, as is the case today, we will be flowing much needed *liquidity* to national and regional markets, and that will mean addidional business for CSDs; we are complementary because we are different!

What other structural market issues do you see surfacing in the new millennium? **AL:** National *legal and regulatory systems* need to adapt to meet the challenges and requirements of global markets.

In the *domestic* marketplace, entities are governed by domestic law and regulatory practice. In the *international* market place, the ICSDs utilise international law and, in the case of Cedel Bank, Luxembourg maintains a highly sophisticated legal framework to govern the custody, transfer and pledging of book-entry securities.

The obligations and interests of depositors of securities in Cedel Bank are governed by the laws of Luxembourg together with our General Terms and Conditions. Let me give some details as it illustrates the type of needs that must be adressed in today's markets.

The centralisation of book-entry securities settlements under a single, thorough and modernised legal regime ensures that customers of Cedel Bank can have confidence in the custody and settlement arrangements. Given the importance of *legal certainty* to interests in securities held and transferred in

Cedel Bank, Luxembourg has continually reviewed and updated its legislation as the needs of the market dictated. Most recently, the situs of securities held in book-entry form in Cedel Bank (in other words the actual place where they are legally considered to be located) has been clarified by explicit legislation which deems such securities to be sited in Luxembourg regardless of the fact that they may be issued or sub-deposited elsewhere.

Cedel Bank is using key features of Luxembourg law to provide as rigorous a legal basis as is possible for the implementation of security arrangements in global financial markets thereby helping financial institutions to cope as well as possible with the variations among domestic legal systems and conflicts of law. In the Europe of the euro, there will be many barriers of that type that will remain and I am using the example of Cedel and of the Luxembourg regulatory framework to give you some idea of the initiatives that will still need to be taken, by private actors as well as by regulators, to overcome the present fragmentation of European markets once the euro is in place.

Our Global Credit Support Service (GCSS) utilises the Luxembourg statute for fiduciary agreements and Cedel Bank as the fiduciary bank to secure the situs of securities collateral firmly in Luxembourg. The *conflicts of law* doctrine (which experts refer to as *lex rei sitae*) provides that the situs of a claim against a fiduciary is the jurisdiction of the fiduciary. Hence, although a customer in GCSS retains his claim to redelivery of securities, the securities are legally deemed to be in Luxembourg. This will greatly simplify transferring interests in securities collateral under international credit support agreements.

The European Monetary Institute has recognised that in a RTGS European market, the cross-border transfer of securities in electronic form ("on a book-entry basis") will be an essential component of providing credit support. Luxembourg law and GCSS takes this basic concept much further since the different types of securities that a given institution can use as collateral are centralised in a "hub" allowing collateral to be homogeneous. It then becomes possible to change its use between credit support, securities lending, repo, sale, etc. through real-time transfer.

All this may sound very technical, but it has a very concrete implication that can be understood by any person contemplating borrowing against a guaranty (like a mortgage "collateralized" by the home being acquired), namely to allow securities held in different countries to be used together rather than separately as a guarantee for financial transactions anywhere, anytime. Again, financial integration is still a challenge!

To conclude, we would like to come back to Europe and ask you how optimistic or pessimistic you are that Europe will overcome the competitiveness gap and develop entrepreneurship as you mentioned? **AL:** For centuries Europe has been the home of excellent scientists, musicians, writers as well, of course, as traders and lawyers. Many pioneering developments and inventions are the work of Europeans. The innovative power was and still is present. I am convinced that the old continent is not "burned-out", as many pessimists claim. We have a good chance to continue to play a decisive role in the future, if we put aside our individual habits and act together with determination. I am convinced that Europe will be a land of peace and prosperity in which this generation and the next can make the most out of their remarkable intellectual capital, around common visions. The euro is a wonderful opportunity to realize how much we already have in common, and to develop trust. I mean trust in our neighbors, trust in our capacity to succeed in the world, trust in people rather than in protections, trust in ourselves. ■

Chapter VIII

The strategic issues *behind the conversation*

Looking at the role of the U.K. in the Europe of the euro, André Villeneuve advises to distinguish very carefully between the British Government, financial institutions in general and the City of London. The positive attitude now expressed by Her Majesty's Government toward the euro is a major catalyst for change but it will take time to translate into fully-fledged participation in the process by large segments of the British financial community which still tends to approach the single currency in operational terms. By contrast, the international community gathered in the City of London is positioning to be at the forefront of the development of these new markets. American banks, in particular, have "little baggage" in European banking as it is now, and they already see the euro in terms of opportunities. Continental financial centers, however, have modernised to the point that any self-complacency would be very risky for London.

Beyond London, the issues addressed in this strategic conversation include the removal of barriers that have prevented the development of a pension fund industry in Europe and the development of an equity culture. Obviously, they also include the role of technology and the impact of the euro on certain types of services such as provided by Reuters. All this is converging toward a vivid description of the consolidation process that will intensify in the European banking and asset management industry.

A.B.

conversation with

ANDRÉ VILLENEUVE,

REUTERS HOLDING PLC

This conversation with André Villeneuve, Executive Director of Reuters Holdings PLC, was conducted by Albert Bressand (PROMETHEE) in London and Paris.

The U.K. may or may not join, but the city of London will be in the euro!

Now André, we are turning to you as the participant from London in this set of conversations to help solve one of the deepest, if not the deepest mystery of the euro. The question is whether the British will be in, out, or somehow in between?

André Villeneuve: To alleviate any doubt, let me begin with something that is certain: whether the U.K. joins or not, the City of London will be in the euro!

London is a place where a large financial community works. That community is not tied so tightly to the British economy and, even less so, the British government. This community, by the way, includes many participants from continental Europe, North America and the four corners of the world. They are used to operating under enlightened regulation with the global market as their horizon.

If you take the *American* banks for instance, you can see that they have very little baggage to protect in Europe because most of them have not been involved so deeply in the domestic economies. For them, EMU holds little threat, EMU is only about new opportunities. And, as they see mainly opportunities in EMU, they are actively building the expertise that they believe will be needed to address these opportunities.

As far as the U.K. is concerned, the mood is changing as the British government has now taken a more positive stand regarding the benefits for the country of joining EMU. True, the British press – much of it by the way is controlled by American and Canadian owners – is often much less positive, to say the least, about EMU. Hence, the importance of the timetable which gives the government time to prepare the public before the next election, in or before 2001.

Speaking of preparing the public, how are they reacting to this combination of rather positive signals from industry and the new Tony Blair government and of the strong anti-EMU current that expresses itself very strongly in the press? **AV:** Most people who think about it now realise that EMU is going to happen. And the longer term problems for the U.K. of staying out are perceived all the more clearly as industry has been more articulate about what it could mean for the U.K. A lot of thinking, however, has to take place regarding the benefits that can accrue to the U.K. as a consequence of EMU. In other words, the *defensive* reasons not to stay out are becoming clearer but the positive reasons to join have not been really very much discussed.

After all, not so long ago, the widely shared assumption was that EMU would not start on time, that it would include only a narrow group of countries and that the U.K. would stay out. In that context one can understand why people have not rushed into detailed discussions of all the good things that they could expect from EMU.

Preparation is not simply about the general mind-set! It is also about a whole set of decisions, large and small, to prepare for what many of our Anglo-Saxon friends still call EMU when for us, on the continent it is already the much more concrete, much more precise euro. Will the U.K. – government as well as financial institutions – be able to prepare not just to deal with that strange process called monetary integration but with the coming of the euro? **AV:** EMU itself is already a complex process. And the British government has to confront the reality of how eleven countries will now run their monetary and economic affairs as one tightly knit group before the British decide to give or not to give the green light for joining. The debate about the so-called "euro-X" council was a telling illustration of this challenge for British policy makers. The U.K. government realises that it cannot play the leading role it aspires to in Europe without full EMU membership. This is despite the compromises reached for the outs on the euro-X council.

A big issue for the British government, in my view, is that until the decision has been taken and a date identified, many people will only work slowly, if at all, to prepare for the euro. Believe me, one will hear a lot about "conflicting priorities", or even about the need to address the "year 2000" challenge first before IT specialists can be freed for the single currency… Many believe that there is no need to commit substantial capital to prepare for the euro before a decision is finalised.

A large part of British industry and even of the British financial sector still thinks about the euro as an *operational* matter. They do not realise yet that it is about a fundamental restructuring in many industries, notably the financial industry. Unfortunately, for them and for the City of London, it is often difficult to identify the full impact of EMU on one's business until one has put together a strong team to prepare for EMU. Usually, such a team begins by looking at the operational impact of the euro: changing machines like ATMs, managing cash flow, adapting banking relationships. It is only after a while that they begin to identify and to understand the strategic issues.

The danger at this point is that many still believe that government will put together a team of very competent, very senior people who will take care of the transition to the euro. This passive attitude toward the implications of a common currency is a source of real danger!

Lord David Simon, European Minister, has begun a campaign to urge British industry to start preparations for the euro early, despite no decision yet.

You have mentioned a couple of times already the danger for the U.K. of being left out of the euro. But in the conversations we have had with bankers and CEOs of stock exchanges on the continent, none of them, as you could see, made the case that London would really suffer. Preparing for an intensified competition with London is what they have talked about. So what are really these dangers? **AV:** You are right that, in the short term, the City of London is not threatened by the euro. Everyday we can see new banks reinforcing their presence here. At least one French bank, for instance, made it very clear recently that they have to expand their trading operations in London because they were in risk of losing their traders to other banks operating out of London. Not only is London a place where levels of remuneration have been driven by U.S. practices, but on top of that some continental countries have such high levels of income taxes that traders and people with valuable expertise are under a strong incentive to leave their home country.

And this is very much a self-sustaining, self-reinforcing process. The large number of international players operating in London create such a large pool of liquidity as to make presence in London even more attractive for the banks that are not there yet as well as for those that have already begun that migration. As if it were not enough, technology also enters the picture on the side of London. It increases the pressure to reduce the number of trading centres at the wholesale level. Citibank, for instance, used to have 32 foreign exchange trading rooms, a number which it has reduced to only 4, thereby concentrating its operations in New York, Tokyo, Singapore, and, of course, London.

All this – and a number of other factors such as the fact that British people are fluent in English, the most international of languages – favours London.

London's Achilles' heel is complacency! The weaknesses that I have just mentioned are real but financial centres on the continent and, notably the Germans, have been very aggressive about building up their strength in preparation to the euro. They start with the disadvantage that financial services in Germany and France have been protected for a long time. This meant that they did not develop as they have done in London. But I am impressed by the progress made over the last two years, in particular in Frankfurt, where the DTB and now the equity markets have made rapid progress toward electronic trading. Paris too has made important progress.

So, even if London is not immediately threatened, over the long run I would not bet against the success of the technology driven efforts coming from Frankfurt and other continental centres. I feel notably that if the U.K. did not join EMU, London could lose significant fixed income activities to the countries which will be primary markets in euro debt.

Several of our participants in this book have described some sort of natural evolution toward a two-hub structure for European capital markets. You also believe that this is the natural point of equilibrium for consolidation for the financial industry in Europe? And do you think the continental hub will be mostly a German one, a Franco-German one, or an even more diverse one? **AV:** I can understand the point because it is not necessarily in the tradition of financial markets to have only one centre. So, I too think that this will be a "two horse race".

Regarding the French financial centre, it is not obvious, however, that this two horse race is necessarily the best scenario for them. In a partnership, there tends to be a junior partner as well as a senior partner, and a junior partner is at risk of being "swallowed" by the senior one. Now, I realise that most people would disagree with me but, let me offer the view nevertheless that the French could probably have benefited from remaining independent if they were able to maintain real agility and flexibility.

But, anyway, does location really matter with the present combination of global-reach-technology and of the Investment Services Directive (ISD) which makes possible to trade in one exchange from another country through remote membership?

AV: It is clear that, with ISD, one does not need to be located in Germany to trade on the German market! So, you can say that location is not an issue, at least, for wholesale financial activity. But if you look at it from the perspective of a financial centre, this is not necessarily encouraging as all banks and intermediaries are now under tremendous pressure to cut their costs and to get out of activities in which they do not really add value. So, these banks and intermediaries are beginning to put pressure on the exchanges so that they become a low-cost place from which to operate. Also, they would prefer not to carry the cost of membership of so many different exchanges. The exchanges have to respond to these pressures.

SBF - Bourse de Paris, in my view, has anticipated these trends correctly and finds itself now ahead of London in fields such as settlement. This is quite an interesting shift!

For financial institutions, change is now driven by three factors: *technology*, the coming of the *euro* and also the greater awareness of *shareholder value*. Until now, concerns about the latter were quite minimal in continental banks, but the trend which began in American banks has now caught up in Europe. The banking industry is now awakening to the fact that the banks which have typically delivered the best shareholder value have often had a narrowly focused product line, and have not tried to be all things to all men.

One competitive asset of the City of London is that the U.K., together with the Netherlands, are clearly ahead of the rest of Europe in encouraging and servicing a growing pension fund industry. Do you feel that the euro can be the catalyst of a catching up by continental countries in this respect? Or will

the continent continue to shoot itself in the foot by putting the interests of the *present* pensioners and the bureaucracies serving them in the present pay-as-you-go systems above the interest of the *future* pensioners [1]? **AV:** More private sector pension funds are inevitable in countries like France, Italy and Germany. It is true that, at this stage, the U.K. has more funds under management than the whole of the rest of Europe. But the driving force will be the people themselves, on the continent like elsewhere.

People have begun to realise that their governments will be unable to meet their pension fund obligations. They know that governments do not always keep their promises, and they are starting to take *individual decisions* that will create a strong expansion of pension funds.

The impact of the euro will remove some of the key barriers that have prevented people from placing their money in another country if this is the best way for them to prepare for their pension needs. So, clearly, the euro will accelerate the growth of the pension industry, and assets will increasingly be invested in other European markets – eventually in global markets.

In particular, we will see a dismantling of the barriers that still keep insurance companies and the pension industry under a strong degree of national control. And I believe this will happen sooner rather than later.

Talking of what one can imagine, this will also go together with a shift away from our continental bond culture toward an *equity culture*, will it not? **AV:** Well, the present French Minister for Economy, Finance and Industry, Mr Dominique Strauss-Kahn, has taken measures to encourage a shift from fixed income instruments toward equities. French capitalism has often been described by French observers as "capitalism without capital". So, a stronger equity culture is certainly in the interest of companies from continental countries.

Individuals are beginning to get used to a *low inflation environment*, which leads them to compare the long term performance of fixed income with equities, and to do so much more scientifically than they could in the past. And, as you know, historically, equities have tended to outperform fixed income product by quite a wide margin over the long term.

---

1. For a discussion of the political economy of pension reform, see "Social Systems, Markets & Democracy", *PROJECT PROMETHEE PERSPECTIVE* n°26-27, November 1995, produced in cooperation with MEFF in Barcelona and notably articles by Dimitri Vittas, Elizabeth Duskin, Dick Taverne and José-Luis Oller.

The issue for financial centres will not be whether they want to encourage fund management and equities, but whether they are able to absorb the money coming to them to be managed!

> Reuters, Globex and the marriage of networks and markets

Having looked, as you have, at these issues from the perspective of European financial centres, it would be fair to discuss with you now the Reuters perspective. But, first of all, what sort of company is really Reuters? The answer may not be obvious as Reuters is a service provider that comes close to being the market place for foreign exchange... **AV:** What is Reuters? Let me see if I can give you a good definition. The way we describe ourselves is, quite simply, that we are the world leading news and financial systems organisation. We do not shy away from observing that the breadth and sophistication of data that we provide to investors, issuers, intermediaries and other businesses is unrivalled. Our products obviously include data but also news in text and video and technical systems for trading rooms. Quite a large gamut of offerings if I may say so, without impinging upon the scientific and objective nature of the conversations in this book!

You asked whether we are simply an information provider or whether we operate markets like a stock exchange does. It is true that 40% to 50% of *spot foreign exchange* transactions, where there are no central market places, are done through Reuters screens and systems. We are probably a useful channel for participants in the market to interact with one another. If you look at *equities*, it is clear anyway that we are *not* the market, because these already exist. Our subsidiary, Instinet, is a *broker* and trades like other brokers do, except that it does so with the full benefit of electronic systems. Instinet is a member of many exchanges around the world, just like Merrill Lynch and others.

We are reminded that, initially, the founder of Reuters used to work for a more traditional news agency, Havas, now operating as Agence France-Presse. The difference is that you have identified the combination of finance and technology as an essential engine for growth. Could we ask you therefore about some impressions regarding this marriage of finance and

technology as well, of course, as its implications for Reuters? **AV:** A keyword is globalization. Markets – or rather people in markets – will become more global, and this will continue to be good news for us.

Banks and other intermediaries rely increasingly on technology and, after a period when they were quite keen on developing their own proprietary systems, they are now looking for generic solutions. At which point I may observe with some satisfaction that Reuters has a 70% market share in the installation of trading rooms as well as a large and growing marketshare in risk management systems.

The present trend toward *outsourcing* is not risk free for banks and intermediaries. They are really entrusting a third party with their quality and brand in the market place! So it does not go completely unnoticed, for customers that do not want to take the risk of being "left out in the cold", that Reuters has been around since the 1850s.

Looking to the future, we can see an increasing demand for systems that help our own clients communicate with *their* clients. This is where WEB based technology now comes into the picture. Our role is to provide the necessary technology, and generic information for products such as portfolio valuation, rather than leave financial institutions already burdened with huge technology demands to reinvent the wheel.

In doing so, the financial institutions working with us are able to preserve their "look and feel" by concentrating limited resources on visualisation. So this is a happy marriage!

All happy marriages do not necessarily evolve for the better however. At PROMETHEE, we followed closely the launch of Globex, an off-hour network linking derivatives markets across the Atlantic: we felt that it epitomised this marriage between networks and markets which we labelled "networked markets" [2]. As you can understand therefore, we are very disappointed, as observers, that Globex is not really doing well! **AV:** Globex may have been a system ahead of its time. Nevertheless, it has performed the ambitious tasks for which it had been designed and, as we are talking, it is still operating.

True, marrying the interest of Reuters as the developer of a global trading system with the more narrow interests of exchanges has turned out

2. For a description of this work, see "Networks & Markets: more than a marriage of convenience", *PROJECT PROMETHEE PERSPECTIVES*, n°21, December 1992 as well as Albert Bressand, "Réseaux bancaires et financiers: une coopération multiforme sur fond de concurrence exacerbée" *Revue d'Economie Financière*, n°33, été 1995.

to be difficult. Yet, MATIF in Paris, and also the CME in Chicago, have been very supportive and, after all, I still think that it was an idea that could have worked in a more spectacular fashion.

What about the transition to the euro? Is it a major undertaking for Reuters? **AV:** The transition to the euro is an issue for us, and quite a costly proposition at that! But it is not threatening or even unusual for us.

We are very active on all aspects of this transition and we aim to be very "euro-friendly" but, in many instances, we depend on decisions by financial centres and communities and there are many market conventions that have to be agreed upon before our systems can be adapted.

In business terms, however, the major consequence for us is not the *transition* itself but the *consolidation process* which the euro triggers in the financial industry.

> The consolidation process among banks

Is this consolidation among banks and financial intermediaries good or bad for Reuters? **AV:** Well, you know, there are good mergers and bad mergers. If I may look at them from the perspective of Reuters, a good merger is one to which financial institutions come with complementary activities either because they are two regional banks operating in different parts of Europe, or because they have clearly distinct activities such as insurance on one side and banking on the other. The most difficult for us is probably the pre-consolidation period when financial institutions are busy "dressing up" their balance sheet – and notably postponing investment – while looking over their shoulder and preparing for the inevitable.

Clearly, in countries like France, the financial services industry has been weakened for having been too late in consolidating. But once stronger banks emerge, the industry focuses again on market opportunities.

What is good for us, really, is when the financial industry looks at the opportunities ahead in fields like pension reform.

So, to come back to your question, the keypoint for us in the euro is its catalytic role in pushing banks and financial institutions to look at the opportunities that they will be able to address. They can do so by looking at the U.S. capital markets to identify those techniques that could find a role in the large and liquid European capital market of the euro era. They can also do it by looking at what is done best in one of the national European markets of today, like securitization in France.

But Reuters will continue to benefit from the huge shift of assets from the public to the private sector in Europe and elsewhere due to pension fund reform and privatisation. Demands for international capital movement and wealth management will continue to grow. Deregulation, particularly in emerging markets, will also be a positive force despite national turmoil. Finally, as our clients revisit fundamental strategic strengths, we hope to benefit from those who feel that they cannot continue to create in-house information and technology solutions for everything they do.

Altogether, the euro already is a catalyst for creativity.

What do you think of the consolidation process for banks themselves rather than from the perspective of REUTERS?

AV: Only a few very large global banks are emerging from this consolidation process. Many have tried only to discover that they could not. Now they have to concentrate on a more focused role for themselves like Lloyds Bank or Bank One. Some have invested very large amounts in acquisitions for this global spree, all the more easily as they were not as concerned as today about shareholder value. Examples included Crédit Lyonnais, of course, but also German banks at a time when they could be managed in a relatively discretionary manner. Now the pressure of shareholders – pension funds notably – is getting stronger and stronger. Witness what happened recently at Dresdner where the proposal by management was voted down. This unprecedented rejection of a proposal from the Board should be seen as a very strong signal... As for British banks, many of them have been acquired and most others have given up their global ambitions. The acquisition of Hambros by Société Générale and the sale of BZW by Barclays were the latest episodes in this process.

If one adds to that the problems faced by Japanese banks, it appears that American banks are the only ones with a global presence in investment banking and that only a few non U.S. banks are in a position to challenge them. Being like Merrill Lynch or Morgan Stanley Dean Witter is a challenge that very few banks contemplate any longer...

On top of that, being global requires a presence in the U.S. market that very few European bankers have succeeded in developing. SBC-UBS is an exception that comes to mind regarding the global reach of European banks, but even they do not yet have a sufficiently strong American base. And it is very difficult to build one now as prices (and salary levels!) are so high. So it is really tough for non U.S. financial institutions to become serious market leaders in America, although names like AXA, Hong Kong Shanghai Bank and SBC Warburg come to mind.

This being said, things are changing rapidly. Expensive mistakes have been made, but many European banks are now looking at the changing environment as a major challenge, and they are approaching it with more emphasis on shareholder value.

What about the many banks that will not become a global player? What are they going to be? **AV:** Even if one assumes that only 8 to 10 institutions will be global, one must bear in mind that this group will not necessarily include the same banks in ten years time! This is a constant tread mill.

So the game of globalization will continue and nothing will be gained for ever. Meanwhile, disintermediation will also continue to intensify.

Indeed, the whole basis of distribution is also changing. Banks can no longer be confident that a network will protect them as their existing networks can be undermined by electronic distribution. Things were much easier when a Frenchman only wanted to buy and bank in French francs! Today, those who believe that their domestic branch network will adequately protect them are placing their faith in a new Maginot line!

To me, therefore, all is now about focus. Some of the medium sized players will have to think in regional terms, but with a simplified product line.

What about *asset management*? Is it on the verge of going the way investment banking has gone, namely disproportionately toward the Morgan Stanley Dean Witters of this world? Will the U.S. power houses leave enough room for European groups to continue to exist or will the consolidation process radically alter the landscape? **AV:** There is a consolidation process going on there also. But it is not clear at all who will really benefit.

True, if funds are tracked *passively*, what you need is the largest liquidity and the lowest cost and having the best individual share pickers will not help a lot. On the other hand, unlike in investment banking, one does not have to put a lot of capital at risk, which means that present players can stay longer. And plenty of investors will continue to support *actively* managed funds where the cost equation is quite different.

Speaking of asset management, it is clear to me that European asset managers are now outgrowing their fixed income culture, and adopting the equity culture that several of the other participants in this project have mentioned. This means, among other things, that they are going to need more sophisticated technology to *track and manage risk* than when they spent much of their time watching the yield curve!

We have talked about globalization, disintermediation, the coming of the equity culture, and the stronger pressures to create wealth and value and to manage risk... How does the euro fit in this global landscape! **AV:** This is, indeed, the world in which the euro will find its place: globalization, technology, shareholder value and the like. Within that world, the euro markets – or rather the markets in euros, not to confuse them with euromarkets – should become stronger, provided that a number of things also happen.

First, the euro itself and the European Central Bank behind it need to establish a solid *credibility*.

Second, the Europeans have to recognize that there are still many differences at national levels that prevent the markets in euros from becoming one market in euros. Among them, as we discussed, are treatment of *pension funds*.

Another barrier may come from the ways in which government debt is issued. Unlike the U.S., where all government debt is issued and managed by the U.S. Treasury, each European government will issue debt with its own ideas of how and when to issue. What René Karsenti told you about the efforts by the European Investment bank to create "euro-tributary" issues by managing different issues in national currencies along the same procedures and same repayment schedules is a good example of what can be done to really achieve *homogeneity* and *critical mass* in such a market.

So, to me, the euro will be a beginning, and much will have to happen to really achieve all the benefits that it can bring about. But it is a promising beginning and a powerful catalyst for change. The markets in euro have the potential to challenge the U.S. dollar markets as a serious alternative for the first time in many years. The City of London is preparing to be an active player and I hope that the public in the U.K. will also understand the benefits of this historic change. ■

Part III

European banking and *the euro challenge.*

Chapter IX

The strategic issues *behind the conversation*

History as well as geography make ABN AMRO one of the few truly global and universal banks. But it is also a bank which gives the greatest attention to national specificities, working in the framework of a complex matrix organization and with a corporate culture emphasizing consensus.

The strategic issues relevant to this situation evolve notably around the "network" which allows to reconcile global reach with local traditions and needs. Technology, the organization of the bank, its use of co-operative networks such as SWIFT as well as its relative reluctance regarding strategic alliances... such are some of the key-factors discussed here.

For European banks, one of the problems in developing a global network is the difficulty of establishing a strong presence in the U.S. With two "domestic" markets – the Netherlands and Illinois in the U.S. – ABN AMRO is an especially important institution to listen to for its views on the link between European integration and globalization. ***A.B.***

conversation with

DOLF VAN DEN BRINK,

ABN AMRO BANK N.V.

This conversation with Dolf van den Brink, Member of the Managing Board of ABN AMRO Bank N.V., was conducted in Amsterdam by Albert Bressand (PROMETHEE) and Hans de Haan (Moret Ernst & Young).

Perspective from a global, universal network bank

For a bank as global as ABN AMRO, is the euro a massive change or just a sort of regional consolidation? Are you approaching this transformation as a bright new beginning or as "globalization as usual"? **Dolf van den Brink:** Your question is about corporate culture as well as finance! So let me answer, first, by looking at how these two levels combine.

As a bank that began operations back in 1824, we have been through quite a set of changes already! We are convinced that the euro will happen, right on schedule and with a large number of participating countries. We see that as a fundamental change for the markets, for the banking industry in Europe and for global finance.

And yet, we feel that this transformation will not change our way of thinking. On the contrary, we see that transformation as reinforcing one fundamental aspect of our corporate culture: our emphasis on cross-fertilization among different perspectives and our efforts to move ahead on the basis of consensus.

Consensus may sound static, but, on the contrary, a strong "consensus culture" is what has helped us accommodate change rather than resist it in the past. We have seen many shocks before as the Europe of the last century and a half has not been a very quiet place indeed. We have been through experiences such as the complete loss of our 30 branches in Iran. But the euro is an altogether different type of shock, one that has been almost three decades in the making if one remembers the Werner plan of 1971 for an Economic and Monetary Union that was confidently scheduled, at the time, for "the beginning of the next decade". And the shift to the euro will take place at a time when almost everything is already changing under the combined impact of globalization, deregulation and technology.

So, as a large bank with operation in over 70 countries, with two thousand branches and a staff of 75 000 persons, we have been moving in directions coherent with these type of changes. We are now readying for the massive transformation that will follow upon the creation of the euro. We are trying to do so with a keen sense of values, things and of perspectives on the world that will not change. In other words, we are ready to remain ourselves in the process of becoming something new: a leading "euro bank".

Does this mean that the banking culture at ABN AMRO will never change? Could you elaborate on this link between what changes and what does not, in your bank as well as in Europe?

DvdB: Of course, while our fundamental principles remain the same, the ways to implement them change, as corporate cultures also evolve even if over a long period of time. Seen from a very large bank based here on the European continent, a clear change is the growing influence of the Anglo-Saxon approach, of the Anglo-Saxon way of conducting banking business. Actually, when you move around this building, here in Amsterdam, you will meet quite a number of Anglo-Saxons. This shows that we have two major "domestic" markets: the Netherlands and Illinois (USA) – and that we do our best to learn from the approaches that succeed in both of these very different environments.

If you look at our recent history, you may also notice that we are taking a much more Anglo-Saxon view of some types of corporate strategy (hostile take-overs being the most striking example) that we had approached only with strong suspicion until the end of the previous decade. But what is not changing is the feeling that these various perspectives should cross-fertilize one another in a way respectful of our basic operating principles.

How will the euro fit in the global financial picture? What is the link between the Maastricht criteria and global financial policy approaches? Is Europe a very special part of the global economy or are we just a few years ahead of the rest of the world?

DvdB: The collapse of the communist system in 1989 was a historic turning point which I personally would like to emphasize. It has created a new level of commitment, a new willingness to change the market place.

There are also changes in the global economic culture. There is now a new consensus, which one can feel for instance at the annual IMF meetings: whether they come from Peru, the Philippines, Poland or Italy, decision makers of all kinds realise that governments, if they have to interfere in the economic sphere, should never do it in an inflationary manner.

In this sense, capital markets are a source of discipline. They are steering the world, so to speak.

Against this background I see the euro process in close interaction with other developments such as the APEC agreement and meetings between the Pacific countries, the NAFTA free trade agreement between Canada, Mexico and the United-States and of course the GATT agreement of 1993. This is one global process.

The reason banks are in Europe so supportive of the euro is precisely that they realise that we all have to compete in this sort of tightly integrated world. NAFTA, MERCOSUR and similar agreements all point in the same direction. Regional agreements such as the one spearheaded by the euro are both catalyst of these global changes and opportunity to learn and adapt a little faster than the rest of the world.

If the horizon is a global one, rather than merely an European one, what do you see as the next steps in this global process of deeper and deeper integration? In particular, do you believe that monetary integration is a natural successor of free trade as the cornerstone of the global agenda? **DvdB:** Considering the level of convergence that has developed among market economies since the fall of the Iron Curtain, I feel that a natural development would be a pact between the yen, dollar and euro zones around low inflation rates and stable currencies.

Such an agreement would be a major force behind further development of trade. Right now, there may be something a bit futuristic about such a pact. Yet, I am convinced that this prospect will appear in a much more favourable light once the euro is in place. Probably, the euro will first have to be "tested". Financial markets will have to grow accustomed to it before global initiatives can be seriously considered and discussed. But some time after 2000 or 2002 this should be the next major issue on the global horizon.

This process of "testing the euro" will not necessarily go without pain and turbulences. How strong do you think the euro will be? **DvdB:** A strong euro depends on the intrinsic value of that currency. The euro can be strong if our countries persist in low inflation behaviours. Meanwhile, in Asia, the U.S. dollar will probably continue to be the currency of choice and, as we have seen recently, the transformation of Asian economies into developed economies is a source of turmoil in its own right.

So altogether, the volatility between the euro and the dollar is hard to predict. Nevertheless, my feeling is that the desirability of more stable exchange rates between these two major currencies will increase. This goes back to my forecast that discussions for global monetary stabilisation will gather steam as part of the governance of a low inflation world.

Moving from global to local, it is clear that a town like Amsterdam is not the same as it was ten years ago. Cultural interpenetration has developed very visibly. In such a context, what does it mean to be recognised as a major bank in all countries of Europe? **DvdB:** It will take a long time before we have a truly European marketplace. We are doing our utmost to move in that direction in ways that are probably most visible in asset management and treasury.

But we always keep in mind this long-term horizon and the various pace at which various groups of clients are moving.

A first goal for us are the top thousand companies of Europe. Although they account for only one or two percent of the total number of European companies, they are very large and for them this European market will become a reality very fast. For such clients, we are preparing to be, quite simply, a leading European bank.

Meanwhile, some 50 000 medium sized European companies with an international orientation will become interested in cross-border standardisation of all kinks of financial services like payments and cash managements products. These companies will belong to our target group as well.

For small businesses, however, the full impact of an integrated capital market in euro, certain as it will be, will take much longer to materialize. Such companies need to prepare for much higher levels of competition than many of them are used to.

Of course we have addressed the strategical aspects deriving from the introduction of a new currency in a number of countries. For certain customer-product combinations, our commercial developments have to be managed on a cross-border basis as well. Hence, our focus on developing our network capabilities.

In addition, as I already mentioned, our two major "domestic markets" are the Netherlands and Illinois (USA), which gives us a stimulating perspective on this integration process! In all other European countries, we are active in only some segments of the market.

What is the general architecture of this global presence beyond your two "domestic markets in the Netherlands and Illinois"? And how is the euro going to modify the present pattern of specialisation? **DvdB:** When we look at the world, we want to make sure that we make the most effective use of the various channels open to us.

We want to make sure that large customers receive "ABN AMRO" products. These customers operate globally and they expect us to provide solutions for their needs that work across borders through each point of contact with them.

Over the long term, we are moving in the direction of providing all of our clients with that global reach under one brand name. This is, so to speak, the ultimate goal.

Yet, moving toward that goal implies acquiring a number of existing banks in countries and markets that we consider important. These banks often have a long history of developing in-depth, trustful relations with their customers in their specific markets. This is an experience and an asset that we respect and value very much. In France, for instance, the NSM bank has no less than two centuries of experience. Behind its acronym, names like Neuflize, Schlumberger, Mallet convey a high sense of caring for their clients in France. The same is true of Banque Odier Bungener Courvoisier also in France.

The culture of ABN AMRO leads us to attach great value to such histories and to the reputation and standards of excellence that have developed as a result.

Hence, the "general architecture", to use your wording, is a relatively complex combination of a strong global brand and of customized local presence through banks with a strong national identity. As I indicated, however, there is a strong common culture holding all these elements together…

Everybody talks about "global financial markets". One of the questions we are asking throughout this book, however,

is how global they really are, or, rather, what is it that is truly global, and what is it that is much less so? ABN AMRO looks like the perfect bank from which to seek insights on this.
DvdB: Of course, we are immersed in global markets and impacted by global trends such as:
– the deregulation of financial markets worldwide, which the recent negotiations and agreements within the World Trade Organization (WTO) will further accelerate;
– the commoditization of many financial services as a result of these high levels of competition;
– the critical role of information technology in almost all aspects of banking and finance.

The banking industry is now following the same route as, for instance, the car industry. Economies of scale therefore come to the forefront.

Achieving substantial economies of scale in all aspects of bank operations becomes indeed the most visible expression of globalization, even for banks like ours which remain attached to the specific traditions and relations established over many decades, in each of the countries where they operate. The investments called for to achieve such economies of scale are very technologically intensive and they often carry price tags in the billions.

The euro and the further dismantling of remaining barriers in Europe is already intensifying these pressures. The search for economies of scale is accelerating to the point that one could say that it has become essential to success and, even, to survival.

To me, there are three subjects that should be considered as tightly interdependent: globalization, the preparation for the euro and the efforts to remain or to become a low- cost producer in each single market. Actually, each of these three trends feeds on the others in a mutually reinforcing manner...

The fact is that globalization is part of all these equations – those of the euro and of investments to lower costs – does not mean that all players are global. On the contrary, you have indicated that a number of banks in your own network do retain a strong national identity, and this must apply to many other banks worldwide. So what would be your short list of truly global players? **DvdB:** It is not really up to me to present the hit parade of global banking; there are quite a few well-informed journals or magazines that offer such lists in a well-researched and detailed manner.

The question that I can answer is a narrower one as it limits itself to the short list of banks that are not only "global" but also universal in the type of services that they offer with a strong emphasis on a retail network.

In this light, the names that come to mind, clearly in a non-exhaustive manner, include HSBC, Deutsche Bank and Citibank, even if the latter no longer defines itself as a "universal" bank.

If I may use your question to explain a little better what is special to ABN AMRO, let me point to the fact that globalization, in spite of all the hype, is not a one way street. Banks or companies that have embarked into efforts to develop a global presence may very well decide, after a few years, that the time has come to concentrate on a more limited number of markets (as well, of course, as on a more limited number of products). So I share your concern that globalization is not something that goes without saying and that would translate into a collective strategy whereby all types banks and companies would expand abroad.

Against the background of globalization, ABN AMRO is one of the few banks that did not retrench but that, maintained and developed a global presence, year after year, decade after decade. Like many others, we did it in fair weather but we also did it in foul weather.

There are countries, such as Malaysia and Indonesia in which we were the first foreign banks. But in all countries, as I tried to illustrate in the case of France, we have endeavoured to find the best combination, the best synergies between global and local.

We can see that you find the term "global" best used in conjunction with other words, and notably with "universal" and, also, with the term "network". ABN AMRO pamphlets and the advertising campaign you have been running across Europe in preparation for the euro have described you as "the network bank". What do you have in mind with this "GUN" combination of global, universal and network? **DvdB:** The "network" is about the combination of the various parts in our bank that allows to bring to our clients those services most adapted to each of them. We are not trying to sell the whole world to each single customer, but if they need some of our products, then we must be able to deliver with the necessary flexibility.

There has to be a balance between being domestic and being global in such a network. This is where the Dutch tradition helps with its emphasis on listening to others. A key point is to be receptive to other cultures: to listen and to adjust.

Again, as we discussed earlier, we are "consensus oriented". The Anglo-Saxon flavor that we are acquiring does imply elements of international competition, but that should not abolish this basic orientation. We are quite capable of being bankers in America in the ways Americans expect. But an American working with us here in Amsterdam at the global level is also encouraged to adapt to our consensus culture. This is a two way street, a street of cross-fertilization among cultures rather than one of cultural imperialism one way or the other.

As far as our strategy to also be a *universal* bank, the explanation is quite simple. We try to fully integrate our *commercial banking* and *investment banking* activities because we strongly believe that there are synergies between the two. These synergies work in the best interest of our customers and of ourselves.

There must be a link between this view of globalization and the rather complex "matrix structure" behind your internal organization... DvdB: Yes, this is a quite complex structure but we are also pursuing complex objectives as we want to be strong globally and to recognize also the role of geography and of local cultures, traditions and market environments. As Hans de Haan was observing a few minutes ago, we also give special importance to lines of business and to the synergies on which they should be able to draw between the different channels at our disposal, whether telecommunication and electronic links or physical networks of branches.

We try to look at our own structure from the perspective of our clients. This means that we must have three types of leading threads: client line of course, but also product lines because we are also competing with specialized banks that will be 100% focused on certain products, and also with emphasis on geography. No surprise then that the structure may be a little complex as we try to find the right balance between these three approaches. Some people find it difficult in terms of time that must be devoted to build the necessary consensus.

What do you expect from technology over the next few years, notably with respect to the euro? DvdB: A lot of the adaptation and transformation will be technology driven. It is clear that IT will be tremendously important to payments in euros. Our biggest project here is called Global Transaction Services GTS, it is focused in the first phase on the euro and it involves major expenditures – about 500 million U.S. dollars at first, growing up to a lot more later.

This is clearly a major investment and it will help us to address, not only the issues narrowly associated with the euro, but also the many other issues that must be addressed to help our clients to treat Europe as a whole as their *domestic* market.

If we may ask you a question of a slightly more personal nature, can you explain why the same person on ABN AMRO's board, namely yourself is entrusted with responsibility over two fields usually seen as very different, sometimes almost opposite: technology and human resources. **DvdB:** Well, I am used to multiple personalities as I have been a commercial banker and then an investment banker... So my real "hat" is that of universal banking.

It is so obvious to me that there are strong interactions between human resources and IT. In the coming years, we will have to take strategic decisions and deploy resources in ways that will depend simultaneously – and very critically so – on human and IT resources. The way people work nowadays cannot be separated from the sort of tools to which they have access. Actually, my predecessor in the Board also had these two fields under his watch.

What role then do you attribute to the large banking co-operatives such as SWIFT, Euroclear, Echo... **DvdB:** We see them as neutral associations. Working through them is much better than the type of approach that was tried in the 1970s through *ad hoc* efforts to team up with a supplier and with one's own customers. That sort of approach, which was tried in various fields, did not work because nobody knew who was in charge. It was adding one level of complexity to our own not-so-simple structure...

Coming back to the euro and technology, as you know, the major project presently underway is the TARGET system for inter-bank payments in euros. But TARGET is meant only for big payments, and it consists mostly in interconnecting national payment systems once they have been upgraded to handle payments in real time and one by one (Real Time Gross Settlement, RTGS, as technician call such networks).

We do not see SWIFT playing a new role either and the local clearing houses will still be around. So Europe will not change very much in terms of infrastructures beyond the type of modernization that was needed anyway.

We have links with all clearing houses and we are approaching all systems with the interests of our clients in mind, with their needs for cost-price advantages and for advantages of speed. Of course, as a global bank we have a keen interest in providing corporate treasurers with real-time information and with the opportunity for "gaining time" as you say, because acting faster is a key competitive advantage. Business-to-business payment are very important in our approach and you may say that only Deutsche Bank and we will be present in all the countries (I mean present in the full sense of the term and not simply through a representative office) so as to provide this sort of service to clients.

Banks have traditionally procured little from outside compared to manufacturer – roughly speaking less than a third against more than two third. Do you see globalization and the euro leading to much higher levels of what André Lussi refers to in this book as "in-sourcing"? What about strategic alliances? Can they really work? **DvdB:** In the long term, it is clear that what you call "insourcing" should be a big trend. Book keeping and payment as well as the move toward on-line paperless operations calls for a set of state-of-the-art expertise and for levels of investment as well as of expertises few can afford purely internally.

As for alliances, our approach so far has been to do as much as we could internally, focusing on the activities for which we are adding value. But nothing is certain for ever and this may evolve and we keep our eyes open to what alliances could bring either to enhance the cost-base or to combine market forces. This being said, big strategic alliances are also a big source of problems.

Discussing with you, we understand a little better what is the GUN – Global Universal Network – behind ABN AMRO self descriptions. Is there one word, may be a more mundane one, that could capture the type of identity that goes with this GUN? And how does it apply to the euro? Might we suggest that this is the word "balance"! **DvdB:** In the end, we have to see how far down market we can compete. A full retail operation is very complex and, even with the euro, we do not foresee a very strong integration of retail banking in Europe.

"Call centers" and other "direct banking" channels will accelerate the trend toward cross-border banking but, at the end of the day, a majority of people want to do business with a bank of their country. Nevertheless, there is a small but important segment of the clientele that thinks in European terms – because of their works, habits or travels. Being panEuropean is justified in a number of segments but one must be aware of the tremendous investments involved, not just in technology but also in marketing the brand as a European brand.

Actually, our big project is to create European business accounts that can be open through one single window in one single country but that will give our clients accounts in as many euro countries as they want, with real time information and consolidation, all this within the same contractual framework and conditions. Beyond this, we use the "alignment of technology" to create an "alignment" of our business all around the world.

Once data bases are linked as they are beginning to be the key issue for a global universal network – call it GUN if you want! – is about knowledge. I mean not just knowledge creation but also knowledge sharing among 75 000 men and women who can be almost anywhere in the world. Ninety per cent of knowledge stays with the person or with the team. The key issue is to share and transfer such knowledge from one place to another. This implies that you can identify the common denominators that give this knowledge universal relevance. Sharing knowledge cannot be identified with overwhelming people with e-mail, it is far more complex, most of which are not relevant. In that sense, yes, the key issue is one of balance.

We are European, we are global and also, we are different. It is important to be different and to welcome difference, within and around the organisation. I believe we should integrate what we can with costs and demand very much in mind. Our strength then lies in finding this difficult, complex but essential balance between what is domestic and what is global. This sense of balance, after the euro just as before, is what I believe is most essential for a group that wants to be, let's put it simply, relevant. ■

Chapter X

The strategic issues *behind the conversation*

A major process of portfolio re-allocation will take place on the way to - and in the aftermath of - the euro. Actually, for asset managers, the pre-euro arbitrages are already in full swing. Hence, the first set of strategic issues addressed in this conversation with Philippe Collas was related to the changes in the markets that asset managers anticipate in preparing for the euro.

"Club Europe", a forum for institutional investors created by Société Générale Asset Management, helps its members identify which changes are already built into investors' decisions and which ones still have to find their way into such decisions.

Consensus seems to be quite advanced regarding the future benchmarks for the "yield curve" in euros. By contrast, preparing for a much broader gamut of risks and for larger spreads among investment-grade-instruments will take more time, even though everyone agrees that the days of the country-fund manager are already gone...

To be more perceptive and more agile than rating agencies and large investment banks will be quite a challenge for fund managers.

Asset managers have begun proposing or testing with their own seed money the products of the euro age. They are also busy putting into place the research capacities and the analytical tools that will be indispensable in order to survive the combination of more volatile markets and of direct competition with the anglo-saxon power houses.

This being said, longer term strategic issues also include the concentration process that will take place in the asset management industry. Will it go the same way as investment banking, with large U.S. firms in a dominant position? Will European banks preserve their present control over distribution networks? Will discount brokers finally succeed in becoming major competitors in Europe? The agenda addressed with Philippe Collas is a broad one indeed! A.B.

conversation with

PHILIPPE COLLAS,

SOCIÉTÉ GÉNÉRALE ASSET MANAGEMENT

This strategic conversation with Philippe Collas, CEO of Société Générale Asset Management, was conducted by Albert Bressand and Catherine Distler (PROMETHEE) and Bernard Nivollet (ERNST & YOUNG) in Paris.

Asset managers already live with the euro!

Is the euro a watershed, a major development or a "non-event" that markets have already built into self fulfilling expectations?

Philippe Collas: Actually, when I thought about this "strategic conversation" that we were about to have together, my first reaction was to feel that you were coming too late! The euro has *"happened"* already, some time toward the end of the Spring of 1997, when the general opinion switched from disbelief to complete certainty. Since then, the markets have taken for granted that the euro would be in place right on time, on January 1, 1999 and that ten or eleven countries would be participating.

Until that change occurred, people could not see the relevance of this great undertaking for day to day matters. Uncertainties were much too high, the German factor was seen as overwhelming, participation by Southern European countries was derided as a *"Club Med"* affair... Then, all of a sudden, perceptions changed radically. From then on, everyone would take for certain that, yes, the euro was on its way. As a result, the convergence among "*yield curves*" (which give the interest rates for each maturity) extended quickly beyond the core countries.

The same shift in perception could be detected outside of Europe. In a trip I took to Asia and North America in early 1997, most people expressed disbelief or disinterest. When I saw them again in the late summer and fall of

1997, the same people were completely convinced that the euro would happen.

As economists, we could probably exchange a few words on the relevance of the theory of "rational expectation" to what you call the "self fulfilling prophecy" behind the euro. Convergence in expectations was clearly at work and played a key role in the process of macroeconomic convergence.

You are not simply observing convergence in expectations, you are also taking some initiatives to foster it, are you not?
Ph. C: I imagine what you have in mind is the "Club Europe". Yes, together with a number of institutional players, we have set up a club in which to think about the implications of the euro for our profession, for the world of asset management. This is also a place where we can brainstorm about the initiatives that we could take inside our various organisations. These discussions have been pursued in two main directions: equity markets and fixed-income markets.

In addition, the electronic networks that are essential to our activity will have to adapt. This is something many of us realised but which was not taken into account at operational level in terms of information systems and of accounting. Logistical problems must be addressed, and Club Europe is also one way to raise the level of awareness about them.

What are the changes in markets that you are discussing and preparing for in this framework? **Ph. C:** National markets today are quite different in terms of some basic characteristics. Italian government debt, for instance, is more on the short term side – three years and less – whereas German government debt leans more toward the longer term side of the curve, with French Treasury OAT somewhere in between. Obviously, in the unified market in euros, a number of re-alignments and re-positionings are conceivable. Everyone also realises that a set of benchmarks will emerge and it is not too early to begin preparing for them.

These sorts of things were relatively easy to identify and we find that market practitioners were quite prepared to discuss them. But there are other aspects of the transformation that call for more radical re-examination, and such rethinking cannot happen overnight.

A fundamental challenge for us is the impact that the euro will have on the *diversity of instruments* and on the much *broader gamut of risks* that asset managers will have to deal with. This goes well beyond the re-positioning of existing instruments in what will be their common environment.

An important aspect of the situation today is that pension funds tend to have more than ninety percent of their resources invested in fixed-income assets. As a result, expertise in asset-management groups has been centered on the capacity, so to speak, of "working the yield curve". *Counter-party risk* was hardly ever considered. The spread between Société Générale and French Government bonds, for instance, was minimal (something like 2 *centimes*) and the difference was so small that few asset managers in their right mind would buy *corporate* rather than government debt. This is clearly going to change with the euro. Spreads will develop between different government debts and, even more so, between government and corporate securities.

As a consequence, asset managers will have to alter quite radically their typical portfolio. In our case, we have begun preparing for such a shift as early as mid-1996, and we have already put in place the information networks that will help us conduct our business and be well positioned in this very different type of market.

The recent currency and market turmoil in Asia has shed crude light on the quality of much of the information about risk that is available to the markets. How is a group like yours dealing with these problems of information and risk evaluation?

Ph. C: Indeed, someone who followed the monetary and financial crisis in Asia could see that ratings tended to be revised *after* rather than before problems had occurred. It is important therefore to strengthen internal capacities within the group to monitor those types of risks and to act upon them more rapidly.

In our research team of forty-odd persons, for instance, we have set up a new unit staffed with five persons to prepare for the higher new levels of analytical capacity that we expect to be necessary. They specialise on European signatures, identifying and evaluating the European debt-issuers in order to be able to assess the future risks and the spreads likely to be attached to each of them by the markets.

We do our best to anticipate these qualitative changes in the nature of markets. In doing so, we bear in mind that the market that will develop will be far larger than the sum of the existing markets in the national currencies of Europe before the euro.

In this respect, one of the interesting developments to watch will be the "euro-euro", or, in other words, the euro-markets in the euro-currency that will develop alongside the euro-dollar, euro-yen and other traditional euro-markets. So we are in the process of looking at all present issuers on the euro-markets in those national currencies that are actively traded today (euro-FF, euro-DM, euro-Luxembourg francs) because they are likely to become active participants in this euro-euro world still to come.

Where will this "euro-euro" market be located, and how will it develop? **Ph. C:** Issuers will be largely Europeans. At this stage, *British* issuers are very prominent in the euro-markets. So I feel that the market will develop, first, around London but what happens after that is wide open. Indeed, one reason for this British pre-eminence is that *pension funds* are far more developed in the U.K. than they are on the continent, with the exception of the Netherlands. As pension funds are likely to develop also on the continent, even if more slowly, one can imagine that a broader *diversity of participants* will develop for the euro-euro.

But this broadening of market participation and the greater diversity of risks that will be brought to the market are not restricted to one particular segment. We should prepare for a very significant, across-the-board increase in the levels of diversity, of risks and of competition. Asset managers will be under very strong pressure to perform and to outperform, even more so than they are now. And this will lead them to expand their horizon very significantly.

Do you see the dawn of an equity culture in continental Europe? **Ph. C:** In conversations that I had with Bernard Nivollet in the past, we could easily agree that investors, whether institutional or individual, are already under major pressures to look at equities in a different light.

A number of institutional investors – such as French insurance companies – find themselves committed to achieving yields that they are no longer able to achieve with government bonds in the present environment of low interest rates and better control of public finance. As you know, they are under *legal obligation* to guarantee their clients with a return of at least 3.5% for contracts in French francs over the long term. In addition, competitive pressures force them to promise higher short term returns. So, altogether they are likely to look for better balanced portfolios with substantially higher investment. Hence, they are looking for performing investments in *equities*. They are now proposing contracts in "units of accounts" rather than in so called French francs contracts. Such contracts are not subjects to the 3.5% guaranteed minimal rate of return and, on top of that, they qualify for a lower solvency ratio (1% against 3%). This also relieves them from some of the constraints that had limited their investments in equities.

A major process of re-thinking has begun, even if it will take a long time before bearing all its fruits. Used as they are to the fixed-income culture, pension plans ("*caisses de retraite*") and life insurers can resort at first to some increases in the contributions; there comes a time, however, when higher performance is the only answer. So the development of an equity culture will be in everybody's interest.

What are the other major changes you anticipate with the advent of the euro? Ph. C: Like others, we realise quite clearly that the days of the country-fund manager are numbered. And so are the days of country-based-benchmark indices. As much foreign exchange risk will disappear with the euro, analysts will be able to focus on the strength and risks of each issuer and on the specific market in which this issuer is doing business. In other words, the *country* perspective will become irrelevant and the *sectoral* perspective will prevail.

This radical shift in the ways we look at securities will imply much more pronounced market fluctuations. We are preparing for the *more volatile* markets that will prevail once the present barriers are removed.

The big strength of an asset manager will be his or her capacity to anticipate changes before rating agencies or brokers' analysts. As you know, large price movements occur as soon as Goldman Sachs or a similar firm makes public its opinion that some problem is developing or that one company that they are following is doing clearly better than another in the same sector. Changes in rating will move huge amounts of capital. This is something that we are anticipating and preparing for. In addition, one can hold for certain that large amounts of capital will be invested, in any case, in the top hundred European companies. Asset managers will need to anticipate these huge flows of money.

On our side, we are working on the development of a Société Générale benchmark that can help us in our discussions with rating agencies.

We are also already working on the rebalancing of our portfolios. To take the easiest example, we are clearly "overweight" on France. We are presently managing 600 billion French francs worth of assets, of which 75 % are invested in France. We know these proportions will have to change drastically. The euro is a threat, but also a tremendous opportunity.

What is the time horizon that you have in mind in preparing for these transformations? Ph. C: What I am describing *is not* for 1999:

the pre-euro arbitrages are going full swing *right now.* When this book appears, you can be sure that the fundamental shift will already have taken place. What will remain to be done will be more like living with the shift and making it a source of profitable opportunities.

Market volatility will increase dramatically among as well as within sectors. The search for quality and high returns will have important consequences. Those French banks that still have insufficient returns will be in risk of seeing investors walk away from their shares, and this market disaffection could be a major problem.

U.S. and U.K. financial institutions include a set of specialized asset-management networks with a good mastery of quantitative analysis and other cutting-edge techniques. By contrast, banks in continental Europe are still controlling this type of activity, often with more modest research and technical capacities. How you see competition evolving at the interface of these two market structures? **Ph. C:** Continental Europeans will display their rational and scientific skills in this new equity environment. We are quite confident that we can be as competitive as British fund managers. But when we look at the U.S. capital market, it is obvious that the Americans have already been through the sort of revolution that the euro will unleash in Europe. We are fifteen years behind - or, if you prefer, we have to catch up quickly.

The present fragmented and relatively illiquid markets that we have in Europe will give way to one large, liquid market. Its depth will be more comparable to that of the present U.S. market. Such a market will attract foreign investors. There is no doubt in our mind that *competition with U.S. asset managers* will be, to use an understatement, quite intense and very challenging…

U.S. investment banks are making for asset management the type of efforts that they had made previously for investment banking. The perspective of these American (and other non-European) actors will become increasingly important, which also raises the issue of the pension fund industry here in Europe. The trend today, in many countries, is to delay adapting our pension systems but I am quite confident that changes will rapidly become unavoidable.

Also, it is difficult to imagine that the financial industry in Europe can remain as fragmented as it is today. The euro will compel all of us to take a fresh look at size, alliances, distribution, market products.

And what are the challenges that you are preparing for in term of products? Ph. C: As I said, we are preparing for the exit of country-fund managers and for a great decline – not total disappearance from the scene, but a strong decline – in country based funds.

The next generation of products will involve higher levels of arbitrage, higher levels of risk taking. It will be much more diverse as the yield curve ceases to define the horizon of asset management in Europe and will be replaced by a similar attention to the various levels of risks.

We have changed our own organization. Our previous structure combined four units: "France", "other developed countries", "emerging markets" and "others". By contrast, our present structure has one "euro-division" in which sectoral analysis can develop for the whole "buy side" of the market.
We still follow the same number of equities – about 400 European ones for the actively traded – but the screening process is now sectoral.

What are you telling your customers? How do you think they will react to the big change that the euro will represent as far as savings are concerned? Ph. C: Our individual clients won't see abrupt change. A first reason is tax, a field in which harmonisation will take much longer than it has been the case for regulatory matters.

As you know, for instance, we have in France savings plans in equities that give special tax advantages to the individual investors, the *Plan d'Epargne Actions* (PEA). To qualify for PEA, funds must be 60% invested in France. So, the average individual investor is not likely to become as European minded as he or she could be in light of market opportunities. Countries are often less agile in tax matters than in regulatory changes. The time horizon for anything involving major changes in the tax structure is usually very long.

Actually, within "our Club Europe", we are organizing round-tables in key euro-countries. From the discussions we hold, it is clear that the French situation looks more like the rule than like the exception and that resistances to change, or simply problems that will take time to be overcome, can be found all over Europe.

Even the Thomas law passed under the previous conservative government to create pension funds in France included limits. This being said, if such limits are not removed, what will happen is that French investors will invest abroad. Once currency risk is removed, people will take a hard look at what they can do to prepare their retirement and they will make their own decisions in what will be the domestic market at that time, namely the whole euro-market.

What about institutional investors? How are you trying to meet their needs on the way to the euro? Ph. C: In early 1996, we created our first "euro fund" for our institutional clients. True, this was initially an eight-country-fund as the Mediterranean countries had not yet converged toward the Maastricht criteria, but such things are easy to correct. Of course this fund will be re-labelled in euros.

Europe Actions is based on eight sectors (finance, luxury goods, construction, "grande distribution" etc.). We have also a number of specialised one-sector funds but, at this stage, we finance them with our own seed-money without offering them yet to our clients. We are working on the learning curve, so to speak.

As far as fixed-income products are concerned, we are now offering a global product. But one of the new developments should be a *mixed equity/bond fund*, with a balance between the two types of instruments that evolves in line with our perception of the market. This type of *hybrid investment* is something very popular in the U.K., but in France, until now, we had tended to select asset managers in terms of their expertise in bonds. So we are breaking away from the old habits and bringing to market the type of products that will be in demand when the euro comes.

To come back to a set of issues that we have discussed in the first part of this book, on which sort of stock exchange do you expect to operate to conduct this massive asset reallocation? Ph. C: An Europe-wide stock exchange would obviously serve our needs well. Today, for instance, Elf accounts for about 8% of the Paris Bourse capitalisation. So it is not possible to be "overweight" on Elf in our portfolios as this would quickly take us above the 10% prudential limit. By contrast, if we were operating on a Europe-wide exchange, Elf would represent a much smaller share of total market capitalisation and we would enjoy a much higher degree of flexibility in asset allocation.

Similarly, there are distortions implicit in the structure of national market capitalisation that do not go well with a global asset allocation strategy. In France for instance, banks and the distribution sector are over-represented.

On the whole, I expect that a pan-European market will develop for the top European companies while "small caps" and "medium caps" will remain traded in national settings.

What about distribution networks then? Are we turning to this issue only toward the end of the conversation because this is the weaker link in the "value chain" that you are busily

adapting to the euro? To which extent do you feel that the concentration of distribution networks in the hands of banks can protect you from foreign competitors? **Ph. C:** On the retail side, it is difficult to be present without a distribution network. We have developed presence in Germany, Benelux, Spain and Italy through distribution agreements but we know that for a long time this will not come close to the network we have developed in France, by far. So, the key issue is competencies. We are like British asset managers, with no major distribution network. Hence, we have to be as performing as they are.

A difference with U.S. is the existence in each of our European countries of insurance companies and banks with a very large number of branches. In addition, as you know, asset management in Europe tends to be done by companies like this one that are owned by the large network-banks or insurance companies. This pattern of ownership will remain a major source of fragmentation after the euro.

Do you envision a separation between asset management and distribution? **Ph. C:** You are right to ask the question as it is very relevant to the long term vision. But we are still at an intermediate stage where the owners of the smaller asset management houses have not yet realised the pressures they will face. Pressures will materialize from the bottom with "grande distribution" and from the top with "electronic delivery channels" targeted toward the upper market.

We are preparing for these two changes. Regarding electronic distribution, for instance, we have just begun in Spain, now, as we are speaking. Italy will come next in March 1998, then Germany in June and so on. When the euro comes we'll be able to access clients electronically in the whole euro region.

On this electronic network, we will act as brokers (*courtiers*). But, we'll try to be smart distributors. We will not offer the whole gamut but a shorter list of products. That list however will not be a static framework as we'll use dynamic asset allocation, *clés en mains.*

Will there be a European Charles Schwab? In other words, will the banks and financial institutions of today be facing competition from new groups of financial intermediaries like the American "discount brokers"? **Ph. C:** This is indeed a key question which we have been asking ourselves repeatedly. Charles Schwab himself tested the waters in France, with no success. They tried with more success in the U.K. Yet the euro will encourage this type of trend.

Schwab is first and foremost a network of brokers. On top of that they have developed an electronic network and electronic accounts faster than others. They can bring technology but cross-border selling is a tough challenge as it involves working with local banks, authenticating clients in a fool-proof fashion, processing payments swiftly… The stakes are very high and we are all keeping our eyes open to these new types of competition.

May we ask you to imagine that you have been offered a long sabbatical to celebrate the coming of the euro and that you come back to asset management one decade later... What will asset management look like in the year 2010? Will you be able to recognise much of what you know today? Ph. C: You are welcome to invite me to these virtual sabbatical moments... but I will not surprise you by saying that the landscape will be hard to recognize for someone who would have really accepted these ten years out of the markets. Many – if not most – middle-sized operators would probably no longer be around, and the large ones would have become very large indeed. More importantly, people would have evolved, and this is probably what would have driven the whole process of change.

For ten years, people will have been searching for *competencies.* And they will have found them: a new class of intermediaries will have developed, many of them working "on the net".

All in all, *distribution* will be the key discriminating factor. And large sums of money will have changed hands in this race toward distribution power and placing power. *Deep pockets* will be needed and, as you know, at this moment there are not many French banks that have been able to accumulate the profits that it takes to play in that type of hard driving game. What may be less often mentioned is that, beyond financial resources, language and culture will also be discriminating factors. All in all, the going will be rough.

The true global players will include some big Americans and Swiss, a couple of Germans banks, ABN AMRO and a few others. Being among those few others will be a tough challenge. Actually, it is *the* challenge on which we are working before, or more probably, instead of this tempting sabbatical years that you have kindly put before my eyes… ■

Chapter XI

The strategic issues *behind the conversation*

The conversation with René Karsenti had really three subjects: European integration as a socio-economic process, the technical change likely to take place in the various compartments of markets after the euro, and the strategy followed by EIB to pave the way for deep and liquid markets in euros and to do so with the long term "sustainability" of the new currency in mind.

Created in 1957 in the wake of the Treaty of Rome itself, EIB is the lending arm of the EU, in charge of promoting "the balanced economic development of the Union". Hence its well known activities in infrastructural and local development projects. Hence also the critical role of EIB in helping the candidate countries in Eastern Europe prepare for membership in the EU. Job creation has become a core dimension of these development objectives. As agreed at the Amsterdam Summit, this is about to take EIB, a "triple A" borrower, into the world of venture capital to the tune of 1 billion euros per year.

Aspects of post-1999 markets in euros discussed include, notably, benchmarks for bond markets, issuance techniques, credit valuation, swaps and the generic AA credit risk, as well as the euromarket in euro and the changing balance between off-shore and domestic... this special section toward the end of this discussion is clearly designed for the expert audience!

But the strategic issues addressed here also include financial relations with developing countries as well as the critical role of EIB in using its 25 billion ECUs issuing power to begin creating liquidity in euros through such preparatory measures as "euro-tributary issues". In other words, the full "guided tour" of the capital markets in the waiting... *A.B.*

conversation with

René Karsenti,

European Investment Bank

This conversation with René Karsenti, Director General, Finance, European Investment Bank (EIB) was conducted in Luxembourg by Albert Bressand (PROMETHEE) and Kenneth Hay, (Ernst & Young S.A., Luxembourg).

A large financial institution promoting financial markets in euros: the European Investment Bank (EIB) perspective

Before we discuss the implications of the euro for banks, and the strategy followed by the European Investment Bank (EIB), may we turn to the seasoned financier you are for some "informed outsider's opinion" on a subject addressed in the first part of this book, namely the impact of the euro on European stock markets? You have worked in London as well as on the continent, and we would appreciate your views on what will happen in these matters. **René Karsenti:** Well, there is a good news and what one might call a tough news. The good news is that more European stock exchanges than "Cassandras" would expect may survive. The tough news is that they will have to do so in a very competitive framework in which each one of them will have to identify its competitive advantages pretty much as any company would do. In addition, stock exchanges will need to achieve and to make available to their members and clients a level of *economies of scale* proportionate to the size of that huge, integrated European capital market that the euro will create.

Currently the European Union (EU) has some 45 stock exchanges – one in each capital plus a number in regional centres – compared with only eight in the United States, where the equity market capitalisation exceeds that of the whole EU.

In my view, the consolidation process should be most severe among exchanges for futures and derivatives. Many contracts on fixed income and foreign exchange products will become redundant and yet futures and options are now traded on some 16 exchanges in the EU, compared with only six in the United States.

Likewise, bond and equity trading will also see more geographical concentration. True, the continuous fall in information and transaction costs is making it feasible for trading to be more geographically dispersed. Yet, other factors like the need for specialised personnel and computer services and the globalization of markets still suggest that trading will continue to gravitate towards very few financial centres.

So, I am convinced that a number of exchanges will have no choice but to explore the possibility of mergers with other exchanges, and that all of them will need to position themselves through appropriate alliances and link-ups in the "new financial geography" that Jean-François Théodore describes in the first conversation in this book. Against this background of "fierce competition and forced co-operation", I imagine that one aspect of your question must have to do with the competition between London and the continent...

Your opinion on that aspect of competition would also be most welcome indeed! **RK:** Here again, let me suggest that there is good news and bad news. The good news is that continental Europe, in my view at least, will have some important competitive advantages. Having the *European Central Bank* in Frankfurt is clearly one of them, and this will create a "magnet effect" of value to Germany and, more generally, to euro-country institutions. Another advantage has to do with the *quality of clearing and settlement systems* and with the capacity of euro-country institutions to settle directly in what will soon be the *second reserve currency of the world.* In addition, the main government borrowers in euros will be based on the continent.

Financial centres may try to protect their market share, both by making their markets more attractive but also through hidden protectionist measures on who can trade domestic issues or sell to domestic investors. If limits would be established on access by London-based banks to TARGET, the euro-payments system under development, clearing and settlement may also become a source of competitive disadvantage for London. Looking at book on "Europe 2012" edited by Albert Bressand, I can see that such a risk will be more pronounced in the "KernEuropa" scenario, namely the one in which the euro is limited to a small number of continental countries...

This being said, the bad news for continental players is that London is likely to keep most of its comparative advantages: it has the world's largest *foreign exchange* market and stands clearly above the others in *international equities* as well as in *eurobonds, swaps, investment banking,* and *global asset management.* Its foreign exchange market is global in nature and depends less on intra-European trading, which makes it less vulnerable to the large loss in business that the euro will entail in that respect.

So, altogether, its high concentration of bankers, lawyers, traders, and accountants and its open philosophy imply that London will retain a comparative advantage over alternative financial centres on the Continent. This suggests that the announcement by the Chancellor of the Exchequer in November 1997 to support the euro but to delay British participation will not necessarily affect London position too much: after all, in the past few decades, London has been able to build up its leadership despite the fall of Sterling as an international reserve currency! This, however, may hold true only for a few years: if the U.K. were to stay out of the euro for much longer, it is quite possible that the role of London would suffer in a much more pronounced manner.

Tax considerations will also be a major element. I agree with what Gérard Pfauwadel says in this book about how hard it is to maintain financial centres of excellence on the continent when it costs financial institutions there between 400 and 450 euros (against 180 euros in the U.K.) to deliver 100 euro of after-tax purchasing power in the form of salaries to their specialists or to their traders. The result is that activities that could be carried on the continent have been moving to London and are quietly continuing to do so.

To speak of the country in which the EIB is located and to follow up on the work you mentioned in which PROMETHEE participated, can you describe the implications of the euro for the financial centre of Luxembourg [1]? **RK:** As that book acknowledges, private banking has clearly played a major role in the first

1. *Europe 2012, Globalisation et Cohésion sociale : les Scénarios Luxembourgeois,* Fondation Alphonse Weicker, *op. cit.*

phase in the development of the Luxembourg financial centre. But, living here, I am impressed that Luxembourg has also developed a whole set of competitive advantages that will be of value in the more demanding environment of the euro. These competitive advantages, include:
– good skills in *fund management*;
– a capacity to work in a *multi-currency environment*, something that is not as usual as one might think in global finance;
– strong *back offices* for the banks themselves and for third parties from all over the world, also its large area of clearing and settlement services through such companies as Cedel Bank and the cooperative recently set-up by four Luxembourg banks to combine back-office services;
– a *capacity to adapt* rapidly which makes Luxembourg less "prisoner of the past" than financial centres in larger countries.

Luxembourg has done its best to attract *listing of issues* and this will remain a competitive advantage on which they can continue to build. The same is true of the quality of back offices as illustrated in your book. The challenge now is probably to build the critical mass of high level expertise needed to address the most profitable aspects of fund management and other financial activities.

> The role of EIB in promoting markets in euros

With these remarks on stock exchanges in mind, it is even more interesting to talk about the European Investment Bank as a major actor in the financial markets. But, first, it could be useful for our readers to explain what sort of institution this European Investment Bank is, what is its role and who are the "stakeholders" that it has in mind in fulfilling this role. The "woman-and-the-man-in-the-street" in Paris, Copenhagen or Madrid are not necessarily very familiar with the "EIB" acronym... **RK:** Anyone who has heard of the Treaty of Rome could have heard of the EIB! Just like the European Union we just turned 40 as we were created in 1958.

Our total lending program exceeds 24 billion ECU per year. In 1997, about 23 billion ECU were borrowed mostly in European financial markets and we do so with the benefits for us and for our clients and partners of being an efficient, "AAA rated", financial intermediary. In other words, a financial intermediary of very high credit-rating able to tap markets in the best conditions.

The EIB's central mission is to promote the "*balanced economic development of the European Union*" – in other words, to support European services economic integration for the benefit of all European regions. We do this by making long-term loans for sound investment projects relevant to our mission. Thus, a high percentage of our lending is for infrastructure projects of all kinds (road, rail, energy, civil aviation, telecommunications etc.). Actually, I believe there are very few major construction projects in the European Union in which the EIB is not involved.

So the man or woman "in the street" that you mention would have good reasons to know us as we are probably involved in financing either in that street or at least in many of the highways to which it leads!

Examples of EIB financed projects range from road and rail networks in Finland and Sweden in the North fast-railway systems throughout Continental Europe and to gas pipelines bringing natural gas from Algeria to Spain, Portugal and Italy. Our lending goes to both the *public* and *private* sectors. Indeed, an important feature of our current activity is increasing involvement in private finance projects. We also lend substantial amounts to *industry*, both directly to large companies and, through the intermediary of banks, to small and medium-sized enterprises (SME).

One feature of our lending is that about two-thirds of it is directed to the less developed areas of the European Union, thus confirming our principal mission of promoting balanced development through economic integration.

To be exhaustive, I should mention that the remaining 10% of our lending – representing a significant 2-3 billion ECUs per year – goes to over 100 countries throughout the world in support of the European Union's external development aid and co-operation policies. The largest amounts go to Central and Eastern European countries and to the Mediterranean region. The former will grow and assume increased importance as a number of those countries move toward accession to the Union.

I cannot resist also adding that all this is done with a staff largely based in Luxembourg, and a budget smaller than almost any other multilateral financial institution. We pride ourselves on our leanness, productivity and efficiency…

You are describing the lending policy of the EIB and the objectives that it serves. But you have not yet answered our question on the stake holders whom EIB has in mind in carrying out this mission… **RK:** Your eagerness to know who our "stakeholders" are does not surprise me in light of the contemporary debates about "shareholder value" and "stakeholder capitalism"! Let me say, quite simply, that there are three "constituencies" that we keep in mind in anything we do: our shareholders of course, our borrowers and our investors.

– Our *shareholders* are the fifteen member countries of the European Union. Unlike what is true of other supranational financial institutions, all of these fifteen countries are also borrowers. These countries appoint our governing board and their support is essential to the EIB;

– Our *borrowers* are governments, public institutions, local governments, companies, financial institutions. To them, we are, first and foremost, an AAA financial intermediary able to raise and lend funds for long periods at very favourable market rates;

– *Investors* in our bonds also have rights that we bear in mind in everything we do. For each ECU we lend, about 90 cents have to be borrowed from them. They have the right to hold solid investment at the highest level of security over long period of times and in full confidence. They probably look at us in terms not simply of our size and staying power (we have been operating for 40 years!) but also in terms of the very prudent, very conservative policy that we follow in our own borrowing and lending decisions.

Just like Alexandre Dumas' "three Musketeers", these three constituencies are really four rather than three, the fourth major stakeholders being our own 950 employees. Their skills and dedication are our key assets.

Are we correct to say that the EIB is the largest supranational financial institution, even if its name is much less familiar to the general public than that of the World Bank? **RK:** You are technically correct: the EIB is now the world's biggest multilateral borrower and lender. In fact, I think we now lend and borrow more than all the other international financial institutions. This year we will lend over 25 billion ECUs, mostly within the European Union, and to finance it we will borrow a similar amount through more than 160 bond issues in some 20 different currencies. With assets of over 150 billion ECUs and outstanding loans of over 120 billion ECUs, our strong AAA status is supported by our shareholders – the 15 Member States of the European Union – and our strong capital base of 62 billion ECUs.

But this is probably not the only relevant way to understand what we really do. So let us move from this brief description of the EIB to one leading thread in this book, namely the emergence of the euro as the second world currency. It is in that perspective that the role of the EIB really takes its full meaning.

Considering the importance you are already giving to the ECU, one might wonder whether the euro is not simply changing the *name* of the currency... **RK:** The answer to this is a straightforward "no". We are anything but a passive future user of the new currency, just as we have been anything but a passive user of the ECU when it was at the cutting edge of European monetary integration.

We are, indeed, one of the institutions committed to making the euro happen. And to do so at the highest level of satisfaction for the citizens, workers, companies and governments of Europe as well as for their partners in the rest of the world.

As I already mentioned, our charter entrusts us with the mission "to contribute by means of long-term loans towards the integration, balanced development and economic and social cohesion of the member countries". And the euro is the cornerstone of "European integration" as defined by all member countries, with the partial and probably temporary exception of the two countries that have asked for an opt-out clause.

Our attention, however, is not limited to the euro but also gives weight to the *enlargement process* that will transform the present Union of 15 into an Union of some 20 or even more than 25 countries. These are landmark developments that will profoundly affect the future of the Union and its relationship with other countries in the world.

Hence, our medium-term strategy is firmly centered on supporting the introduction and sustainability of the euro while also laying solid foundations for enlargement. This is an essential part of what "integration" means in Europe today.

Could you elaborate on what it means for the EIB to define its medium term strategy as that of supporting "the introduction and sustainability of the euro"? **RK:** This involves both our lending and borrowing operations.

Insofar as *lending* is concerned, our central task of promoting economic integration in the *less prosperous areas* assumes even higher relevance as countries struggle to avoid being left out of the euro. The budget stringency necessary to attain the Maastricht convergence criteria will remain a critical factor of the European economic scene. In this matter the EIB will have a crucial role in sustaining sound investment both within the member countries about to switch to the euro and those – for example, Greece – still striving towards membership. Creating financing partnerships with the private sector will be a very important element of this renewed effort to help the less advanced regions of the Union catch up with the rest.

This role was strongly endorsed and vindicated by the Amsterdam Summit meeting of European Heads of Government on June 16-17, 1997. In a major new Resolution on Growth and Employment – a key support to EMU and its accompanying Stability and Growth Pact – they called on the EIB to step up its lending activities in a number of key areas, such as *infrastructure* and *small and medium-sized enterprises,* especially in the *high technology* sector.

How to combine growth with stability, is indeed the question for post euro Europe!

This is an important challenge for the EIB, and we are already implementing an *Amsterdam Special Action Plan* (ASAP) to respond to this task that Heads of Government have given us as part of their effort to make sure that stability and growth would go together in a way that contributes to job creations in Europe.

What about the borrowing side of your strategy? **RK:** The EIB has an even more directly relevant role in promoting the development of the euro, the new single currency. With an expected annual borrowing requirement in euros of well over 20 billion euro, we can, as we did with the promotion of the ECU and other European currencies in the 1980s, do a great deal to establish a large and liquid euro market.

In fact, we are not waiting for the euro to exist to put it at the centre of our borrowing strategy. In January 1997, we launched the first euro bond issue, a 1.3 billion euro 7-year issue. Until the euro is created debt service will be performed in ECUs at the rate of 1 ECU for 1 euro. Thereafter, it will be repayable in euro. In addition, we have launched a number of *"euro-tributary" bonds,* denominated in the present European Union national currencies, but reimbursable in euros after January 1999. So far, more than 5 billion ECUs have been launched. These issues have been denominated in Dutch guilders, French francs, Portuguese escudos, Luxembourg francs, Deutsche marks and Italian liras.

By ensuring that these and future issues are due at regular intervals, we aim to establish an euro benchmark "yield curve", adding to the flexibility and attractiveness of the future liquid euro-bond market. Thus, we expect that EIB bonds will become major benchmarks which meet the needs of investors worldwide.

Listening to you, one has the feeling that the EIB has already moved beyond the present set of national European currencies and has begun to work with some strange currency that few people have even heard about and which you just referred to through this description of "euro tributary" issues. Could you please explain what that strange "euro-tribe" currency is?

RK: Nuclear physicists have grown accustomed to strange particles that only exist during brief periods of time, as transitions between more stable forms of matter. I can see that PROMETHEE and Ernst & Young are ready to extend that view to the no less surprising field of currencies in which the "euro-tribe" would briefly coexist with francs, marks and euroguilders! Seriously, and very concretely, we do our best to manage our present operations in national European currencies in a way that will pave the way for the euro and enable the markets in euros to begin with a sizeable pool of issues.

Actually, it is quite true that with our "euro-tribe" we have begun to look at national currencies as precursors of the still-to-come euro.

It may be worthwhile to come back to what the EIB has been doing to support the development of markets in ECUs to get a sense of the type of contribution you are now making to the emergence of an efficient and sustainable market in euros...

RK: The EIB has always made a significant part of the loans it grants in ECUs. For instance, the amount granted in ECUs during 1995 (2 billion ECUs) places the ECU fourth in the ranking of EU currencies in the disbursed EIB loans. Total loans granted in ECUs by the EIB add up to some 13 billion.

Because of the amounts the EIB disburses or receives from its clients to cover interest or capital reimbursements, the EIB will be a very significant participant in the constitution of the critical mass in euros.

You seem to give special importance to establishing the EIB as a benchmark issuer in euros. This is not a complete surprise to us, as many of our guests in these conversations have also expressed their interest in providing a benchmark, or at least instruments as close as possible to a benchmark, in the

financial markets of the euro era. How exactly are you approaching that aspect of your responsibilities? **RK:** Anyone interested in this issue of "benchmarks for the euro" would probably tell you that EIB decided *not* to issue in one of the major European currencies in the early fall of 1997 because we felt that conditions in that specific market led to a spread over government bonds that we found excessive, although it would have been in a single digit number of basis points. So, yes, we do pay very precise attention to how we are perceived and ranked in the markets!

But the real story is not about benchmarking for the sake of benchmarking. It is about the low costs which we feel committed to making *available to our borrowers* for long periods so that they can pursue their own development objectives in the best financial conditions. In other words, benchmarking is not about some macho pecking-order out there in financial markets; it is quite simply about the cost of money for the clients of large financial intermediaries like ours.

In that respect, we want to stick with the very prudent – or let me say very conservative – policies that we follow like our gearing ratio (namely the fact that our loans will not exceed 250% of our capital), our liquidities, the guarantees we seek and all the measures we take to limit and control financial risks. If you look at our balance sheet you will see for instance that we have no less than 10 billion ECUs in liquidity (11 billions US$). Total outstanding debt represents more than 100 billion ECUs, putting it as the fifth largest issuers in Europe as compared to sovereign issuers. This will provide an important pool of liquidity in euros when such borrowings are converted from ECUs into euros.

As the largest international issuer, the EIB is therefore particularly well-positioned to launch and feed the market with benchmark issues denominated in euros. We are preparing ourselves: our current funding strategy reflects these objectives very clearly!

What does it take for an issue to be a benchmark ? **RK:** "The good features" that make benchmark issues include quality and financial *soundness* of the issuer, *liquidity* and good standing of the bonds on the secondary market, significant *size*, diversity of *maturities* along the yield curve. We pay the highest attention to them.

The increasing importance of *credit differentiation in the bond market* should further enhance the relative status of the EIB and therefore its competitiveness. EIB bonds should continue to remain the best complement to EU government bonds in Europe but also with U.S. and Asian investors.

> Entrepreneurship, venture capital and job creation

Life however cannot be simply about benchmarking which, as you said, is only a means to an end! This continent is often seen as too "risk-adverse" and a number of the contributors to this book – such as Werner Seifert and André Lussi – have called for more risk-taking, for a more entrepreneurial attitude here in Europe. So, what about the "Silicon Valley benchmark"? Does the EIB contribute to risk-taking and entrepreneurship in Europe? **RK:** There is no contradiction between doing the utmost to protect our AAA status as an issuer and lending to entrepreneurs who are ready to take *risks*. On the contrary, the cost of money to them will be a direct reflection of the prudence of the intermediaries on whom they can rely for access to the markets. It is, however, our responsibility to deal with these risks in a way that remains compatible with our own low-risk status.

True, a very large share of the EIB loan portfolio is in the field of infrastructures (transport, telecommunications, pipelines, etc.), yet individual loans to industry and loans to small and medium size enterprises (SME) through financial intermediaries now account for almost a quarter of the 23.2 billions ECUs that the EIB has lent in 1996. Over the past five years, the EIB has financed no less than 42 000 SMEs as well as 5 400 local authorities, a far cry from exclusive attention to very large AAA borrowers!

We are fully aware that growth, competitiveness and *job creation* are at the forefront of the European union priorities. Strengthening the competitiveness of SMEs is one of the most appropriate ways of dynamising the productive base and combating unemployment. Between 1992 and 1996, we have channelled no less than 11 billion ECUs to the 42 000 SMEs which I just mentioned.

Meanwhile, the 7 billion ECUs that we have lent to 5 400 local authorities have contributed to creating the *infrastructures* that are a prerequisite for business activities, notably in the less advanced regions.

If you analyse our patterns of disbursements you can see that this support to entrepreneurial activities emphasises as much as possible *cross-border partnerships* in accordance with our role as the financial institution of the European union. You may also notice that a good number of these projects have a high R&D component and that we pay special attention to introducing or supporting *non-polluting technologies.*

In line with the emphasis the newly elected French government has placed on employment and job creation, the Amsterdam summit of June 1997 has called for strong action in favour of small companies and high-tech entrepreneurs. It did so by entrusting the EIB with the responsibility to make good on these promises which a number of political parties, such as the French Socialists, saw as the indispensable counterweight to the tough disciplines of the Stability pact. How is EIB going to play this role of venture capitalist? **RK:** As you know very well, the full name of the Pact is "Stability and Growth". What I earlier called financial prudence or conservatism is a good foundation for growth.

As I mentioned it briefly earlier, the EIB is now working intensely on three initiatives adopted at Amsterdam, as a contribution to the social cohesion necessary to make the euro a success.

– first, we have been asked to strengthen our contribution to *Trans European Networks* (TENs), something for which our loans backed by our AAA issuers status are well adapted;

– second, we have been asked to develop our activities into new fields such as *education* and *health* with *job creation* a major perspective;

– third, and this is where your concern for entrepreneurship comes in, we have been asked to do even more for SMEs, particularly in *high-tech sectors.*

To implement this third initiative without putting in jeopardy the thrust of our intermediation strategy, we will earmark no less than 1 billion ECUs *of our financial surpluses* for this type of operation.

Obviously, we don't have the ambition to become the European Hambrecht & Quist, in other words, a venture capital fund. Therefore, we will essentially operate in close co-operation with our affiliate, the European Investment Fund (EIF) which will invest on our behalf in venture funds and therefore act as "a manager of managers".

> The working of financial markets in euros

Now that we understand the impact of the euro on EIB and its operations a little better, could we ask for your views about the broader impact that the euro will have on financial markets? We realize that this will involve a set of relatively technical issues of great interest to financiers that some of our readers may see as a little esoteric. So we could begin

with the broad view, after which we will be ready for technical questions regarding bond markets, swaps, derivatives and the like. And, if you agree, we will conclude with the international aspect of the role of the euro... **RK:** To speak first of the general impact, the euro is likely to speed up the impact in Europe of the four trends that are changing the global financial landscape – deregulation, institutionalisation of savings, information technology, and globalization.

Competition is likely to increase among providers of intermediation services: banks, institutional investors, exchanges, and financial centres.

The euro will remove a major part of the information advantage but it will not eliminate all comparative advantage as domestic firms will retain their national *distribution networks* and should remain best informed about local needs.

The euro implies an effective opening up of retail banking markets; its impact could be similar to the surge in mergers and acquisitions that followed the introduction of inter-state branching in the US, although the two areas have key structural differences.

Monetary union is likely to increase the pace of *consolidation* among European banks which we are already observing as they try to benefit from the opening up of markets, cut costs, gain economies of scale in trading and underwriting and react to the consolidation of *corporate treasury functions.*

At the same time, cost pressures – caused by the introduction of a single currency and the loss of commissions and trading revenues from intra-euro-zone trading – will increase competition. The costs associated with conversion to the euro have been estimated at some 2-3% of banks annual operating expenses over the full 3-year transition period. However, these costs will not be entirely a burden as it will force banks to upgrade their information technology and thus give them another tool for gaining competitive advantage.

Competition will become most intense in the underwriting and trading of domestic bonds as access to local-currency information matters most for these.

The euro will induce banks' corporate clients to organise treasury and risk-management functions on a European scale and thus automatically put more banks in competition with each other. A consolidation among clients will put pressure on banks to do the same thing.

What will be the implication of the euro for institutional investors from the rest of the world as well as from Europe?

And will financial intermediaries be ready for them?

RK: The trend towards *private pension funds* will have a profound impact in the European investors landscape. The euro will probably increase the trend towards lower-cost, passive, index-based asset management, similar to what has already happened within the U.S. market.

But it will also result in a much higher level of competition among financial intermediaries. For one thing, large companies will have better possibilities to access capital markets directly, to "dis-intermediate" banks and intermediaries. The latter will need to be even more innovative than today. Until now, the multiplicity of currencies had acted as a break on financial innovation: the European financial industry of the era will be under strong pressure to become as innovative and as agile as its counterpart in America. Financial techniques such as asset-backed securitization will probably be adopted much more rapidly and on a much larger scale than has been the case until now.

Furthermore, the euro should improve the competitive position of institutional investors – such as mutual funds and other asset managers – relative to commercial banks in the intermediation business. Differences in *tax and legal treatment* will nevertheless slow down this process. The position of issuers such as the EIB may very well be strengthened as EIB products will provide greater liquidity and first-class credit. On this large market in euro, the "critical size" for intermediaries will increase substantially.

Banks and intermediaries that are "big" by the present standards will be "small" by the euro standards: a bank with a 10% market share in France today will find itself with a market share of only 2% or 3% in its wider "domestic" market in euros. Achieving the "critical size" will be a major challenge and I do not see how it could be met without a much higher level of cross-border consolidation. To quote my friend Pierre Richard chairman of Dexia which is the result of a merger between, notably, Crédit Local de France and Crédit Communal de Belgique, what is needed now is a genuine "*European capitalism*".

The progressive disappearance of national financial markets will certainly imply more rather than less of the type of alliances and "strategic interconnections" that are discussed in the first set of these "strategic conversations"! Presently, as I mentioned, there are 45 stock exchanges in Europe against only 8 in the U.S., and 16 futures markets against 6, and this is probably not the best possible conditions of financial globalization! Technology however can allow the present exchanges to catch up in a more flexible fashion than outright mergers, through *remote membership* and networks for electronic trading.

We can see it as decentralized, automatized trading allows the Luxembourg Stock Exchange to be an active player in the euromarkets.

> Technical issues

May we now ask to pursue this analysis for our more market savvy readers?... Many would certainly be grateful for a "guided tour" of the market in euros still to come in the company of one of its architects. **RK:** I believe that the single currency will have a profound impact in at least three areas by allowing to: complete the *single market* in goods and services, lock-in the major progress made toward a world of *low inflation* and promote economic *growth*, and do so on a continental scale. This will have of course a set of important technical implications for the working of market. As for EIB we do have therefore what you might call a "vested interest" in the single currency as we had for the ECU: we are a lender, borrower, investor, user of derivatives in ECU; our accounting is in ECUs and our lending and funding is essentially in European currencies.

Perceived robustness of the *legal arrangements* and other factors affecting market credibility will be the key to the market for the euro. These issues can be divided in three areas: legal issues, operational issues and relationship with non-participating member states.

There are major legal changes that we need to take into account. During the transition phase from January 1999, the euro and participating member currencies will co-exist: the euro will be designated as the single currency from the start, with national currencies becoming non-decimal denominations of the euro. Indeed, during the transition, the French franc and German mark will simply be different expressions of the euro which are legally equivalent rather than separate currencies. Unless otherwise specified, or mutually agreed by counterparties, *existing contracts* denominated in a national currency would continue to be fulfilled using that original denomination.

Similarly, EC regulation deals with the question of *legal continuity* as one concern is achieving continuity between contracts denominated in ECUs, such as swaps, and the euro. The European Council in Madrid declared that continuity between ECUs and euros would be one for one. The EIB unambiguously stated after such council that its ECU debt will be serviced at 1.1 in euros, which EU regulation has now confirmed officially. The key concern to market participants seems to be whether the Union has the ability to influence different interpretation of contracts not subject to the law of European member states.

For market participants, the EMU will bring benefits by reducing economic inefficiencies. In particular cross-border trade flows will increase, as foreign exchange risks, interest rate risks and cross-border investments risks are all substantially reduced.

Indeed, monetary union will remove the existence of different currencies, monetary policies, and perhaps to some degree *fiscal policies* as a factor segmenting European financial markets. It effectively brings about a merger of the capital markets of the countries that joint in EMU. Without currencies to differentiate themselves, issuers and investors will have to look at other factors – such as credit and liquidity – to search for value in markets.

The most striking change will probably be in the bond market. Could you guide us through what you think will be the key changes in terms of credit risks and of key techniques?

RK: Monetary union will create one of the world's largest government bond markets. Let me offer just a few numbers to illustrate this:

– If one combines the J.P. Morgan Government Bond Indices for the countries most likely to participate in the euro as early as January 1999, one ends up with a total market value of over 2 trillion dollars, compared to 2.6 trillion dollars for the U.S. and 1.1. trillion dollars for Japan;

– If one adds to that group the "opt-out" and higher-yielding government markets, the figure adds to a combined market value of 2.6 trillion dollars, equal to the U.S. market.

However, unlike the U.S. and Japan the euro government debt market will not be nearly as homogenous, as it will still consist of many issuers with different issuance procedures and liquidity. This should have implications for credit valuation, issuance techniques.

Credit valuation is probably where the most striking changes will first materialize. Today, government bonds issued in national currency carry no default risk. Once the euro is in place, participating governments will lose the ability to use central bank reserves to support their public debt. National governments, effectively, will become "local" governments for credit analysts. To some extent, they may be comparable to U.S. municipalities and Canadian provinces even though these borrowers are within one sovereign federal state.

However, the initial market impact of this big change in perspective is likely to be relatively small. The main debt-rating agencies are likely to re-rate domestic debt taking also into account their external debt rating. Also, as initially all government bonds of participating members are likely to be accepted as *collateral for repurchasing operations* by the European Central Bank (ECB), distinctions between the different issuers at the short end of the curve would be blurred.

Further domestic investors are initially likely to favour national debt. However, longer term credit valuation will become important, especially if a member state starts to encounter structural problems after the euro. The change in credit valuation will also complicate pricing/valuation of non-government debt as none of the euro government bond markets will continue to define a "risk free" yield curve.

Regarding *issuance techniques*, it is clear that competition between participating member governments to attract capital will be intense. With currency differences removed, *liquidity* and *credit* risk become the key factors in relative pricing. For the larger markets there would be an incentive to follow the U.S. model, as France has done, creating a more transparent market structure, with primary dealers and with regular issuance cycles in a wide range of products: money market instruments, very-long bonds as well as offering Strips and index-linked structures.

Governments of smaller countries may find it difficult to follow this route without compromising the average issue size and liquidity of their issues. Instead, we could see a number of smaller countries follow the Swedish approach, concentrating issuance in a small number of benchmarks to create bonds, for example, at specific segments of the yield curve.

Sovereign debt issuance should immediately switch to *"domestic"* vehicles. However, the offshore *Eurobond* structure should continue to keep its appeal to non-government *corporate* issuers (usually U.K. law, Luxembourg listing, bearer structure). Indeed, most issuers will be keen to tap the markets through the logistically simplest and cheapest issuance vehicle. *Unless* domestic issuance becomes considerably less onerous from a documentation perspective and turnaround time, this will often mean offshore Eurobonds.

A reduction in *sovereign* eurobond issuance is likely, as historically, sovereign borrowers have tapped non-domestic markets to access additional pools of capital essentially when their domestic markets were too small.

What does this mean for corporate issuers? **RK:** EMU is likely to strengthen the development of a corporate bond market and the EIB will be ready to diversify its products to accompany its clients in the bond markets.

Development of *corporate bonds in euros* is also going to witness some interesting changes. Unlike the U.S. corporate bond market, the eurobond market has been segmented by currency which has inhibited the development of deep credit markets. Almost 50% of non-sovereign issuance is AAA in the European currencies segments of the Eurobonds. In continental Europe, a large portion of corporate financing is done through banks rather than bond issuance and this situation is unlikely to change quickly. However, the euro will bring *better liquidity* with many more issues trading in the same currency for a given issuer; this suggests that we are likely to observe a greater appetite for *lower-credit issues.*

The total outstanding size of the eurobond markets (excluding sovereign issuers) that would make up a broad monetary union is 0.6 trillion dollars, about the same size as the euro-dollar market and considerably smaller than the U.S. corporate market which stands at around 1.9 trillion dollars [2]. Again, the EIB is the largest international issuer with more than 100 billion dollars outstanding debt.

For supranational issuers such as the EIB, it is likely that issuance will have features closer to government bonds.

Foreign exchange markets ("Forex" as practitioners are fond of calling them) are probably where the impact of the euro will be felt in the most spectacular – perhaps the most brutal – way as a number of markets will disappear overnight. What will this mean for European financial centers? **RK:** Well, if we begin by looking at London, we can see that Forex activity (either spot or forward) is unlikely to be affected very much as only a small proportion takes place among currencies of the euro countries. A much greater impact would be in the continental Forex markets where trading in the local currency, both versus EMS and non-EMS currencies, makes up the bulk of turnover (50% in Paris for example).

A wider monetary union could ultimately mean that the volume in US dollar/euro and Yen/euro could well be *higher* than the current sum of the US dollar/EMS currencies and Yen/EMS currencies turnover.

We know you have been taking a special interest in the swap markets since you were involved in the very first swap deal to have been reported, the famous IBM-World Bank swap agreement of 1981. May we ask the swap experts in you to

2. excluding MBS, ABS and municipals (source: J.P. Morgan)

come to the forefront and tell us how he sees these markets to be impacted by the euro? **RK:** It's nice of you to mention this memorable 1981 which saw IBM borrow Deutsche marks so as to benefit from the low cost made possible by its low exposure in that market and then "swap" these DM liabilities with dollar liabilities of the World Bank. In this spirit, before answering your question, I would like to elaborate a little on why swaps are important, not simply for financial experts but for anyone interested in, or affected by, the globalization of financial markets.

To understand the importance of swaps, we have to think of what was implied before 1981 by the fact that a company or a bank could not borrow in one national market without having to operate in the currency of that nation. Of course, one could sell that currency if it was not needed (and if it was fully convertible!) but there was a cost and a future currency risk in doing so that meant that currencies were important barriers between markets. By contrast, the possibility to borrow in one market and to "swap" the money thus raised with another institution operating in another market allows a much higher degree of integration among markets.

Borrowers now have the freedom to separate *currency consideration* from the *considerations of cost* and conditions of *access to funds.* In so doing, they can shop around for the best solutions, which is good for them. They also provide other market participants with very efficient ways to compare prices and credit valuation in all of the large financial markets of the world, which is good for capital markets as a whole.

Now, coming back to your question, let me offer some more technical considerations on what the euro will mean for swap markets in Europe. It is first useful to compare the swap market with its underlying cash bond market.

Today, total swap outstandings for core European currencies add up to some 3 trillion dollars (end '95) compared to the largest individual core government market, Germany, at 0.67 billion dollars equivalent, almost five times the size. (It is however fair to note that current swaps include intra-EMS swaps). In contrast, swap outstandings in the U.S. (4.3 trillion dollars) are only 1.6 times the size of the U.S. government bond market. The swap market can be also thought of as representing a *generic AA-bank credit risk.* Consequently, following monetary union, swap markets of participating countries should become perfectly fungible unlike government bonds. This could result in a swap market that is larger and more liquid than any of the underlying government markets.

Such enhanced liquidity is likely to accelerate the use of swaps outside of the banking sector. Advances in *collateralisation* and *mark-to-market agreements* should allow a new range of participants, such as fund managers and insurance companies to access the market. As in the U.S., a key barrier will be regulatory restrictions, but the relative size of the euro swap markets compared to the alternatives should be a significant attraction.

Absolute turnover should ultimately increase following monetary union, despite the loss of cross-currency swap activity. Furthermore, the creation of the euro swap market will boost activity and liquidity in other derivatives instruments such as euro-swaption, cap/floor markets.

This "tour d'horizon" would not be complete if we did not say a word about the derivatives markets. **RK:** Following monetary union, many of the current futures contracts would share very similar specifications. This is likely to lead to a number of structural changes:

First, one may expect improved liquidity in money market futures. Following monetary union, money market futures contracts of participating member states would become almost interchangeable, the only real difference being the location of the underlying fixing, such as LIBOR or PIBOR. As a result, liquidity is likely to concentrate in a single contract which should enhance liquidity, making it more comparable to the 10-years currently available for the euro dollar contract.

Similarly, monetary union greatly reduces differences in bond futures. In time, a single bond future may very well emerge. Similarities between euro government bonds suggest that turnover is likely to concentrate through time in a single contract. At the same time, there may be an attempt to establish a contract where deliverables include a range of different government or supranational issuers (such as the EIB).

We have already discussed equity markets when we asked you, initially, for your views about stock exchanges. Can we come back to this topic now in term of equity *operations*? **RK:** The euro will eliminate many of the remaining barriers that limit intra-European equity holdings. Currency risk and transactions risk would be eliminated. Price quotations in the same currency would raise *transparency*. And many of the restrictions on foreign shareholdings by institutional investors would not be operational anymore.

Correlations at returns across the equity markets in participating countries should increase. Greater competition in intermediation services and more intense capital flows would help markets behave more as one. And the elimination of intra-EU currency fluctuations would eliminate an important source of differences in corporate earnings across markets.

> Beyond 2002…

Thanking you for this detailed analysis of the markets in euros, let us come back now to the broad picture: what about the status of the euro as a reserve currency? **RK:** The technical changes we just discussed mean that the market in euro will offer a range of opportunities that will be wider than the current European markets. The euro is likely to become an important reserve currency as a result of enhanced liquidity and a broader range of instruments. In fact, the market will be greater than the sum of the existing financial parts. As a genuine European market will begin to replace the present fragmented, national markets the role of the euro will develop beyond the sum of the present roles of national European currencies. Non European institutional investors as well as non European central banks will probably use it in a prominent manner in the next round of financial diversification.

Consequently the role of the U.S. dollar can be expected to decrease in relative terms. The pace of change, however, will be conditioned by the pace at which European banks and intermediaries will be able to achieve the "critical size" and the higher levels of product innovation that we just discussed.

Beyond all these changes, what do you think is going to be the deeper impact of the euro? **RK:** As many of the other participants in these "strategic conversations", I believe that the euro is a historic opportunity to accelerate change in Europe. True, the European Union, with its 350 million inhabitants still accounts for a little more of the world's production than the U.S. (29% against 27%). But it is also a continent of 18 millions unemployed still looking for the adequate division of labor between the public and competitive sectors. With the exception of the U.K. and of the Netherlands, it is also a continent in which a rising share of the future earnings of the younger generations has been quietly mortgaged to pay for the pensions of the present generations. Accelerating change is therefore the key priority, and this is how I would like to conclude this discussion about the euro.

"The world does not belong to us, it is simply lent to us by our children". This is something that the previous generation – that of Robert Schuman, Jean Monnet, Konrad Adenauer and other visionaries – had understood. The euro is an opportunity to ask "which Europe are we going to leave to our children?". Will it be a prosperous, active Europe able to find its place in the tough global world out there? Or will it be a declining Europe, obsessed with the status quo and lending a complacent ear to the old demons of protectionism and nationalism? Already, Europeans represent only 5% of world population, a proportion that will be halved in the next thirty to fifty years. Will this be simply a relative decline? Will it be an absolute decline? Or will we seize this historic opportunity to make it coincide with a new European renaissance?

The present paradox, in Europe as well as in the rest of the world, is that globalization goes hand in hand with a general increase in defensive attitudes, a *"raidissement général"* to speak in my mother tongue. This can take the form of hatred, xenophobia and fanaticism, or simply as a set of negative attitudes toward the rest of the world. Globalization is not perceived as a good thing by those who fear that it will displace them, deprive them of their cherished ways of life and submit them to uniform standards. And yet, globalization is also an extraordinary coming together of different peoples, an extraordinary opportunity to share not just images but also emotions and aspirations. Maybe we need a form of globalization, a form of universality that does not appear so distant and so uncontrollable. Maybe we need what the great writer Amin Maalouf calls "a universality of proximity".

This is where being European appears to me as a precious asset in this difficult effort to combine globalization and identity, being open to all others and to be oneself. The identity of a given nation is built on multiple belongings. The feeling of "European belonging" is not in competition with other feelings of belonging, whether national or religious. It is something different, something which we are lucky to share with countries of the West *and* countries of the former "East", with countries of the Northern shores of the Baltic *and* of the Mediterranean region, with Christians as well as with Jews and Muslims.

Are there many other such belongings that can bridge so many divides? I hope the euro and the European enlargment to the East will help us understand how precious such a link can be in preserving peace, prosperity and competitiveness for our children when our turn will come to leave them this Europe that they have lent to us… ■

Part IV

The global integration frontier **and** *the euro.*

Chapter XII

The strategic issues *behind the conversation*

European convergence for the euro builds on two global trends:
- Interdependence, a reflection of cross-border flows,
- Governance, a reflection of private and public efforts to set the framework.
Catherine Distler and Albert Bressand briefly present some of the tools developed by PROMETHEE to track strategic developments and challenges in these two arenas.
For interdependence, they start from the four flows of People, Goods, Money and Information (P,G,M&I) and discuss the integrative role of technology by looking at networks as "linking machines".
Governance can be analysed in terms of four "layers". The first two are centered on corporations and competition law ("co-production") and on traditional inter-governmental processes ("co-ordination") while the two higher layers imply stronger ties ("co-regulation") or the pooling of sovereignty ("co-sovereignty"). The experience of Europe is less exceptional than one might think, both in terms of the hybrid nature of EU governance and of the elements of co-regulation and even co-sovereignty in the global economy at large.
Concrete examples of co-regulation are then discussed in short conversations with eminent national regulators.
The first guest is Jean Saint-Geours, former chairman of COB and until January 1998 a member of the governing council of the International Accounting Standards Committee (IASC). The discussion continues with René de La Serre, Director General of the CCF bank and Chairman of Conseil des Marchés Financiers (CMF) and Bertrand de Mazières, Secretary General of CMF. Both Jean Saint-Geours and René de La Serre are also Vice-Chairmen of PROMETHEE.

CATHERINE DISTLER AND ALBERT BRESSAND,
PROMETHEE

Presentation of the analytical framework behind this project, by Catherine Distler and Albert Bressand, and short conversations with Jean Saint-Geours (IASC Advisory Council) and with René de La Serre and Bertrand de Mazières (Conseil des Marchés Financiers - CMF).

Convergence at the intersection of interdependence and governance: the euro and the multi-tier map of globalization.

As the moment approaches to conclude these "strategic conversations" on what painter Victor Krotov calls "PlaNet euro", let us invite our readers to step back and reflect on the "global integration frontier" of which the euro is about to become a major element.

The picture of *integration* that emerges from Europe as it prepares for the euro is, at the same time, more and less than conventional pictures of globalization might lead to expect. *More*, as no other region in the world grants as many rights to citizens and companies of other countries. *Less*, because the abolition of national currencies will give prominence to yet another level of differences between national markets that were never thought of as barriers – they are just ways-of-doing-things – but that will now be perceived as obstacles.

The map of integration that the euro brings to light is, to put it simply, a complex one. This complexity feeds notably on two types of overlaps: the overlap between local, national and global, and the overlap between "*micro*" and "*macro*". These overlaps and paradoxes are an invitation to refine – sometimes to rethink – the conceptual map with which corporations, governments as well as experts approach globalization in general and European integration in particular.

Local foundations, global architectures

In each of these free wheeling discussions, we have seen European considerations combine with *global* and *national* ones. Like the far-right and the far-left in politics, the two extremes of "very global" and "very local" tend to be surprisingly close to one another, with technology introducing more and more "short-circuits".

Listening to Luc Bomans and to André Lussi, whose organizations were born in the off-shore global world of eurobond markets, one hears simultaneously about complex chains of transactions that circle the world in seconds *and* about very specific features of Belgian and Luxembourgian laws. The latter, local as they are, play an essential role in creating *legal certainty* for traders crossing many jurisdictions at the push of a button. In that sense, some local decisions have global implications through the type of "architecture" that companies and individuals can put in place to support their own efforts to globalize. The same is true in the field of technology as the development of norms or tools (like "navigators", HTML and Java for Internet) can have system-wide implications.

Micro decisions, and macro convergence

Asking what makes a "strong economy" (a more appropriate question in his view than that of a "strong euro"), André Lussi observes that it must feed on two complementary forces: "corporate competitiveness" and "collective governance". This combination of "micro" and "macro" forces is an essential aspect of the present globalization frontier.

At the present stage, the move toward the euro involves thousands of banks as well as political leaders, computer programmers as well as central bankers. Should one of these groups fail to reach their objectives, the whole transition would be compromised. More strikingly, the "micro" decisions taken by the thousands of private banks and companies are a major force behind the "macro" capacity of the member States to transform the challenge of the euro into the *self-fulfilling prophecy of the euro*. We had a vivid illustration of these synergies at a meeting convened in the mid 1990s by Shell International in London to discuss scenarios of European integration:

British participants were discussing pros and cons in terms of high politics, until Dr. Stephan Schuster from Deutsche Bank began describing the wealth of concrete programs already well under way in German banks for the transition to the euro; all of a sudden, London-based participants realized with amazement that the process at work on the continent was also backed by a set of bottom-up, mutually-reinforcing initiatives in the market place itself or just behind it...

This complex combination of local and global, of "micro" strategies and "macro" policies can be summarized under two headings: interdependence and governance.

Interdependence, technology and the P,G,M&I paradigm

Interdependence is a diffuse form of influence best understood in terms of cross-border flows. *Trade flows* and *flows of capital* are those most commonly discussed. But *flows of people* and *flows of ideas and knowledge* are just as important in challenging the closed and self-centered nature of national economic spaces.

Referring to these flows as "P, G, M&I" (People, Goods, Money and Information), we have called attention in previous work to the *integrating impact* that technology has come to play *among* them. This additional form of integration can be compared to the shift from an "analog" world in which voice, data and images flow in completely distinct networks to the multimedia convergence made possible by digital technology.

Indeed, digital technology is now leading to attach an "electronic image" to any person, any goods, any sum of money and any bit of information flowing through the economy and society. These electronic images lend themselves to powerful forms of management that have become essential to the creation of wealth and of competitive advantages. We have analysed them beginning with concrete examples like the SABRE computer reservation system, electronic stock exchanges, credit-card networks and bar-codes, Walmart type of distribution systems and other "linking machines"[1].

In the tradition of Alfred Chandler[2], our analysis has emphasized the role of *distribution* in the present economic transformation. While here is not the place to dwell at length on these new paradigms, many of the conversations in this book have illustrated the importance of electronic

---

1. See Albert Bressand and Catherine Distler, *La Planète Relationelle,* Paris, Flammarion, 1995.

2. Alfred Chandler, *The visible Hand, the Managerial Revolution in American Business,* The Belknap Press Of Harvard University Press, Cambridge and London, 1977.

distribution in transforming financial intermediation. This is true notably of cross-border integration among stock exchanges[3]. *Interactive distribution* is the second "visible hand" of capitalism.

From I-tech to R-tech: "Linking Machines"

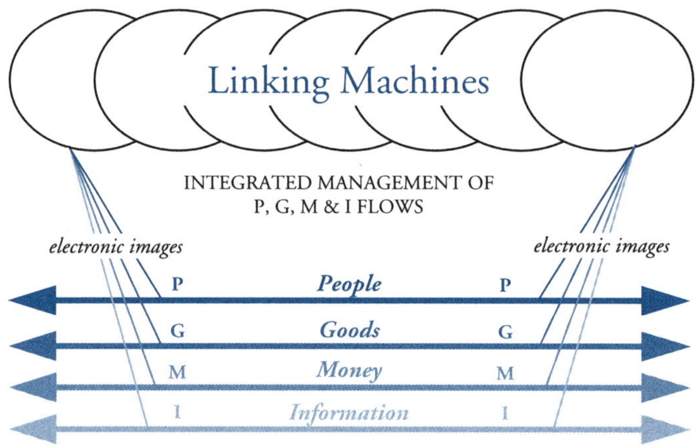

Measuring interdependence, however, is an increasingly difficult and elusive undertaking because of qualitative changes that come from globalization, especially at the high level of openness that exists now in Europe. The "internal market" put in place in 1992 has led to the removal of check-points at the border making it more difficult if not impossible to keep track of cross-border trade. Similarly, the Schengen Treaty means that one cannot know with precision how many people cross borders every year. Globally, the importance of *services* in wealth creation also makes it almost impossible to put a value on what is crossing borders in the form of disquettes, phone conversations and "human capital" not to mention what is transferred from one side of the globe to the other via *Internet.*

The *statistical data* included in the last chapter of this book provide a number of important measures of these various aspects of interdependence (this is the first step in a research program in co-operation with *Eurostat* that will continue to focus on quantitative analysis of the global integration frontier and of Europe's place in it).

3. This work on electronic distribution and electronic commerce has been discussed with PROMETHEE members at Abbaye de Royaumont in October 1997 as part of the "Corporation 2020" program that PROMETHEE conducts in cooperation with EDF, Ernst & Young and Shell.

Networks as linking machines

Interdependence is, first, a function of the *size* of P, G, M&I flows. As such, it is usually measured in terms of trade ratios, of investment flows and of shares of foreign investors in the capitalization of national markets and in the holding of national public debt. It also involves people-centered flows like travel and tourism as well as mobility of workforce across borders, share of employment provided by multinationals etc. Last but not least, flows of information are a fundamental aspect of interdependence and of the working of global markets.

But interdependence is also a function of the tightness of the web that global "*linking machines*" allow to develop - whether the "networked markets" described by Jean-François Théodore, the clearing and settlement networks of Euroclear and Cedel Bank, the news and financial-quote networks operated by Reuters, the remote banking capacities put in place by ABN AMRO or the distribution networks for asset managers like Société Générale Asset Management.

Interdependence reflects the developement of P, G, M & I flows *and* of the ways in which they can be managed and leveraged with the support of "information highways" and "linking machines". Listening to Jean-François Théodore and Jörg Fischer, one realizes that networks like those centered around Euronext and Eurex play a critical role in the management of such flows. Interdependence patterns are a function of the infrastructures and legal frameworks provided to market participants – more generally to companies and individuals using networks of all types. And discussing the shift to the equity culture as several of our guests have done, one can also see that the deeper impact of P, G, M&I flows on society – on risk taking for instance – depends of the type of *expectations* that preside to their use in society as large.

In this spirit, as could be detected in the questions behind a number of these conversations, PROMETHEE has put forward the definition of networks as *"linking machines"* or "*relationship management machines*" presented at the end of Chapter I, a definition that combine three dimensions.

The first dimension is the technical one in which an infrastructure allows to establish *contact* among network users.

The second dimension is a legal and regulatory one in which a combination of public and private rules ("infostructure") allows participants to *contract* with one another.

The third dimension is of a cultural and strategic nature as it relates to the shared set of expectations and behavioral norms ("infoculture") that provides a framework for *commitment* among participants.

These three dimensions of contact, contract and commitment allow to identify "*best practices in networking*" and to shed new light on the role of networks in wealth creation[4]. These dimensions help us better understand what is taking place around the networks put in place within and among stock exchanges. Our conversations with André Villeneuve, Werner Seifert or Jörg Fischer provide concrete examples of what is at stake behind *infrastructures* such as Globex, Xetra, NSC as well as important differences in the "infostructures" of EURO NM, Euronext and other networks well described by Jean-François Théodore. The different levels of relationship management ("R-tech") are also critical to global integration as it develops around Internet.

Governance and the taming of the "co"

Governance, meanwhile, is also a combination of four different layers that we have suggested to label co-production, co-ordination, co-regulation and co-sovereignty.

The first two layers are those usually emphasized by analysts of globalization as they center on *corporate strategies* (co-production) and on the traditional *intergovernmental processes* (policy co-ordination) taking place in such fora as the OECD. The last two "layers" are those in which Europe finds itself in the position of a vanguard as the level of opening implied goes well beyond the concept of free trade embodied in agreements like NAFTA, APEC or the WTO. *Co-regulation* and *co-sovereignty*, however, gradually find their way into global patterns as interdependence challenges the capacity of nation States to regulate, if at all, in other ways than jointly. Sylvia Ostry and others have well analysed this gradual shift in the international agenda from merely "removing barriers" to looking at national policies as a set of mutually connected decisions that no country can take in isolation from the others, except at its own risks[5]. Let us comment briefly on these four "layers" of governance.

Co-production: corporate strategies go beyond traditional comparative advantages (e.g. low labour costs) and attempt to integrate "value chains" across borders. This is true *inside* multinational companies: 60 % of Franco-German trade is now intra-corporate trade. This is true also *among*

---

4. PROMETHEE has also conducted a set of "strategic conversations" among its corporate members on excellence and quality in networking in its E=mc^3 program on Excellence in networking as the Mastering of Contact, Contract and Commitment. Meetings on "best contact", "best contract" and "best commitment" have been hosted by, respectively, Groupement Informatique de l'Assurance in Paris, Euroclear in Brussels and Shell in London.

5. Sylvia Ostry, *Council on Foreign Relations*, New York

companies as they are not simply trading and specialising, but jointly producing the same services or products.

Co-ordination: this first level of policy integration is the central activity of organizations like OECD. The "G7" process (now G8 as *Russia* is included) has come to be seen as the cornerstone in this level of co-ordination. It is also relevant to the EU policy dialogue outside of the (expanding) fields in which the common European institutions have a mandate: at this stage, a critical issue for European governance is whether *tax policies* still belong in this intermediate level or whether the creation of the euro implies that tax matters be gradually addressed as part of the other, more demanding, layers of European integration.

Co-regulation: the growing integration between manufacturing, finances and services, as well as the move toward "co-production" give increasing importance to differences among national regulations as obstacles. Much of the "Europe 1992" program was about regulatory convergence rather than about trade, but the BIS prudential ratio also are about co-regulation. The short conversation with René de La Serre and Bertrand de Mazières here below provide a very concrete example of how national regulatory structures now dovetail into a European one while allowing for a diversity of national approaches.

Co-sovereignty: the euro is the most striking example of this highest level of integration, but it is not an isolated one. Other examples include countries that have to submit to IMF adjustment programs (as approved by the other governments of the world according to IMF weighting and rules) as a condition for continued participation in the global economy. The Stability and Growth Pact approved at the Amsterdam Summit of June 1997 puts budgetary policy partly in this domain, as governments must respect a common discipline regarding the balance of their budget.

Dealing with these four layers – these four "co" – is the real challenge for nation States today. The view that States will simply disappear, attractive as it is to some, is in contradiction with basic market values, investors-protection, fight against corruption, prudential oversight and the like *and* with fondamental needs of democratic society. Rather, States just like corporations are engaged in different forms of interactions that put higher premium on working together. Let us look therefore succinctly at the four "co" layers.

Co-production and co-ordination:

As everyone realises, private actors play a major role in the development of an interdependent global economy, to the point where analysis like that by

Kenishi Ohmae leads to talk of a "borderless world" in which States could simply vanish. In reality, the need for governance *increases* in proportion to the development of interdependence and private actors play a role in its development. The latter do not do so, however, in substitution to States but as part of hybrid governance systems and networks that bring public and private actors in closer and closer relationship.

Anyone familiar with the reports of the *Group of Thirty*, which brings together eminent financiers, realise the importance of the proposals that they make quite regularly regarding the prevention of systemic risk and, more generally, the governance of international finance. Our conversation with Luc Bomans provides insights into this important form of co-operation between practitioners and regulators around such notions as elimination of "pipeline risks" but also quality and integrity of information.

As illustrated in the Euroclear-sponsored report *Beyond G30* [6], interconnection and division of labor among networks is a key aspect of well functioning global markets. More generally, the role of corporations in governance broadly defined does not stop at policy proposals but includes the much more visible process of co-operation and integration known under such names as strategic alliances, joint ventures, cross-borders M&A and more generally the restructuring of business activities in ways coherent with the global nature of markets. One might dispute that such behaviour really belongs in the field of *governance* but the latter, in our view at least, should not be restricted to formal processes in which government officials take decisions. On the contrary, what matters is the impact of countless decisions, some public and many private, in shaping the global system and in providing a framework in which the issues that it raises can be addressed.

Cross-borders M&A are both a higher form of interdependence *and* a force behind the *hybrid nature of governance* as private decisions – such as the proposed merger between Ernst & Young, our partner in this book, and KPMG – are scrutinised by competition regulators in the U.S. and also in Brussels (DG-IV) and EU countries, thereby fostering along complex patterns of integration[7].

In this sense, we do suggest to include *co-production* as a fully fledge layer of global governance in which corporations play a key role but do so in

---

6. Cross-Border Clearance, Settlement, and Custody: Beyond the G30 Recommandations, Morgan Guaranty Trust Company of New York, Brussels office as Operator of the Euroclear System, June 1993.

7. See Catherine Distler, "Convergence & Conflicts over Competition Law" *PROJECT PROMETHEE PERSPECTIVES*, n° 15, January 1991.

a framework that public authorities can influence even if in increasingly subtle and market oriented forms. A few years ago, this co-production layer would have included *industrial policy* but the latter is increasingly confined to a few specific sectors such as the U.S. military aerospace industry (which often happens to be civilian too!), the "European" defense industry as the latter is still exempt from internal market discipline, and co-operative R&D programs in fields like semi-conductors (*Sematech* in the U.S.) and information technology (the ESPRIT, EUREKA, IMPACT, RACE and successor programs in Europe)[8] as well as Japanese program like the *Fifth Generation Computer* and the *Human Frontier* programs.

As for *co-ordination*, it has in common with co-production to let nation States interact in whole sovereignty, at OECD or in fora like the G7 summits. This is well known enough for us to simply refer the reader to the large literature on interdependence, calling her or his attention to the notion of "*regime*" as developed by Joseph Nye and Robert Keohane[9] in the 1970s when interdependence was first conceptualised. For them, a "regime" is a set of norms, rules and expectations shaping interactions in a given domain. The notion is still very valid although our next two layers now call for more focused attention on those regimes where national sovereignty is shared rather than exercised in the traditional manner.

Co-regulation: the mutual recognition benchmark

The degree of openness that EU countries have granted one another is well beyond anything written, or even discussed, in the North American Free Trade Agreement (NAFTA), the ASEAN forum, APEC, GATT or WTO. A central element of the "Europe 1992" freedom is the principle of mutual recognition.

Mutual recognition implies much more than free trade. It implies accepting rules and regulatory decisions of other countries as legitimate on one's own territory. Mutual recognition can be seen at work in the Single Banking Passport and the Investment Services Directive (ISD) that have transformed the competitive environment in which all our distinguished guests operate, as a license granted by any of the eighteen EEA member countries becomes a passport for doing business anywhere else in the Union and EEA without the need for additional national licences.

---

8. See Catherine Distler, "Networking in the Knowledge Galaxy" PROJECT PROMETHEE PERSPECTIVES n° 17, June 1991.

9. Joseph Nye and Robert Keohane *"Power and Interdependence: World Politics in Transition"*, Boston, Little, Brown and Co, 1977.

The principle is not without limits and presupposes significant work in common to lay out a set of "minimum criteria" that all countries will adhere to in developing their own regulations. But, precisely, this process of permanent discussion and of nitty-gritty co-operation is a driving force at the service of European integration along the "Monnet method".

The political economy of trust

The *internal market* set up in 1992 and the *Schengen agreement* to let people cross borders without having to stop at police check-points are major achievements made possible by mutual recognition. The key ingredient is trust. This trust can be supported by advanced electronic networks such as the Schengen data base and network which allow a police officer from any member country to let a non-European enter the whole Union (except Denmark, the U.K. and Ireland which still have to heed André Villeneuve's suggestion to join this borderless Europe). But trust is what really allows levels of openness and integration beyong the old benchmark of "free trade". Indeed, euro bank notes could carry a map of Europe with the motto "in this human community we trust".

A currency is the reflection of mutual trust among members of a community. It is supported by elaborate systems of control and police but if trust comes to vanish, the currency turns into an empty shell. Hence, the European Central Bank must be seen as the tip of a much larger "iceberg of trust", formed over decades of integration by a slow process of accretion.

The euro revolves around a superior level of trust – not just in policies but in the "mindset" of the policy makers and of the electorates to whom they are responsible[10]. It is supported by the big stick of the Stability and Growth Pact which commits member countries to deposit a full 0.2% of their GDP (yes, GDP) for each 1% of GDP in their deficit above the 3% limit. As Yves Franchet observes here below, however, the real underlying mechanism is the "changes in the mindsets" that have occurred in the transition to the euro.

Leading German figures have described quite explicitly the type of transformation that they saw taking shape around the euro. Karl Lamers – spokesman of the CDU Parliamentary Group – together with Wolfgang Schäuble – a possible successor to Chancelier Kohl – Michael Glos – leader of the Bavarian CSU – and Rudolf Seiters (CDU) pinpointed the results of

10. The reader is of course referred to Francis Fukuyama, *Trust : the Social Virtues & the Creation of Prosperity*, New York, The Free Press, 1995.

the convergence process and "the attractiveness of the Maastricht Treaty that has helped Italy in a decisive manner in renewing its old political system which is now changed quite radically by reform of its own Constitution"[11].

Co-sovereignty as a long term global beacon

The last of our governance layers is the most demanding in terms of integration as countries pool sovereignty to exercise it jointly rather than separately. This whole book is tracking some of the impact of this major step toward co-sovereignty which Europe calls the euro. By now, the reader must see clearly that this was neither the first nor the last step on that road, preceeded as it was by the "single banking passport" established by the *Second Banking Directive* and the cross-market freedoms of the *Investment Services Directive*. Already the Stability and Growth Pact and the first decisions taken at the Luxembourg Summit of December 1997 on tax policies indicate that this road is still a long one on which the journey is continuing.

Even for Europe, co-sovereignty remains very partial. Politically, since the Maastricht Treaty, Europe has called itself a "Union". Yet, a full and genuine Union it is not. The Amsterdam Treaty was negotiated to adapt the institutional framework left unchanged by Maastricht to the twin transformation of the *single currency* and of *enlargement* to Eastern Europe. Progress registered at Amsterdam included making respect of human rights a pre-condition for rights of vote in the Council of Ministers and some strengthening of the role of the President of the European Commission. But the conference failed to clarify the key institutional issues. On the contrary, the contradiction is growing between the genuine element of federalism implied by an independent European Central Bank (ECB) and the efforts by national governments (the French often siding with the British) to prevent any move beyond the inter-governmental process. Centered on the Council of Ministers, this process puts national executives in the strange situation of acting as the *legislative* branch of the Union as if the French, among others, still had to read Montesquieu.

Majority voting would be the natural way to go for countries that will submit to the independent authority of the same supranational ECB. And yet, the Amsterdam Treaty left pending a democratic definition of majority voting accommodating people as well as States. It will extend majority voting only very marginally to three areas (R&D programs, establishment's right and

11. *Le Monde*, September 18, 1997.

a totally cryptic third area). Also at a time when trade negotiations centre more and more on intellectual property and on services of all types, including banking and financial services, the governments meeting at Amsterdam preferred not to draw the lessons from the existence of the internal market and have kept the negotiating power at a national rather than an European level. This will not prevent some of the same governments from calling for a Europe able to "speak with one voice" in the field of Foreign Policy and Security, as it went without saying that the "one voice" in question can only be theirs…

Such contradictions remind of the famous bottle that is half empty – if one thinks of the decisions that present leaders are leaving untaken – but also half full – as the same governments combined forces to protect the move to the single currency from countless reasons to shelve it for better times.

"One compass with fifteen needles": such was the image, in recent work for the Alphonse Weicker Foundation in Luxembourg, to describe the Intergovernmental Conference that concluded at Amsterdam and is what it reveals about the long term objectives of European integration. Using two axes – one about the nature of European *governance* (from completely inter-governmental to fully federal) and a second about the *external implications* (Europe merely a market or a power on the world scene) – we found that national preferences were distributed so perfectly in all possible directions that governments could all be pulling with maximum energy for many more years, with a high risk their efforts would cancel one another or lead only to complex technical compromises rather than more Europe in a direction that the general public could clearly understand.

The compass with fifteen needles: the IGC countries pulling in all directions

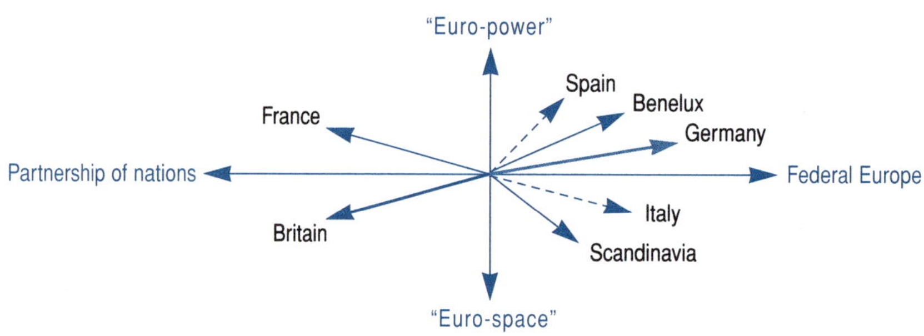

Source: "Europe 2012", op. cit.

Subsidiarity, an accelerator or a brake?

The governance of Europe is still a hybrid system in which a few key supranational institutions – most notably the European Court of Justice and soon the European Central Bank – coexist with an *inter-governmental* decision process. The European Parliament has seen its role of "co-decision" strengthened a number of times – most recently in the proposed Amsterdam Treaty – but remains incomparably weaker than the Congress in the U.S.

In the spirit of co-sovereignty, the euro will strengthen the federal part of this hybrid system by transferring all powers to make monetary policy to the independent European Central Bank that will come to life on July 1, 1998. But below the policy level, all operational matters will still be under the responsibility of the ten or eleven *National Central Banks* (NSBs) in the European Central Bank system. Similarly, the *TARGET system* for large payments in euros is being created by interconnecting as many national payment systems, all based on the advanced technology needed for real-time gross settlement. In the same spirit, Sir Michael Butler, the British diplomat in charge of the U.K. negotiation team for Maastricht, argued in vain for a *hard ECU* that would have made its way on the scene in competition with, rather than as a substitute to, national currencies.

Few of our guests have not described examples of *subsidiarity* of one type or another. Subsidiarity is a fundamental principle in European governance whereby all matters that can be dealt at one level – usually the national level or the level of länder in Germany and provinces in Spain – should remain at that level. The principle can be the best or the worst depending on whether it is used to *preserve diversity* in a common undertaking or simply to *resist change* by depriving the European levels of the means needed to discharge its responsibilities.

The proposals by the CDU-CSU Parliamentary group in 1994 to move more swiftly toward political union have remained unanswered – pushing Germany to defend her national interest a little more like all other countries[12].

Co-sovereignty includes the euro and monetary policy but not – or not yet – many of the other policy domains that would be critical for a true "union". In particular, the Common Foreign and Security Policy (CFSP) set

12. This text is reproduced in "The Next European Big Bang", *PROJECT PROMETHEE PERSPECTIVES.* n° 24-25, May 1995, p35-42 together with "A German Proposal Still in Need of a French answer", a reaction by the French branch of the European movement prepared by Dominique Bocquet in cooperation with, notably, Michel Albert, Jean-Louis Bourlanges and Jean François-Poncet analysing "the French dream of a strong Europe with weak institutions".

up in the Maastricht Treaty is most remarkable for its failures in Yugoslavia, Central Africa and even the Aegean Sea. For all the rhetorics surrounding it, the true CFSP of the EU is its commercial policy and some common reactions to U.S. commercial unilaterism like the Helms-Burton law and other efforts to apply U.S. laws extraterritorialy. The driving force behind the self fulfilling prophecy of integration is not the CFSP but the good old Common Market and its more ambitious successor the borderless "internal market". In today's information-intensive and services-intensive economy, *a genuine common market* calls for common approaches and *common regulations.* These can be the gateway toward a true "community of people" going well beyond free flows of goods and capital.

Convergence: market forces, policy decisions and strategic interconnection.

Convergence is measured in numbers, and the drafters of the Maastricht Treaty did a good job at limiting the explicit task to a set of five "indicators" related to inflation, interest rates, exchange rates, public deficit and public debt and a sixth indicator of commitment in the form of two years of belonging in the strengthened ERM-II (something the U.K. seems to object to).

In many ways, this book explores the critical zone between treaties and mindsets, between the sort of disciplines laid out in the Stability and Growth Pact and the pure goodwill in which trust may also express itself. The latter may not be enough to preserve the convergence behind the euro, and the first might appear as too much for sovereign countries (and democratic electorates) to swallow. Yet, in between these two levels lies the world of networks, alliances, mergers, cross-memberships, shared tools, common products...

We will come back to this essential issue of convergence in a conversation with Yves Franchet, the Director General of the institution in charge of keeping track of the Maastricht convergence process. Before turning to convergence however, we would like to present the perspective of key regulators or former regulators regarding, of course, co-regulation. Let us turn therefore to Jean Saint-Geours for a discussion of the search in progress in the framework of IASC for common approaches to accounting standards. We will then turn to René de La Serre and Bertrand de Mazières for a short conversation on the way in which the present French institutions in charge of market oversight fit within a broader European regulatory structure for European financial markets.

> International Accounting Standards for the Global Markets: Harmonizing, but around what?

This short conversation with Jean Saint-Geours, former Chairman of COB and of the Technical Committee of IOSCO and member of the Advisory Committee of IASC took place in the framework of the "Corporation of 2020" program led by PROMETHEE with EDF, Ernst &Young and Shell. IASC is the International Accounting Standards Committee. IOSCO is the International Organisation of Securities Commissions that brings together regulators of stock exchanges.

Can accounting standards help us relate the *value* of a corporation – as assessed through the now famous shareholder value – and the *values* held by various stakeholders? And how close are we to uniform standards? **Jean Saint-Geours:** A clean corporation has to be built on a high level of transparency. But how can one speak of the same thing without a common language?

Uniformity is not the goal but the present situation regarding standards is like a currency system without exchange rates, let alone a common currency.

Four years ago there was no German company listed on the NYSE. Then Daimler Benz applied for a listing: their profit turned into a loss several times larger because of the different accounting norms used in the two countries.

The key difference is between U.S. and Europe and, also, between FASB and the proposed IASC: the new FASB chairman has identified 250 differences between those two, and apparently would like them settled by convergence to the U.S. standards. FASB is now pressuring the SEC to take a much narrower view of the type of departure from present U.S. practices that would be acceptable and *The Economist* in its January 17, 1998 issue finds it natural that convergence be nothing more than the adoption of Anglo-Saxon standards…

What are the steps taken, and what is the time horizon now for IASC? **JSG:** This all started with the 1984 Big Bang in London, which triggered a set of similar "bangs" in other places…

Two major shocks gave these "bangs" a more worrisome flavour:
– the first one was the "crash of 1987",
– the second was the collapse of one of the most ancient British bank as a consequence of major failures in market oversight.

Barings was not a very large player but was a very famous English bank trusted not just by the British banking community but also by the U.S. financial institutions.

The British way of regulating was put under less than favourable light...

An informal meeting of regulators at Windsor called after the Barings failure in 1994 led to a detailed set of recommendations and principles about co-operation between stock exchanges and regulators.

You seem to give special importance to the Paris program...?

JSG: The key document is the 1995 "Paris treaty" between IOSCO and IASC, their "common program". The objective was to finish the work of adopting the same accounting standards in the world, agreed upon in this program by March 1998. It seems now that this was a bit too ambitious but everyone is doing her or his best.

The real issues raised by harmonized or identical accounting standards are not technical. They have to do with capitalistic structures, financial cultures and fundamental national rules.

The main stumbling blocks toward a global agreement are where the core of the corporation is in question:

– the valuation of financial assets,

– the treatment of intangibles, some of which are amortized over forty years in France, five years in the U.S.

R&D costs also raise major issues and the same is true of employee benefits.

The proper valuation of financial assets (and notably the more difficult cases of derivatives, options, hedging funds and the like...) is the most difficult issue. Americans insist on the "fair price approach" so as to capture at any given point in time all potential losses and gains regarding the financial assets held by a given corporation. In spite of a few minor differences, this "fair price approach" is very close to the mark-to-market approach. The latter raises more problems in countries like Germany in which the stock market plays a much smaller role in the overall financing of corporations and enjoys less visibility and legitimacy in society as a whole.

It has been proposed by the IASC staff, in early September 1997, to adopt the U.S. approach as the agreed solution but on a temporary basis only. This would have enabled IASC to reach agreement in time for the March 1998 deadline as the other thirteen points on the agenda are less controversial and less difficult to solve than these matters of financial assets valuation. But the Board rejected the proposal of the staff and asked it to build an intermediary IASC norm on financial assets valuation before March 1998.

What is the relation between IASC, IOSCO and the Basle Committee? **JSG:** The Basle committee is the "crown jewel" of a system that began to take shape in the 17th Century when the Bank of England was created. But it dealt with credit risks only and it is only recently that it has begun to look at the market risks that are developing now as a result notably of securitization and deregulation.

IOSCO by contrast is a ten year old baby. It is a forum for eighty or so regulators with no mandatory power: its influence is based on the likelihood that accountants of the world will follow its recommendations. The two institutions have now convened to recommend that the rules that apply to market risks and credit risks equally apply to banks and to financial intermediaries.

What has been done in the way of crisis prevention?
JSG: The Basle committee and IOSCO have focused on four types or measure that can contribute to crisis prevention:
– Capital requirements,
– Internal controls,
– Disclosure,
– Reporting.

Again, the agreement covers not just banks but also intermediaries. In the meantime, the European Union has adopted directives on capital requirement and on investment services.

Are these binding disciplines, or just recommendations?
JSG: There is no obligation to follow these recommendations but the central banks will in fact exercise their surveillance on the basis of this grid of provisions.

Meanwhile, we are moving clearly toward "real time" control (every 15 minutes at MATIF) and each stock exchange has put in place "circuit breakers". They worked well in 1989 and have been used since then when price movements are above pre-defined thresholds. This allows market participants to take the necessary measures thereby enhancing liquidity.

This agenda does not raise simply technical issues but fundamental issues about culture and the different sets of acceptable principles, with IOSCO/IASC providing bridges between national perspectives. But there is also the global investor and if his role continues to increase we may be pushed toward the global approach.

Convergence needs to take place among national standard setters.

In France we are creating a new "Conseil National de la Comptabilité" (CNC) and a "Comité National de la Réglementation" (CNR). Nevertheless, the objective should not be uniformity, but to present options to choose from. Eleven firms in France have adopted IASC. Meanwhile, Deutsche Bank has convinced a number of German companies to opt for IASC.

We need less administrative rules – called in French *réglementation* – and more adequate *régulation* to monitor the system through tighter rules for transparency, for control of counterpart risk etc.

To conclude, would you say that the IASC vision is that we are moving toward a set of global standards? **JSG:** This is probably not yet a really shared vision. Japanese institutions for instance, say they are in favour, in principle, but will be very slow in moving in this direction. Germany also has its habits, and they are closely related to tax matters very specific to that country.

Globalization is heightening the need for *harmonization*, but this is like water dropping from our hands: the more we want to harmonize, the more difficult it is to give a value to what is being regulated! It is in the nature of the system to be volatile, creative and reactive. Market participants do not stay idle in face of new rules but they take new risks, new initiatives. Harmonization has a moving target, it is *"une course poursuite"* in which, if I may say so, true and fair accounting values can only be achieved at a high price. To me this is fine because this is the way the world is, and because truth and fairness in accounting is worth a very high price indeed!

> National regulators in the age of the single European capital market

Conversation with René de La Serre, Chairman, and Bertrand de Mazières, Secretary General of Conseil des Marchés Financiers (CMF) in Paris.

Anyone who has followed the regulatory scene in Paris can only be struck by the magnitude of the changes that have taken place with the strengthening of the Commission des Opérations de Bourses (COB) and the creation of the Conseil des Marchés Financiers (CMF). To what extent has this transformation been related to the move toward economic, financial and monetary union in Europe? **René de La Serre:** Indeed, the regulatory framework for financial services has been profoundly renovated by the *law of July 2, 1996.* This was conceived from the beginning as part of the European process of financial integration. Incidentally, the Europe of financial markets includes not only the EU but its three partners in the European Economic Area (EEA).

Key principles in this law are freedom of *establishment* and freedom of *delivery of services.* We now have a completely integrated European financial market in the sense that any financial institution established in any of the member State of the EEA can operate freely in any other member State just as it would in its domestic market.

Obviously, a key pre-condition is appropriate *supervision.* Therefore, the law has set up a fully-fledged system of control, in terms of *institutions* as well as of *rules.* These rules are firmly grounded in European law. In this sense, France is now part of a broader European regulatory area.

What are the central features of this new institutional framework? And to what extent has there been convergence to a common European regulatory structure? **Bertrand de Mazières:** Three institutions or three sets of institutions co-operate to implement these responsibilities:

– The first one centres around *Banque de France* and is ensured by specific committees (Commission bancaire, Comité des Etablissements de Crédit…). They are in charge of licensing and prudential supervision.

– The *Commission des Opérations de Bourses (COB)* is in charge of the surveillance of the proper functioning of financial markets, with emphasis on the availability and the quality of *financial information* provided to investors and with control over all portfolio-management firms.

– And then, our own institution *CMF* is in charge of overseeing the good organisation and behaviour of financial intermediaries from the moment when they take orders until the custody of financial instruments. Consistent with this overall mission, CMF defines the organisational and operating rules that regulated markets must observe and regulates public tender offers.

These three levels of rules – prudential, market transparency, professional and good conduct – are the same in all EEA member States but each one of these States can choose the institutional setting most appropriate to its traditions and specific conditions. In the U.K. there existed several different institutions as professional surveillance was carried out by specialized SROs, but they are now evolving towards a more unified structure. Meanwhile, in Germany, one finds a bipolar structure with a strong element of federalism …

In other words, the single currency will not be accompanied by a single supervisory structure, there will be no European SEC? **RdLS / BdM:** The European experience already shows that a single market for financial intermediaries can operate without the establishment of such federal-type structures. This should be no surprise, at a time when means of communication of all sorts enable various authorities to work together within what is, in the end, a *regulatory network* in lieu of a regulatory body. Granted, the building of centralised European institutions remains a choice open for the future. But the alternative of a network approach has as much chance of remaining the right answer. Indeed, a network allows more flexibility than one integrated authority, where the huge size is, inevitably, a source of complexity that blunts effectiveness. And a big European structure would have, anyway, to operate within a network connecting to institutions in other parts of the world...

What has been achieved in the year and a half since the new structure was set up in Paris? **RdLS / BdM:** Obviously, the priority has been full implementation of the principles laid out in the French and European statutes. We have now reached the stage where financial institutions can make full use of their freedom to operate in other countries because we have put in place the institutions and procedures necessary for appropriate oversight.

This has been accompanied by a process of thorough preparation by *market participants* and *market organisations.* Financial intermediaries of all sizes have streamlined their structures with a view to better identifying and allocating responsibilities within their organisations. Meanwhile, the regulated markets in France have evolved towards a coherent, more tightly integrated structure through, in particular, the decisions that you have discussed in this book with Jean-François Théodore and Gérard Pfauwadel.

Professional associations have also been very active in liaison with their international networks as well as with us, here at CMF. The co-operation between all parties involved has been organised in the framework of the *Schéma de Place.*

CMF clout and reactivity were put to the test immediately after its creation by an unprecedented bout of cross-border take-overs, providing yet another proof that Europe as a one economic entity is a reality.

Looking to the future, what do you think will be the critical regulatory challenges once the euro is in place? **RdLS / BdM:** The first challenge, to be very pragmatic, is that national institutions continue to develop their dialogue and their co-operation. You can see that this is actually taking place in a very natural way along the three levels we have mentioned:

– Central banks have a long experience of co-operation.

– COB is involved in the Forum of European Securities Commissions (FESCO) which has just been created by all EEA members under the able chairmanship of Tommaso Padoa-Schioppa. A small permanent secretariat is housed in Paris.

– On our side, we maintain close relationships with our counterparts through many informal meetings with no need for much additional arrangements. Here also, our preference goes to a "network approach".

For the longer term, we must remember that regulatory change is merely the accompanying process of a deeper *economic* transformation.

A first key issue is therefore the adaptation of this framework to the cross-border nature of economic activity which raises questions still in need of further elaboration such as the relationship between *nationality* and *territoriality*. As you have followed the discussions around the draft EU "take-over directive", you are aware that responsibility still has to be precisely allocated between authorities of the *home country* where a company is registered, and those of *host countries* where its securities are listed.

Other issues have to do with *corporate governance*. Europe has now become a very active participant in this essential international debate. There is the need to identify common concepts and common approaches that will allow, for instance, clients to be protected in an homogeneous manner throughout Europe, as well as protect the rights of minority shareholders. One of the problems is that financial institutions as well as their customers are no longer easily defined in terms of nationality as they operate across borders through increasingly sophisticated networks. Another field where this has to be considered is the implementation of the *rules of good conduct*. Their administration by host-country authorities is in the interest of the protection of the client, but some investors with cross-border operations are perhaps less keen than others on territorialy attributed protection.

On all these issues, CMF is preparing to contribute to the development of the common European approaches that will provide the regulatory foundation and the common "financial culture" that are two essential dimensions of what PROMETHEE calls the "networked markets" behind the Europe of the euro. ■

Chapter XIII

The strategic issues *behind the conversation*

"To learn from one another" such is, at heart, the essence of the Monnet method for Yves Franchet. And from him too, we learnt a great deal in discussing the Maastricht process as a learning experience for economic policy makers.

The "convergence in mind-sets" has been the true foundation of what statisticians measure under the name of macro-economic convergence. Political signals find their way into economic trends, and the experts in charge of qualifying countries for the euro have been impressed by the role that they can play in overcoming the stalemate of vested interests. Maastricht and Thatcherism are strange bedfellows indeed in this exclusive group of sources of political signals strong enough to make expectations and behaviours converge!

Strategic issues addressed here have to do with the sustainability of the euro as well as with the next steps in policy and economic convergence that will follow. As in the conversation with Luc Bomans, the quality of information is also one essential issue discussed, in the perspective of a global networked economy. Like a number of our guests, Yves Franchet gives emphasis to pension systems and to labour markets. But he also takes some non-conventional views as to the lags and differences in business cycles that are said to prevent the U.K. from joining the eleven "first wave" euro countries before 2002.

Again, convergence does not just "happen". It results from a subtle web of interactions between the world of markets, the world of policy making and the deeper world of human aspirations. As an economist, Yves Franchet helps us conclude this set of strategic conversations on the spirit beyond the letter and criteria of convergence... A.B.

conversation with

YVES FRANCHET,

EUROSTAT

This conversation with Yves Franchet, Director General of Eurostat (Luxembourg), was conducted in Luxembourg and Paris by Albert Bressand (PROMETHEE).

Measuring economic convergence: the euro as catalyst of global trends and the need for certified information

Let me first express our gratitude to Eurostat for the co-operation that has developed around the quantitative analysis of the move toward the euro. Let me also ask you about your *personal* impressions regarding the convergence process. Have you been surprised by the curves and figures that have accumulated on your desk – and if so, what is it that makes the euro more than just a change in the way we measure money? **Yves Franchet:** Yes, I have been surprised just like most economists have been during this long march to the euro. We all had certain ideas and perceptions about what a typical set of macroeconomics data in Europe would look like, at least in terms of basic differences among countries. So, looking at the convergence process in countries like Ireland, Portugal or Italy, most of us were surprised by the magnitude of change and the speed at which it has taken shape. In other words, most of us had been led to think, looking at the past, that the deadline of January 1, 1999 would be too hard to meet for a number of countries. It turns out that we had overlooked the fact that policies are not given but adapt to deadlines and constraints.

If one thinks twice, however, one realises that this convergence is taking place not just as part of European integration but also of globalization. A global economy means competition. In a more open world, at a time of rapid technological changes, countries and companies have to compete. In such an economy it is not possible to have major discrepancies with respect to basic macroeconomics performances like inflation and public finance, and this also helps to understand why countries are ready to go out of their way to be part of the "first tier" of euro countries.

This convergence, however, is a matter of medium term performances and it has been accompanied by instability. This instability can take the form of turbulences, sometimes violent movements in the markets as happened on the foreign exchange markets in Europe in the summer of 1992 and 1993 or as happened to the whole macro-economic environment in Asia in the fall of 1997. It can also involve slower but powerful movements, as we have seen with government deficits in the wake of German reunification. What matters most, however, is the overall picture and the medium term trends. And this is where global pressures and European integration combine their effects.

Countries are under pressures to adopt the "right" policies. But giving up the old habits runs against important national vested interests. Adjustment to the global reality seldom happens simply as a result of spontaneous forces. Strong and clear political signals are needed. In Europe, we have had two series of strong signals of that type in the recent past.

One was the political philosophy of the Thatcher era, and it was a source of very strong pro-market signals indeed! The signals were about the need to take a fresh look at many established policies, with the efficiency of market mechanisms as the new benchmark. Obviously, the speed of adjustment has to be balanced against its social costs.

The second source of political signals is the European integration process itself. Europe is not just a "common market", it is also a shared vision of the direction in which our countries should move, and this vision has proven to be, at least during some periods, a powerful – even if diffuse – source of political signals.

In this decade, we have had two major illustrations of that role of the Union as a source of political legitimacy.

First, we had the single market signals of 1992, a set of "signals" sent from Brussels that allowed a whole set of barriers to be dismantled, at record speed, within the highly visible *"Europe 1992" program.* The European Union and notably the Commission, which are often described as "bureaucratic" entities, were a major source of political legitimacy: by putting their weight behind the internal market program, they enabled national governments to stand up to the many special interests that benefited from all these barriers. Then we had *the march toward the euro* accompanied by the commitment to achieve the transition by a specific date, namely the January 1, 1999. Here also, strong signals have allowed countries to gather the strength, and governments to develop the legitimacy, that allowed to carry out reforms. Major opposition also exists, but so far, the political signals have clearly been in favour of integration.

Change is about politics as well as economics, as PROMETHEE knows well. The economic price for change is often of a global nature, whereas political forces are better harnessed at the European level. In other words, the stage for the convergence process is set *globally*, but the Union is a major catalyst for change.

Does not this put the Union in the uncomfortable situation of being blamed for the negative aspects of globalization?

YF: Indeed, the Union can be used as a scapegoat, as governments find it quite convenient to blame the pains of adjustments on "Brussels".

On the other hand, the political legitimacy of Europe is high enough for this scapegoating to remain, most of the time, only a side-show. Governments of all shades can use the legitimacy of European co-operation and integration to carry out unpopular changes. To take one recent example, as a source of strong political signals, Europe integration process has led a socialist government in Greece to implement an orthodox economic policy and to use this opportunity to modernise, that is to say to adjust to the new world situation.

Other examples include *monopolies* in telecom and *pension systems*. The technological revolution of the twentieth century and the speed of adjustment it requires make the government monopoly in telecom inefficient. Financing the pension systems in a situation of ageing population and public deficit reduction requires new financing schemes.

As we know, competition between nations has become a competition between their non traded elements, e.g. their infrastructures, education systems, communication facilities, social protection systems, etc. Governments need a legitimate framework in which to challenge national policies which have become at odds with the reality of a global economy and to prepare their countries for global competition.

You have just given three examples of this catalytic role that the Union can play: sound *macro-economic* policies, dismantling

***telecommunications* monopolies and reform of *pension* systems. It is easy to see your point in the first two cases, but is not the third one in a very different stage in which there are more talks than results?** **YF:** Yes and no. Just a few years ago, it was not even possible to discuss such issues. Now, by contrast, someone who followed the Employment Summit, here in Luxembourg in November 1997, could detect a strong convergence in the ways member States are now approaching these issues. Regarding pensions, the state of the debate, as you describe it in this volume, is also rather encouraging. After all, not only can talks lead to actions, they are usually a prerequisite for action!

It is true, however, that social policy is the third stage of the convergence process catalyzed by European integration, and it is clear that the debate on social matters has not yet moved in the same way as it has regarding macroeconomic policy.

But what matters, over the long run, is not so much where we stand right now but how far and how fast we are moving. The reality is that the European integration process is first and foremost a learning process. Decision makers – be it in governments or industry – are confronted quite frequently with colleagues in other countries and with a common set of facts that calls for common answers. Gradually, divergences tend to subside and the decisions taken by each of them individually tend to be better than those they would have taken if they had not had the benefit of this dialogue.

Is this the end of the welfare state? Is Europe converging toward "the Anglo-Saxon model"? **YF:** The Union is not about reducing social protection; rather it is about a different approach to social protection, about a different approach to the *financing* of social protection.

What impressed me most during the recent Luxembourg Employment Summit was the consensus reached on this analysis, in spite of very different material situations. The guiding principles that were adopted at the end of that summit focused on the means and best practices to fight unemployment. The fact that national plans will be presented and discussed year after year may not lead to immediate reductions in unemployment. Yet, over the medium term, it means that the Union will be a source of pressure on policies which will trigger new levels of convergence.

Basically, you are saying that the process of integration matters as much as the objectives. Is that simply a reexpression of the Monnet method? **YF:** The common element between the early age of European integration and what we see now is, indeed, the "step by step" approach. A key difference, however, is that in the time of Monnet, the global pressures were in no way as strong as they are today.

Hence a key difference is that we now need to go much faster along that learning curve because the global realities are much stronger than in the past.

The first reaction to the figures we have discussed together and of the short selection that the reader will find in this book is to say that countries in the European Union converge *because* of Maastricht. The reality is that these countries are converging because they have to. Actually, they are not so much *converging* as they are *catching up* with the new conditions now prevailing in the global economy.

In a sense, the integration process that is developing around the euro is not changing the direction but speeding the learning process. I have had discussions with statisticians from the Mercosur countries (Brazil, Argentina, Uruguay and Paraguay) as they wanted to learn whether our experience is relevant to their own integration efforts. My answer has always been that it is difficult to adapt to the global economy but that doing so as part of a group of like-minded countries makes it easier.

In a way, one could say that the conduct of European integration has come to rest on a re-expression of the Monnet method in the context of a more competitive global world economy. The spirit is still there, but the letter can no longer be simply European!

As an economist trained at spotting long term trends from short term signals, are you under the impression that the convergence achieved on the way to the euro is a sustainable one? Will it really stick once the euro is in place? Or is not the Stability Pact a straight-jacket from which countries will want to free themselves? **YF:** The key step is *not* convergence in macroeconomic figures, it is the change of mentality. This is the truly difficult part. Once this has been achieved – as it has been now – a new dynamics, can develop. Negotiating the Pact of Stability and Growth was a real challenge. In the next few years, Europeans will have the benefit of having met this challenge and it will be a matter of remaining faithful to it.

Now I do realise that the media tend to present the Stability Pact as a straight-jacket. This is because they fail to see that it is, first and foremost, a framework for an ongoing process of discussion. As you know, the Stability and Growth Pact implies that beyond 1997 countries within the euro area have to continue a policy limiting public deficit and debts. Large penalties will be paid by those countries that do not respect these criteria. Actually,

I do not expect penalties to be imposed, or very seldom so, because the bulk of the adjustment process will already have taken place. The framework needed for the convergence process to feed upon itself will be in place. Breaking the old ways of thinking, especially in countries like France and Italy, such was the difficult part!

Differences in business cycle across the Channel have been mentioned as another source of divergence. Does the U.K. still belong in an economic environment different from that of continental Europe? **YF:** I believe that the issue of divergence between the U.K. and the continent has been slightly overblown. The business cycle and the fact that the U.K. had been growing for a longer period has now come to the forefront of preoccupations. When they perceive convergence, markets tend to reinforce it.

Actually, I have mixed feelings about this business cycle focus. My feeling is that there is an element of self-fulfilling prophecy in these discussions, either negative or positive. As one could see every time the British governments have made important announcements about the participation of the U.K. in the euro, markets have reacted to convergence signals by strong moves in exchange rates and interest rates that tend to accelerate convergence.

So I would not be surprised to see this issue gradually wane away.

Beyond the business cycle, however, lies another tougher issue: that of *labour market flexibility*. It is a very complex set of issues touching on fundamental values and including the issue of mobility of workers across the Union. This is a topic where the Employment Summit may have seen some progress on the road to convergence. In the U.S., after all, different States are often in different stages of the business cycles, but the higher levels of mobility and flexibility that exist in the U.S. make such divergences much more bearable.

In my view, the key challenge is not associated with the business cycle but with two other issues. There is a narrower one, and there is a broader and deeper one:

First, the more specific issue of the level at which the British pound will join EMU once the U.K. also adopts the euro. As we have seen in the past such level needs to be set right if we want to avoid major disappointments and problems. The fact that the pound had to leave the EMS in 1992 was, in no small part, the reflection of the unsustainable rate at which it had joined in the first place. Not repeating that mistake will be a critical aspect of the relationship between the U.K. and the euro countries after 1999.

Second, a deeper issue is the need to move toward better performing labour market. I am quite confident that the process which started at the Luxembourg Employment Summit will enable fruitful discussions on the issue in the coming months.

Convergence, however, is better understood if it can be measured. And the measurement is the responsibility notably of Eurostat. Could you explain what is the exact role that you are playing in this process? **YF:** It is important to realise that Eurostat is a network institution. There are 60 000 statistic officials in the member countries, but only 700 at Eurostat. So the role of Eurostat *cannot be* to substitute for these 60 000 national statisticians. Rather, it is to help them work in coherent, co-ordinated manners, to have a common language and produce comparable and reliable statistics.

We need for instance comparable ways of measuring inflation, GDP and public deficits. These are not abstract issues for economic historians, because financial contributions of member countries to the EU budget are based on such numbers. Comparing levels of GDP in a mutually satisfactory manner is a prerequisite for all countries to accept the financial contributions asked from them on this basis as fair and legitimate.

This leads to another issue, that of *quality of data.* I remember that at the end of a Monetary Committee meeting the chairman Sir Nigel Wicks made the point that the credibility of the whole convergence process was highly dependent on the quality and on the credibility of the statistics on which it is based. He was absolutely right: the stakes are very high, and countries are very demanding in terms of the quality of information.

Eurostat produces statistics. And, whether we like it or not, statistics are always *estimates.* So we are dependent on the process that we run internally to achieve the high levels of integrity needed for our statistics to be accepted as a legitimate basis for financial contributions.

The process involves national statistical institutes together with the Central Banks and the European Monetary Institute (EMI). In addition, it is very important that we make our decisions transparent to the users, the governments, the Parliaments, the media.

We are moving toward the point where we may be able to certify the process along which our figures are certified, with norms of the ISO 9000 type, as is the case for processes within a private company aiming for a "total quality" label.

Is your reference to the "ISO 9000" standard merely a metaphor or is Eurostat actually rethinking its whole internal functioning? If so, could you elaborate on what is implied? **YF:** This is not merely a metaphor. We have as our goal to certify some of our data producing processes along the ISO 9000 norms, and to do so by 1999. The credibility in a data which is essential for the key issues, will be enhanced by this procedure.

Eurostat has been at the center of a controversy regarding the legitimacy of the inclusion by the French Government of financial receipts related to the pension funds of France Telecom in its revenues for the year 1997. The fear was that this was merely window-dressing and that Eurostat was lending a much too complacent ear to this French effort to produce the data needed to qualify for the euro on that very important year. The same is applicable for decision on other issues like the Italian "Euro tax" and the treatment of German hospitals in national accounts. Have you really been complacent? **YF:** This was probably the most highly mediated and the most controversial of our decisions. Indeed, Eurostat was criticized because it was widely seen by the press as turning a blind eye to a few large continental countries that were taking decisions to lower their official public deficit in order to gain acceptance in the first tier of euro countries.

For one thing, it is clear that our communication process was not conducted professionally enough. This episode had begun with the French government announcing that such a decision would allow France to keep its public deficit at or below the 3% limit and with the German Bundesbank immediately objecting. At which point we were called upon to pass a judgement, with many hopes and counter-hopes pined upon our decision… Our failure was to announce our decision without explaining enough what our mission was, without making it clear enough what exactly we were asked to certify and how we did it.

We need to explain what our role is. Our role is *not* to certify the sustainability of a budgetary process (something which falls under the responsibility of the Commission and of the European Monetary Institute). We are in charge of certifying the consistency of the data presented with a statistical methodology and framework known as the European system of accounts, and, therefore, their comparability.

According to the Maastricht Treaty, national data must be certified to have been developed in compliance with the *European system of accounts*, in its version of 1979. It is the first time ever that the member States of the EU are required to produce comparable estimates of their public debts and deficits. Until now, the figures that have been used in such fora as the Commission, OECD and IMF have been developed along national definitions, which may differ substantially. Our figures have to be reliable and compatible with one another to the point that countries and tax payers can accept them as a sound basis to measure contributive capacities and to share the financial costs of their common institutions and common policies, as well as a basis for the measurement of the compliance with the Maastricht criteria.

The initial controversy you are alluding to revolved around a large transaction between the French government and France Telecom regarding the pensions of France Telecom employees. The issue was to know whether it was a capital transaction – which does not modify the deficit of the governments – or a financial transfer. If it were a capital transaction, then it would fall "under the line" and would not qualify as a government receipt. By contrast, a financial transfer, according to well established definition, falls "above the line" and qualifies as government receipt.

We checked and consulted quite intensely our counterparts in Central Banks, in national statistical institutes, in the European Monetary Institute, and it occurs to us that a large majority of statisticians considered this type of transfer as part of government receipt. As a result, we took the decision and announced it.

Those who disagreed did it because they saw it as a one shot, highly opportunistic and specific transaction that was presented, quite explicitly, as helping the French government meet the deficit target for the critical year of 1997. Their point was that this type of measure could not be repeated and would not correct the underlying financial imbalances in a sustainable manner. This is an important debate in its own right, a debate on long term stability in which the Commission and the European Monetary Institute (EMI) may want to engage member governments. But this was not the debate for which Eurostat input is requested by the Treaty.

Actually we have had to take about twenty decisions of that type, and this was the one that really caught the attention of the media. It did so, first, because of what was at stake and, second, because of the lack of clear explanation on our part regarding what we were asked to certify. I agree that this is a complex process, and I find it extremely important to explain our role more clearly. It was our failure to do so rather than the transaction itself that gave rise to controversy. For the subsequent decisions, we had learnt our lesson and followed a more structured, more professional communication process; and no controversy materialized!

Actually, the challenge for an organization like Eurostat is not just measuring this or that aspect of economic reality, it is also about finding a new role in a broader economic and political integration process. You are really describing a process whereby the production of information – including statistics – is increasingly left to the market, with organizations like yours engaged in the increasingly complex political economy of certification... **YF:** It is true that one cannot talk about the Maastricht criteria without also talking about the role of national statisticians and about the process of cooperation among them that Eurostat, among others, are presiding over. And these roles have changed immensely.

Twenty years ago, there was a scarcity of "micro" data, and there was a *de facto* monopoly of official statisticians. By contrast, today, we have a very large supply of micro data as the remotest supermarket generates disquette after disquette of sales and inventory data. One now finds statistics all over the place. Hence official statisticians are drawn toward a different type of role. The issue is no longer the *existence* of data but the *quality* of data.

The comparative advantage of official statisticians is not that they can produce data, which they do, but that they are able to certify the quality of data and more specifically their independence from vested interests. And this is becoming the essential part of their role.

In addition, however, certification must be done in a timely fashion, as rapidly or almost as rapidly as private actors are producing "micro" data. If they fail to do so, national statisticians will simply disappear from the scene. If they succeed, they will play an important role in the type of global networked economy that PROMETHEE has often described.

How is Eurostat itself adapting and changing? Is Eurostat affected by these global changes that you have described? And how are you adapting to these more subtle changes in the role of statistics and statisticians? **YF:** We are already what you call a networked organisation. We are doing our best to also become a knowledge institution. In that sense, the movement toward the euro, here also, is a catalyst which will improve partnership within the Union, within a network of interdependent national institutions.

For Eurostat, the move towards the euro is, first and foremost, a *learning process.* We are no longer simply exchanging statistics or information, we are exchanging best practices. We do not co-operate simply to facilitate our work, we are also learning and benefiting from this process of exchange.

We are well on our way on the road toward the global networked economy, and for us also the euro is another powerful catalyst for change in this global context.

Here again, this may be the Monnet method in a new shape. A method to learn from one another. ■

Chapter XIV

MEASURING INTEGRATION

This section has been put together in co-operation with Eurostat and will be expanded in future volumes. We express our gratitude to Eurostat for their co-operation and claim responsibility for any error or shortcoming as well as for the succinct nature of the developments that were possible in the time available.

EUROPE, CONVERGENCE AND THE WORLD

A QUANTITATIVE OVERVIEW IN CO-OPERATION WITH EUROSTAT*

Table of contents

1 - Production and purchasing power standards

1.1 - Gross domestic product 1992-1996

1.2 - GDP, yearly growth 1992-1996

1.3 - GDP and GDP per capita at current prices and current exchange rates

1.4 - GDP and GDP per capita at current prices and current purchasing power standards

1.5 - GDP per capita of candidate countries, 1996 (except Cyprus), nominal and corrected for cost of living

2 - Trade and investment in commercial services: the EU performance

2.1 Basic trends regarding EU trade in services

2.2 - World exports of commercial services

2.3 - EU, USA, Japan: trade in commercial services (1995)

2.4 - Cover rates of trade in commercial services for EU, the USA and Japan (%)

2.5 - Foreign direct investment (FDI) in the service sector and globalization - A brief comparison between the European Union and the United States
2.5.1 FDI (outward flows)
2.5.2 FDI (inward flows)

3 - European convergence to the Maastricht criteria

3.1 - EMU convergence criteria: harmonised indices of consumer prices (%)
3.2 - Short-term interest rates: the road to convergence
3.3 - Long-term interest rates: the road to convergence
3.4 - EMU convergence criteria: long-term interest rates (%)
3.5 - EMU convergence criteria: general government deficit (% of GDP)
3.6 - EMU convergence criteria: general government debt (% of GDP)
3.7 - General government consolidated gross debt as % of GDP (selected countries)
3.8 - General government deficit as % of GDP (selected countries)
3.9 - Impact of debt interest payments on the deficit: the primary surplus behind general government deficit (as % of GDP)
3.10 - Fourth ACP-EC Convention - Financial protocol 1995-2000
3.11 - EU development cooperation with ACP countries (including EIB loans) (million ECU)

4 - Integration in the European Union: the budgetary side

4.1 - Expenses of the European Union Institutions (EUI)
4.1.1 - EUI expenses
4.1.2 - Average weight of the different EUI expenses
4.1.3 -Extra-EU transfers
4.2 - EUI loans
4.2.1 - Loans of the European Investment Bank (EIB)
4.2.2 - Other loans of the EUI

5 - Competitiveness and labour productivity

5.1 - Share of OECD production - total manufacturing
5.2 - Unemployment rate, as share of the total labour force
5.3 - Labour productivity, level (at market exchange rate)
5.4 - Labour productivity, value added per hour worked
5.5 - R&D per capita (current ECU)
5.6 - Per capita spending on information technology (ECU)

6 - Financial markets of the Union:

Capitalisation, returns and pension funds: section and text by Thomas Rabe (Cedel Bank)

6.1 - Financial market and market capitalization
- 6.1.1 A - The European Union (EUR15), the likely euro countries (EUR11), the U.S. and Japan (A)
- 6.1.1 B - Comparing the financial markets of the European Union (EUR15), the likely euro countries (EUR11), the U.S. and Japan (B)
- 6.1.2 - Stock markets' size (domestic equities) 1996

6.2 - Differences in rates of return of equities compared to bonds
- 6.2.1 - Annual real rates of return in domestic currency (1967-1990)
- 6.2.2 - Annual excess returns of equities over bond markets in domestic currency (1981-1995)
- 6.2.3 - Annual returns of equities on the U.S. market (1926-1984)
- 6.2.4 - Annual returns of equities and gilts on the U.K. market (1919-1993)
- 6.2.5 - Annual returns of equities and fixed income products on the Belgian market (1959-1994)

6.3 - Demographics, pension funds and mobility of labour in the euro era
- 6.3.1 - Contribution of each pillar to pensions
- 6.3.2 - Assets of life insurance companies (1995)
- 6.3.3 - Pillar 2: coverage level
- 6.3.4 - Assets of life insurance companies (1995)
- 6.3.5 - Distribution of pension funds assets (as % of total assets)
- 6.3.6 - Life insurance assets (as % of total assets in 1994)
- 6.3.7 - Main national regulations on pension funds portfolio
- 6.3.8 - Main national regulations on life insurance companies

*

* *Further readings: International trade in services, 1986-1995. Eurostat 1997; European Union Direct Investment Yearbook. Eurostat 1997.*

1 - Production and purchasing power standards

1.1 - Gross domestic product 1992-1996

Dec. 1997	Volume indices (yearly growth in %)				
	1992	**1993**	**1994**	**1995**	**1996**
Austria	1.3	0.5	2.5	2.1	1.6
Belgium	1.5	-1.5	2.4	2.1	1.5
Finland	-3.6	-1.2	4.5	5.1	3.3
France	0.9	-1.4	2.7	2.0	1.2
Germany	2.2	-1.2	2.7	1.8	1.4
Ireland	4.6	3.6	7.8	11.1	8.6
Italy	0.6	-1.2	2.2	2.9	0.7
Luxembourg	3.7	4.1	3.8	3.2	2.6
Netherlands	2.0	0.8	3.2	2.3	3.3
Portugal	1.8	0.3	1.1	2.5	3.3
Spain	0.7	-1.1	2.1	2.6	2.3
Likely "out" and "opt out" countries					
Denmark	0.2	1.6	3.7	2.5	2.5
Greece	0.5	0.2	2.2	2.0	2.6
Sweden	-1.4	-2.2	3.3	3.6	1.9
United Kingdom	-0.5	2.1	4.3	2.8	2.3
EUROP. UNION 15	**0.9**	**-0.6**	**2.9**	**2.5**	**1.8**
Countries negotiating accession with EU in 1998					
Cyprus	9.3	0.4	6.3	5.8	–
Czechoslovakia	-3.3	0.6	2.7	5.9	4.1
Estonia	-14.2	-8.5	-1.8	4.3	4.0
Hungary	-3.1	-0.6	2.9	1.5	1.3
Poland	2.6	3.8	5.2	7.0	6.1
Slovenia	-5.5	2.8	5.3	4.1	3.1
Other candidate countries					
Bulgaria	-7.3	-1.5	1.8	2.1	-10.9
Latvia	-34.9	-14.9	0.6	-0.8	2.8
Lithuania	–	-30.4	1.0	3.0	4.2
Romania	-8.8	1.5	3.9	7.1	4.1
Slovakia	-6.5	-3.9	4.9	6.9	7.0
Total 11 candidate countries CC11	**–**	**1.0**	**4.0**	**5.4**	**4.5**
Island	-3.4	1.0	3.7	1.0	5.2
Norway	3.3	2.7	5.5	3.6	5.3
Switzerland	-0.1	-0.5	0.5	0.8	-0.2
USA	2.8	2.4	3.7	2.4	2.8
Japan	1.1	0.1	0.5	0.8	3.5

Source: EUROSTAT dissemination data base New Cronos.

1.2 - GDP, yearly growth 1992-1996

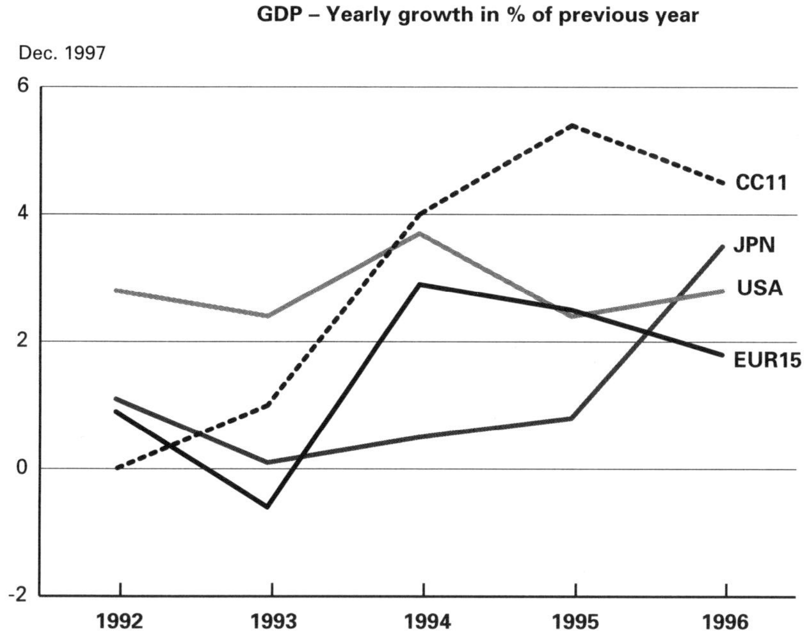

Source: EUROSTAT dissemination data base New Cronos.

After slowing down in 1992 (0.9%) and 1993 (-0.6%), the economies of the European Union have returned to a sustained growth path in 1994 - 1995. The milder growth of 1996 has been followed by a rebound in 1997 to about 2.5% that is expected to carry into 1998 in spite of Asian problems. This is favorable to a smooth start for the euro although the larger core-countries appear more dependent on exports than the small countries and opt-out countries.

1.3 - GDP and GDP per capita at current prices and current exchange rates

Dec. 1997	Total - Mrd ECUs					
	1992	1993	1994	1995	1996	96/95 in %
Austria	144.7	156.0	165.4	177.1	180.3	1.8
Belgium	173.6	183.1	195.7	209.0	211.3	1.1
Finland	82.1	72.0	82.5	96.3	98.6	2.4
France	1,020.1	1,063.4	1,119.2	1,169.1	1,204.7	3.0
Germany	1,523.8	1,633.8	1,729.4	1,846.4	1,854.6	0.4
Ireland	40.3	41.4	45.4	49.4	55.7	12.8
Italy	941.7	842.0	855.7	831.4	956.4	15.0
Luxembourg	9.8	11.0	12.3	13.2	13.4	1.1
Netherlands	248.9	267.3	284.6	304.1	312.0	2.6
Portugal	71.1	70.1	71.5	76.9	81.9	6.6
Spain	449.3	412.0	410.7	430.9	460.9	7.0
Likely "out" and "opt out" countries						
Denmark	107.5	113.0	120.0	129.4	134.7	4.1
Greece	75.6	78.6	82.5	87.4	96.8	10.8
Sweden	191.4	158.5	167.1	176.3	197.1	11.8
U.K.	809.3	806.0	858.9	846.4	908.4	7.3
EUR 15	**5,889.2**	**5,908.3**	**6,201.1**	**6,443.1**	**6,766.8**	**5.0**
Countries negotiating accession with EU in 1998						
Cyprus	–	–	6.7	–	–	–
Czechoslovakia	–	29.4	33.4	38.6	43.9	13.9
Estonia	–	1.4	2.0	2.8	3.3	20.7
Hungary	28.7	33.0	34.9	34.2	32.9	-3.6
Poland	65.0	73.4	77.8	91.0	105.9	16.4
Slovenia	9.6	10.8	12.1	14.3	14.2	-0.6
Other candidate countries						
Bulgaria	6.6	9.2	8.1	10.8	7.4	-31.4
Latvia	1.1	1.9	3.1	3.4	3.9	15.3
Lithuania	1,2	2.0	2.9	3.5	4.9	42.6
Romania	15,1	22.5	25.1	27.3	23.1	-15.3
Slovakia	–	10.2	11.6	13.3	14.5	9.4
CC11	**127.3**	**193.8**	**211.0**	**245.8**	**254.2**	**3.4**
Island	5.3	5.2	5.2	5.3	5.7	7.3
Norway	97.6	99.1	103.6	112.1	124.2	10.7
Switzerland	188.3	202.2	220.3	235.8	232.0	-1.6
USA	4,643.5	5,411.6	5,646.1	5,374.3	5,776.8	7.5
Japan	2,872.9	3,653.1	3,948.8	3,924.1	3,622.2	-7.7

Source: EUROSTAT dissemination data base New Cronos.

Dec. 1997	**PER CAPITA - ECUs**					
	1992	**1993**	**1994**	**1995**	**1996**	**96/95 in %**
Austria	18,285	19,522	20,599	22,006	22,367	1.6
Belgium	17,286	18,156	19,349	20,613	20,806	0.9
Finland	16,284	14,220	16,223	18,857	19,247	2.1
France	17,780	18,445	19,331	20,109	20,638	2.6
Germany	18,907	20,126	21,239	22,610	22,647	0.2
Ireland	11,347	11,617	12,726	13,779	15,470	12.3
Italy	16,265	14,495	14,690	14,249	16,337	14.7
Luxembourg	24,850	27,576	30,454	32,273	32,168	-0.3
Netherlands	16,391	17,483	18,504	19,673	20,101	2.2
Portugal	7,209	7,097	7,223	7,751	8,245	6.4
Spain	11,517	10,541	10,491	10,989	11,736	6.8
Likely "out" and "opt out" countries						
Denmark	20,792	21,776	23,058	24,747	25,607	3.5
Greece	7,325	7,571	7,911	8,362	9,252	10.6
Sweden	22,080	18,184	19,029	19,970	22,289	11.6
U.K.	13,953	13,851	14,709	14,442	15,454	7
EUR 15	**15,959**	**15,936**	**16,669**	**17,268**	**18,081**	**4.7**
Countries negotiating accession with EU in 1998						
Cyprus	–	–	–	10,431	–	–
Czechoslovakia	–	2,842	3,230	3,733	4,254	14
Estonia	–	939	1,306	1,855	2,263	22
Hungary	2,780	3,202	3,401	3,339	3,230	-3.3
Poland	1,694	1,909	2,020	2,359	2,742	16.2
Slovenia	4,833	5,436	6,080	7,208	7,154	-0.7
Other candidate countries						
Bulgaria	776	1,089	965	1,290	889	-31.1
Latvia	400	718	1,204	1,352	1,574	16.4
Lithuania	325	525	784	933	1,332	42.8
Romania	662	989	1,106	1,203	1,022	-15
Slovakia	–	1,924	2,161	2,471	2,698	9.2
CC11	1,440	1,838	2,001	2,320	2,418	4.2
Island	20,398	19,685	19,680	19,946	21,274	6.7
Norway	22,773	22,989	23,887	25,722	28,343	10.2
Switzerland	27,127	28,927	31,311	33,307	32,643	-2
USA	18,179	20,962	21,659	20,427	21,762	6.5
Japan	23,119	29,315	31,615	31,264	28,719	-8.1

Source: EUROSTAT dissemination data base New Cronos.

1.4 - GDP and GDP per capita at current prices and current purchasing power standards

Dec. 1997	Total - Mrd PPS					
	1992	1993	1994	1995	1996	% EUR 15 in 1996
Austria	136.0	142.1	149.6	154.3	162.7	2.4
Belgium	176.7	184.1	193.6	199.0	208.3	3.1
Finland	69.3	73.4	77.3	85.1	91.1	1.3
France	1,006.4	994.6	1,034.5	1,071.7	1,118.9	16.5
Germany	1,377.9	1,394.0	1,495.6	1,557.7	1,632.8	24.1
Ireland	44.4	46.9	52.5	57.6	64.8	1.0
Italy	952.3	936.7	993.7	1,036.8	1,079.9	16.0
Luxembourg	9.6	10.4	11.3	11.9	12.3	0.2
Netherlands	245.1	252.4	268.9	287.1	305.0	4.5
Portugal	99.4	104.7	110.9	114.9	122.4	1.8
Spain	479.6	486.9	500.3	522.1	545.9	8.1
Likely "out" and "opt out" countries						
Denmark	84.9	90.5	96.7	102.2	108.5	1.6
Greece	101.5	106.1	112.6	118.4	125.6	1.9
Sweden	136.0	136.3	143.8	153.5	160.4	2.4
UK	896.3	914.1	960.0	973.6	1,029.6	15.2
(1)	**74.2**	**35.7**	**0.6**	**-1.2**	**161.3**	**-**
EUR15	**5,889.2**	**5,908.3**	**6,201.1**	**6,443.1**	**6,766.8**	**100.0**
CC10*	–	496.8	529.7	568.9	611.8	9.0
USA	5,740.7	5,870.5	6,224.5	6,484.9	6,926.4	102.4
JPN	2,370.8	2,404.7	2,459.4	2,539.8	2,730.2	40.3

** CC10: Candidate countries except Cyprus*

Source: EUROSTAT dissemination data base New Cronos.

(1) Statistical discrepancy due to the equality 1 PPS = 1 ECU at Union level. This adjustment has been performed for EUR12 to 1993 and for EUR15 from 1994.

Dec. 1997	PER CAPITA - PPS					
	1992	**1993**	**1994**	**1995**	**1996**	EUR 15 = 100 in 1996
Austria	17,181	17,779	18,631	19,171	20,194	111.7
Belgium	17,592	18,254	19,136	19,629	20,508	113.4
Finland	13,744	14,494	15,194	16,668	17,788	98.4
France	17,541	17,252	17,867	18,433	19,168	106.0
Germany	17,096	17,172	18,368	19,075	19,937	110.3
Ireland	12,510	13,152	14,711	16,069	17,998	99.5
Italy	16,449	16,126	17,061	17,768	18,447	102.0
Luxembourg	24,577	26,103	28,074	29,048	29,500	163.1
Netherlands	16,144	16,510	17,484	18,567	19,648	108.7
Portugal	10,076	10,596	11,197	11,585	12,315	68.1
Spain	12,296	12,456	12,780	13,317	13,902	76.9
Likely "out" and "opt out" countries						
Denmark	16,414	17,433	18,572	19,555	20,625	114.1
Greece	9,837	10,223	10,799	11,322	12,001	66.4
Sweden	15,691	15,633	16,372	17,386	18,147	100.4
UK	15,453	15,708	16,440	16,613	17,516	96.9
(1)	-	-	-	-	-	
EUR15	**15,959**	**15,936**	**16,669**	**17,268**	**18,081**	**100.0**
CC10	-	4,711	5,025	5,402	5,819	32.0
USA	22,474	22,740	23,878	24,649	26,092	144.0
JPN	19,078	19,297	19,690	20,236	21,647	120.0

Source: EUROSTAT dissemination data base New Cronos.

1.5 - GDP per capita of candidate countries, 1996 (except Cyprus), nominal and corrected for cost of living

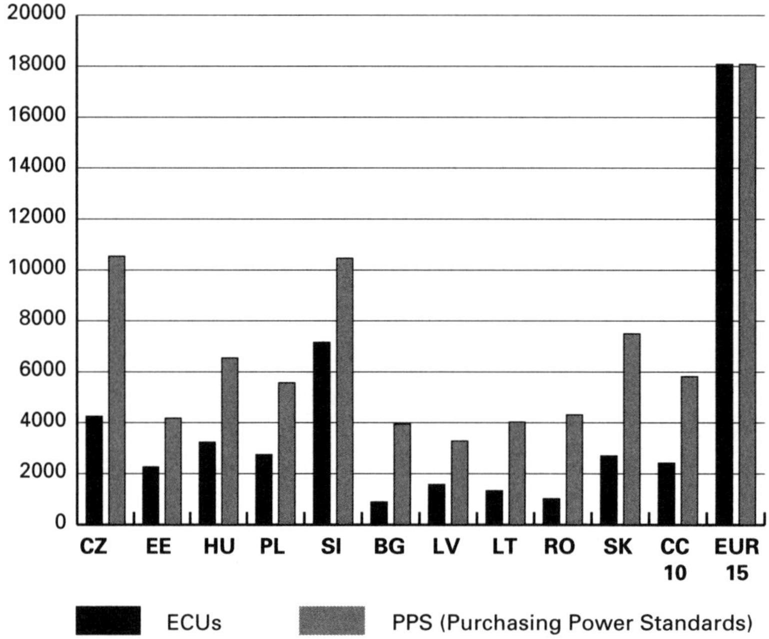

Source: EUROSTAT dissemination data base New Cronos.

2 - Trade and investment in commercial services: the EU performance

Concerning the position of the EU in the world economy, we have chosen to emphasize the services sectors, in line with their role in contemporary wealth creation as well as of their importance in the WTO "Tokyo Round" agreement and in the "Europe 1992" internal market.

2.1 - Basic trends regarding EU trade in services

Commercial services generated 682 billion ECU of cross-border trade in 1995, by which time world commercial services exports were almost twice greater than in 1986.

The EU is the world's largest exporter of commercial services, accounting for 26% of the total, followed by the U.S. with a 22% share and Japan with a 7% share.

In fact, a sectoral analysis shows that the EU is a leader in the export of services except for *Travel* (or Tourism) and *Royalties and license fees*, in which the U.S. is the main exporter.

The performance of Japan appears to be weaker than that of the EU and U.S. However, in the case of Royalties and license fees, the relative performance of Japan (size of exports brought to GDP) is comparable to that of the EU. Exports of Royalties and license fees accounted for 0.10% of GDP for the EU, 0.12% of GDP for Japan and 0.37% of GDP for the U.S. in 1995.

These results seem to highlight that fostering more investment in the R&D sector is needed for the EU.

However, the EU cover rate (expressed as the ratio of exports and imports) has dropped considerably. In 1986 receipts from commercial services covered 126% of commercial services expenditure, but this fell to just 104% in 1995.

Over the same period, the U.S. recorded a striking rise in the cover rate of trade in commercial services from 116% in 1986 up to 160% in 1992, falling to 154% in 1995.

The position of Japan is different: the country is a major net purchaser of external services and has a significant deficit in trade in commercial services, with a cover rate that has changed slightly from 56% in 1986 to 53% in 1995.

In addition to the apparent loss of competitiveness vis-à-vis the U.S., certain services, particularly in the financial domain, may have migrated to off-shore centres. This makes it difficult to analyse the performance of

European services on the basis of trade alone, as many of the companies registered in off-shore centres are subsidiaries of European companies whose international operations thus consist in investments and investment income.

2.2 - World[1] exports of commercial services[2] (Million ECU)

	1986	1992	1995
EU*	111,111	159,548	177,068
USA	75,074	130,419	152,659
Japan	21,957	38,063	49,053
Rest of World	168,538	183,790	303,232
World[1] Total	376,680	534,060	682,012
EU as % Total	29%	30%	26%

** EUR 12 for 1986; EUR 15 for 1992 and 1995*
Source: EUROSTAT (balance of payments)

1. World (IMF figure) excluding Intra EU exports
2. Commercial services = Services - Government services

2.3 - EU*, USA, Japan: trade in commercial services (1995) Exports by sector (Million ECU)

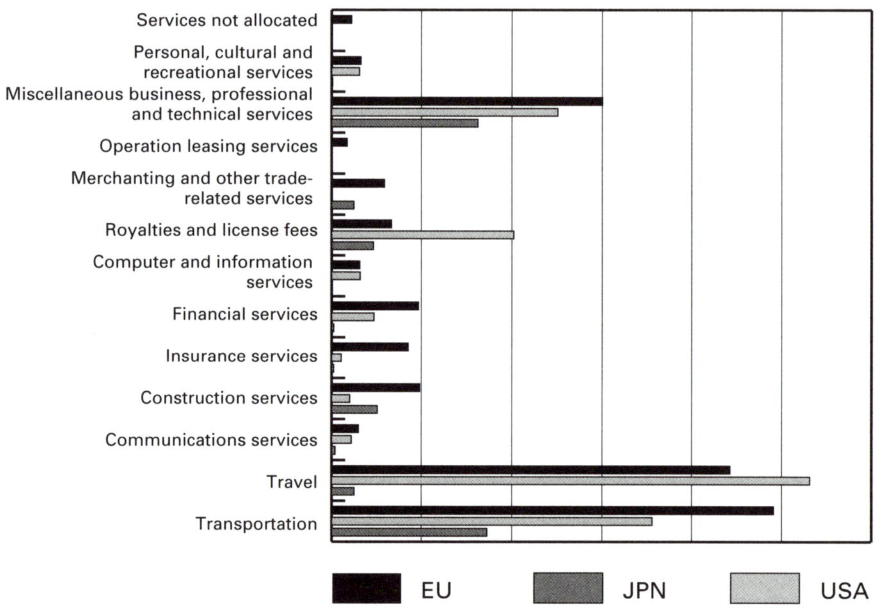

** For the EU (15 Member States), Intra EU exports are excluded*
Source: EUROSTAT (balance of payments)

2.4 - Cover rates of trade in commercial services for EU*, the USA and Japan (%)

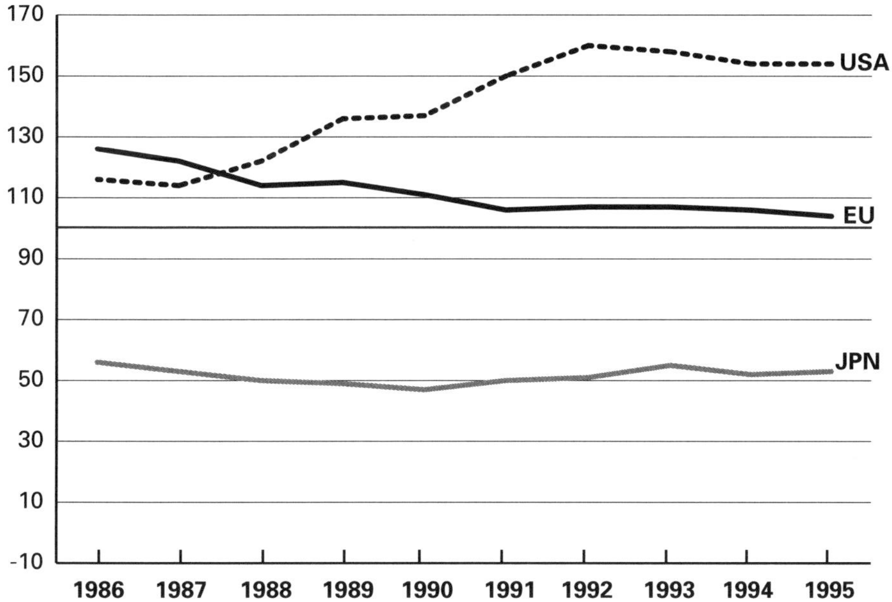

** EUR 12 for 1986-1991; EUR 15 for 1992-1995*
Source: EUROSTAT (balance of payments)

2.5 - Foreign direct investment[1] (FDI) in the service sector and globalization - A brief comparison between the European Union and the United States

2.5.1 FDI (outward flows)

The total outward FDI flows of the Union underwent a dynamic growth between 1992 and 1995, increasing by a factor of roughly 2.5. In that year, the last for which comparable figures are available, the flows of the Union outpaced those of the US by 13 billion reaching ECU 44 billion.

1. FDI knows three sub-components: equity capital, other capital (inter-company loans) and reinvested earnings. As only about half the EU Member states currently report reinvested earnings the comparison is based on equity and other capital only. If reinvested earnings were to be included the observed results might differ substantially.

Foreign direct investment flows (equity and other capital) of the EU* and the U.S. 1992-1995, in million ECU

	1992	1993	1994	1995
EU				
Outward flows to the world	17,828	24,157	24,129	44,472
of which services**	53%	56%	17%	53%
USA				
Outward flows to the world	20,301	35,106	17,657	31,375
of which services***	46%	70%	31%	29%
EU				
Inward flows from the world	22,760	21,504	21,814	37,706
of which services**	54%	58%	62%	47%
USA				
Inward flows from the world	23,872	43,061	38,038	35,891
of which services***	65%	65%	44%	52%

**) only extra-EU flows,*
***) EU services include the NACE groups trade and repairs, hotels and restaurants, transports, communication, financial intermediation, real estate and business activities, and other services*
****) US data for hotels and restaurants, transport and communication and other services is among the non allocated*

Structural weight of services in total outward FDI flows

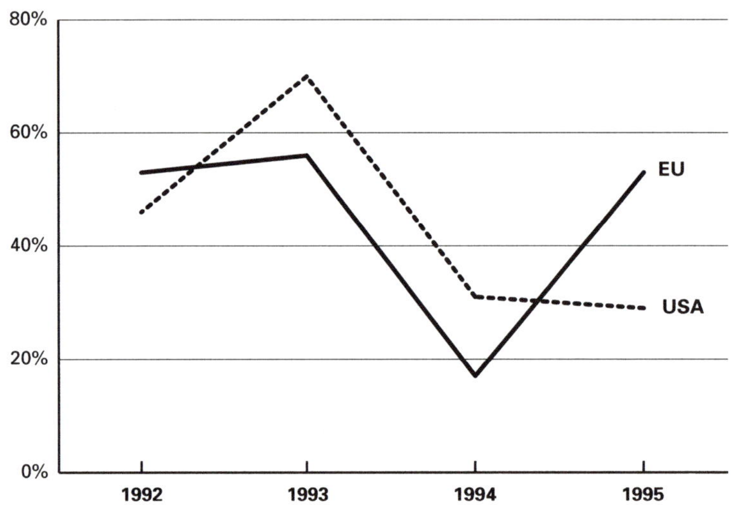

Source: EUROSTAT (balance of payments)

2.5.2 FDI (inward flows)

The slowdown of foreign direct investment entering the EU that may be observed for 1993 and 1994 was clearly halted in 1995. With ECU 38 bn the observed increase of EU inward investment (+73%) in 1995 was strong enough to leave the US behind, but clearly not as markedly as with the outward flows.

Structural weight of services in total inward FDI flows

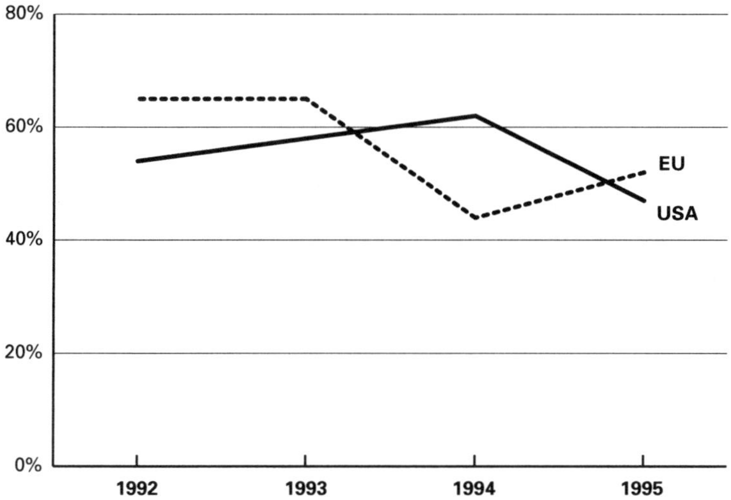

Source: EUROSTAT (balance of payments)

Whereas US inward flows in 1995 still exceeded the value invested abroad the opposite applies for the Union.

3 - European convergence to the Maastricht criteria

3.1 - EMU convergence criteria
Harmonised indices of consumer prices (%)

Maastricht objective: less than 1.5 percentage points from the average of the three lowest rates.

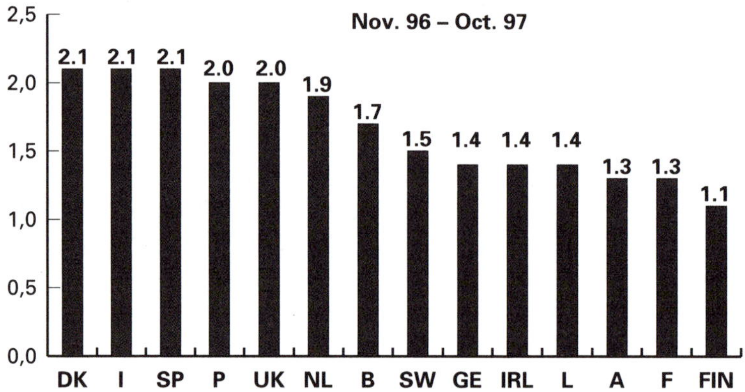

Greece average of available data since january 1997: 5.8%

Source: Autumn 1997 Commission forecasts

3.2 - Short-term interest rates: the road to convergence
Money market rates of EU member states*

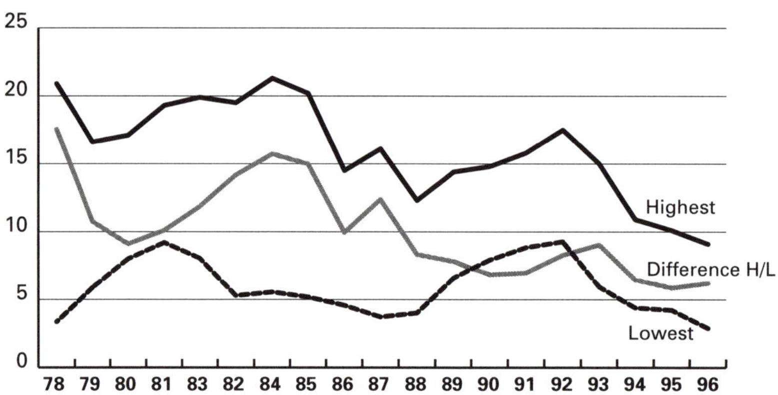

** data exclude Greece* *Source: EUROSTAT*

3.3 - Long-term interest rates: the road to convergence Government bond yields*

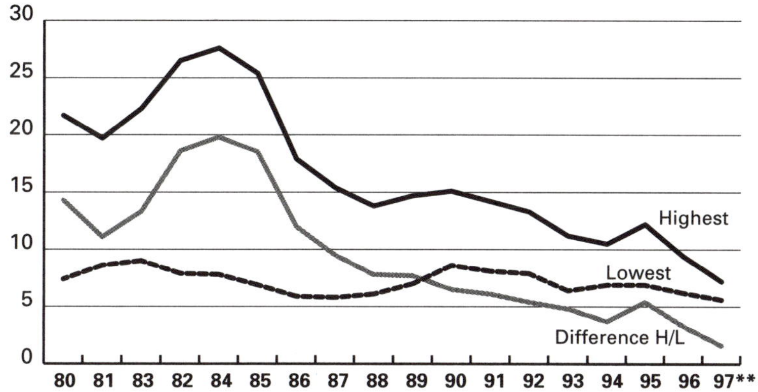

Some earlier data not available for Finland, Sweden, Austria
** excludes Greece (data not available)*
*** first ten months*

3.4 - EMU convergence criteria: long-term interest rates (%)

Maastricht objective: less than 2 percentage points from the average of the three countries with the lower inflation rate.

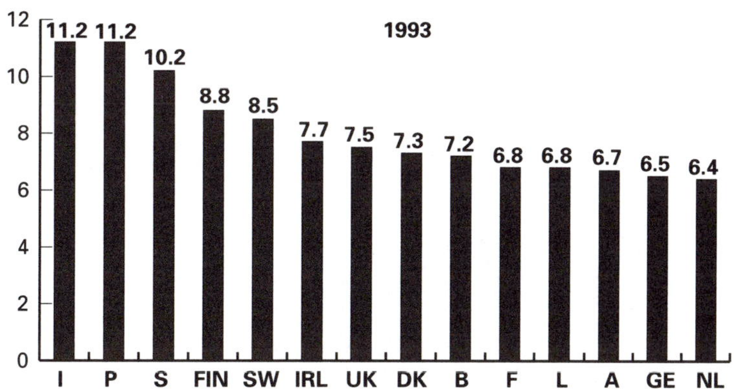

Greece 1993: 23.3% *Source: EUROSTAT*

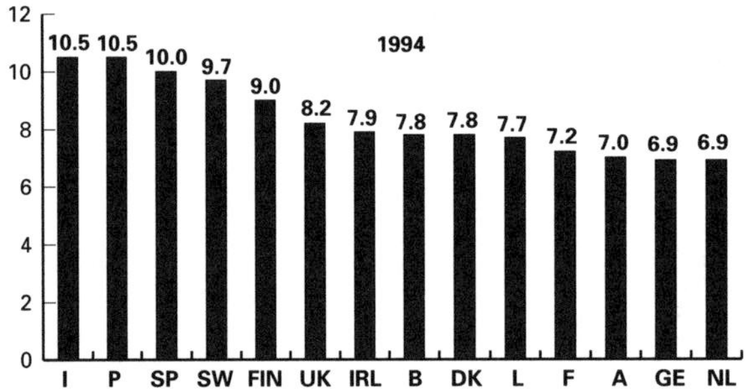

Greece 1994: 20.8%

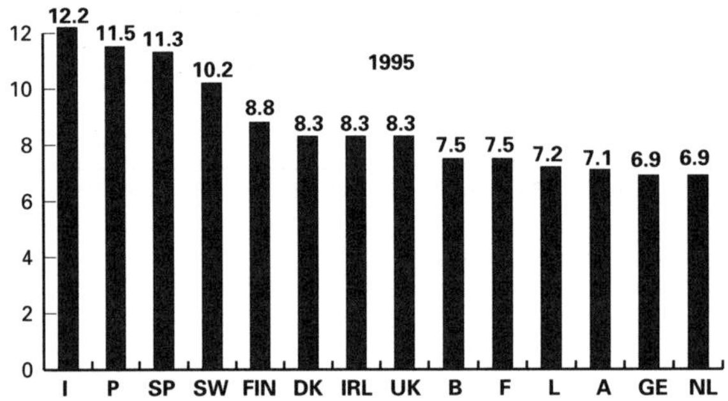

Greece 1995: 17.4%

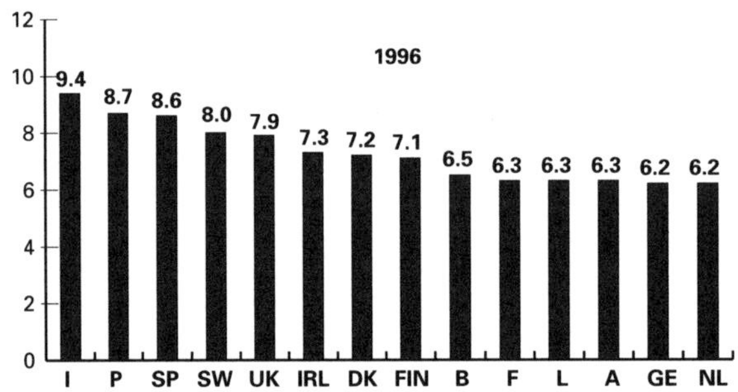

Greece 1996: 14.8%

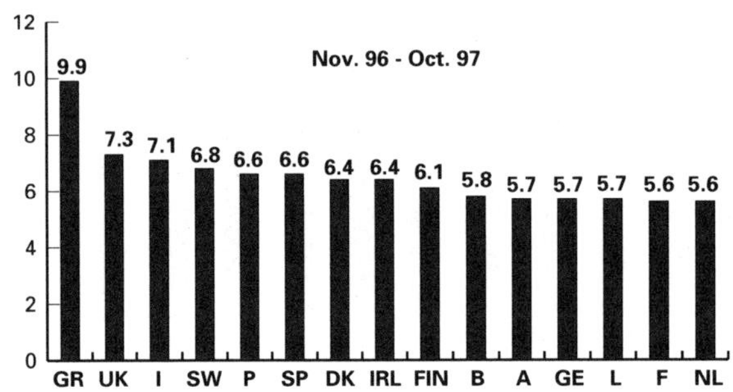

Source: EUROSTAT

3.5 - EMU convergence criteria: general government deficit (% of GDP)

Maastricht limit: 3% of GDP

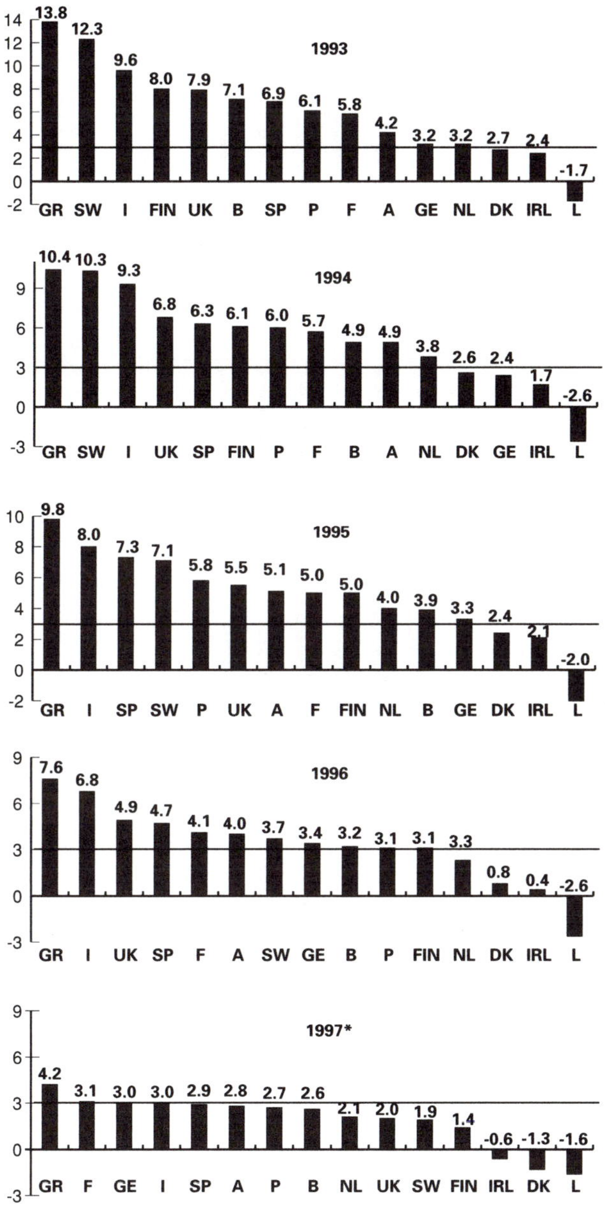

** Autumn 1997 Commission forecasts*

Source: EUROSTAT

3.6 - EMU convergence criteria: general government debt (% of GDP)

Maastricht limit: 60% of GDP

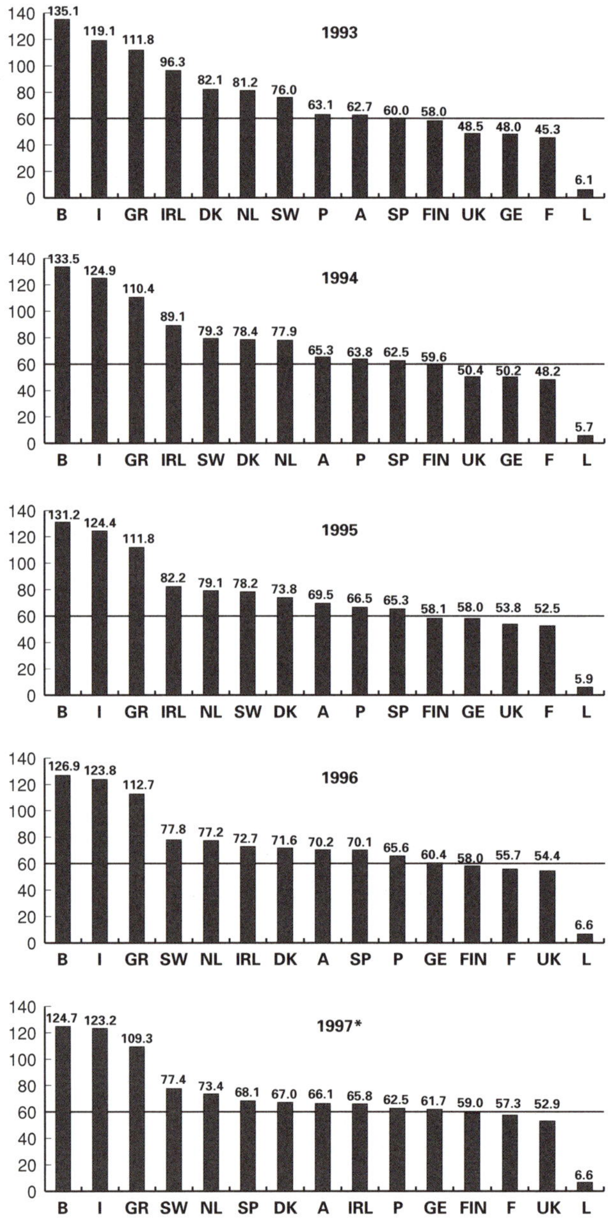

** Autumn 1997 Commission forecasts*

Source: EUROSTAT

3.7 - General government consolidated gross debt as % of GDP (close up on selected countries)

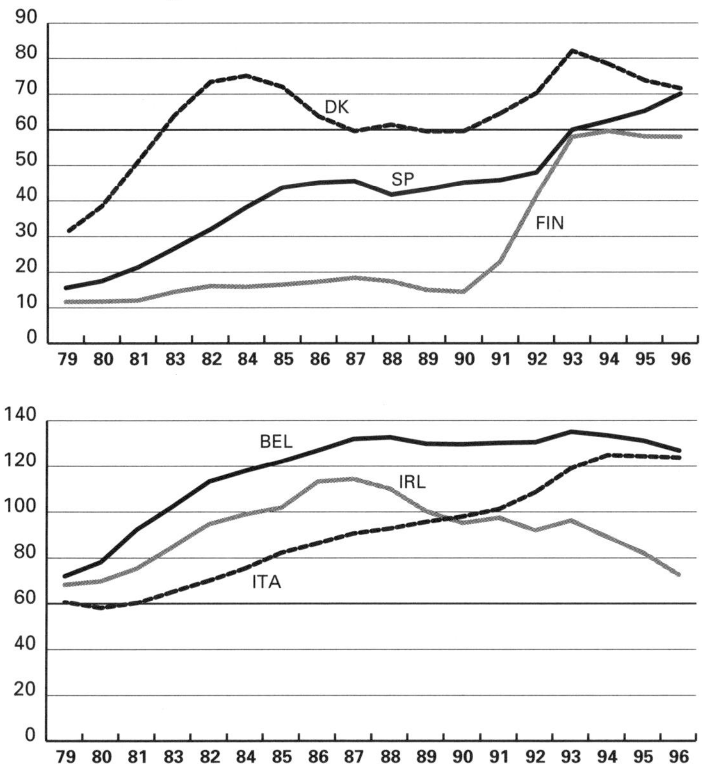

Note: Maastricht definitions apply to these data from 1992 onwards.

3.8 - General government deficit as % of GDP: close up on selected countries

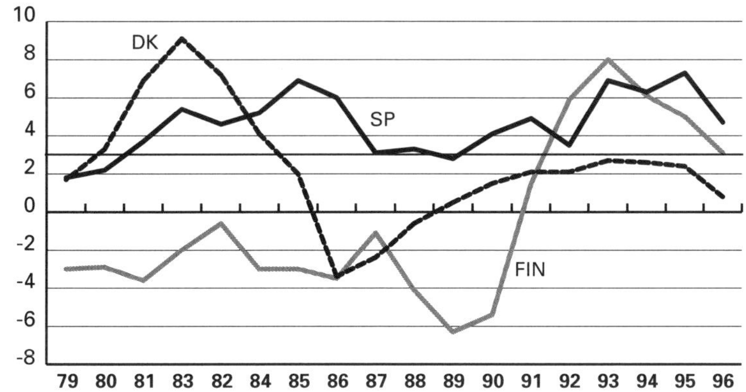

Source: EUROSTAT

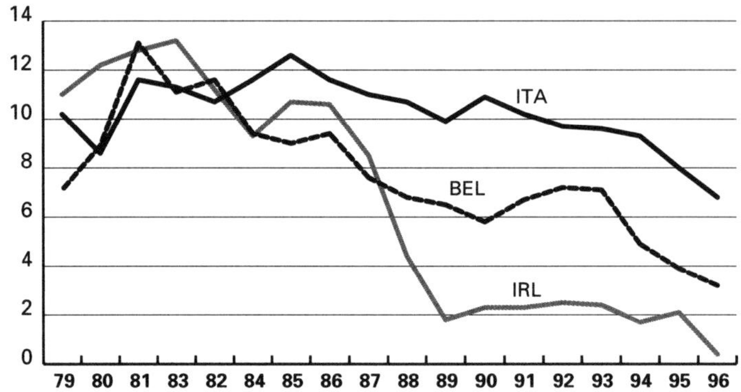

Note: Maastricht definitions apply to these data from 1992.

3.9 - Impact of debt interest payments on the deficit: the primary surplus behind general government deficit (as % of GDP)

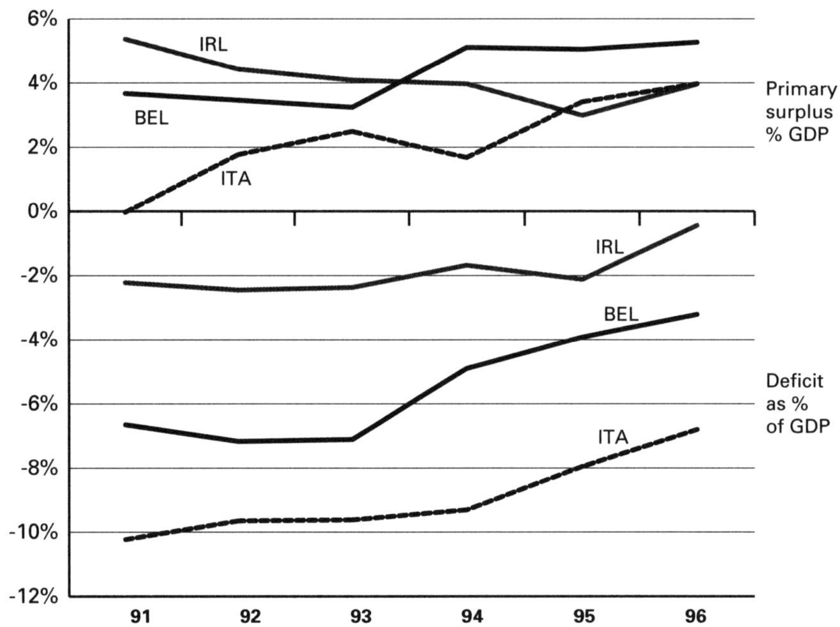

Note: Difference between general government deficit and primary surplus represents debt interest payments.

Source: EUROSTAT

3.10 - Relations with Africa, Caribbean and Pacific (ACP) countries: fourth ACP-EC Convention Financial protocol 1995-2000

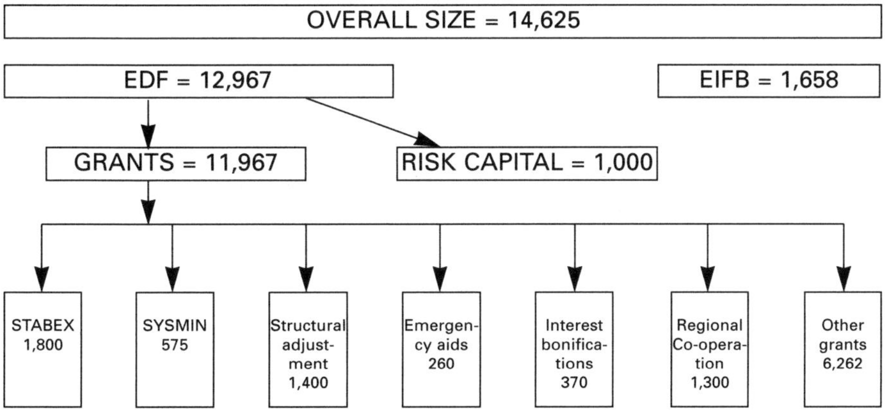

The purpose of STABEX is to stabilize the prices of a set of commodities that play a critical role in the exports of ACP countries. SYSMIN pursues similar objectives for select minerals of interest to the poorer countries.

3.11 - EU development cooperation with ACP coutries (including EIB loans) (Million ECU)

		Total AID
Rome	1958-63	581
Yaoundé I	1964-69	730
Yaoundé II	1970-75	933
Lomé I	1975-80	3,514
Lomé II	1980-85	5,439
Lomé III	1985-90	8,854
Lomé IV	1990-1995	12,000
Lomé IV-rev	1995-2000	14,625

Source: EUROSTAT

4 - Integration in the European Union: the budgetary side

4.1 - Expenses of the European Union Institutions

The expenses of European Union Institutions (EUI) fall into five main groups:

1. Common agricultural policy.

2. Structural actions with a view to ensure the economic and social cohesion of the European Union.

3. Extra-EU policies notably aid and cooperation actions toward the African, Caribbean and Pacific countries (ACP), Central and Eastern European countries (CEEC), Mediterranean basin and Asia/Latin American countries.

4. Research and development actions that follow notably on the ESPRIT program and its many specialized programs.

5. Operating expenses of the EUI.

The total amount devoted to the EUI activities grew sharply over the 1987-96 period, doubling between 1987 and 1996. Within this general upward trend, the main point concerns the development of the two major components of the European Union instruments: the EAGGF Guarantee fund at the center of the Common Agricultural Policy (CAP) and Structural Funds. The weight of EAGGF Guarantee has fallen by about 19 points since 1987, whereas that of the Structural Funds has risen by 13 points. Structural Funds which aim at promoting the development of less prosperous regions as well as overall ajustment and integration. One should also take note of the important rise in R&D expenditures (+ 2 points).

Source: EUROSTAT (balance of payments)

4.1.1 - EUI expenses (Million ECU)

	87	88	89	90	91	92	93	94	95	96
Guarantee (1) (agriculture)	23,708	27,651	26,521	26,588	32,665	32,713	34,531	33,606	34,500	39,083
%	*65.6%*	*62.4%*	*58.8%*	*56.3%*	*56.1%*	*49.8%*	*51.2%*	*50.7%*	*47.5%*	*46.9%*
Structural Funds (2)	6,024.3*	8,159.6*	9,926.9*	11,334*	15,168.4*	17,916	20,460	16,226	19,775	24,717
%	*16.7%*	*18.4%*	*22.0%*	*24.0%*	*26.1%*	*27.3%*	*30.3%*	*24.5%*	*27.3%*	*29.7%*
EDF transfers and external actions (3)	1,260.7*	1,905*	1,725.3*	2,380.6*	2,154.5*	3,791	3,632	4,669	4,938	4,984
%	*3.5%*	*4.3%*	*3.8%*	*5.0%*	*3.7%*	*5.8%*	*5.4%*	*7.0%*	*6.8%*	*6.0%*
Miscellaneous intra-EU transfers (4)	1,743.8*	1,812.7*	2,055.9*	1,431.1*	2,453.6*	4,464	1,539	3,912	5,130	5,747
%	*4.8%*	*4.1%*	*4.6%*	*3.0%*	*4.2%*	*6.8%*	*2.3%*	*5.9%*	*7.1%*	*6.9%*
Total transfers	32,737	39,528	40,229	41,733	52,441	58,884	60,162	58,413	64,342	74,531
%	*90.6%*	*89.2%*	*89.2%*	*88.4%*	*90.1%*	*89.7%*	*89.1%*	*88.1%*	*88.7%*	*89.5%*
R&D	487	677	825	1,082	1,050	1,674	1,923	2,185	2,267	2,677
%	*1.3%*	*1.5%*	*1.8%*	*2.3%*	*1.8%*	*2.5%*	*2.8%*	*3.3%*	*3.1%*	*3.2%*
Operating expenses	2,911	4,115	4,064	4,382	4,705	5,086	5,400	5,731	5,957	6,043
%	*8.1%*	*9.3%*	*9.0%*	*9.3%*	*8.1%*	*7.7%*	*8.0%*	*8.6%*	*8.2%*	*7.3%*
Total	36,134	44,320	45,118	47,197	58,196	65,643	67,486	66,329	72,566	83,251
%	*100.0%*	*100.0%*	*100.0%*	*100.0%*	*100.0%*	*100.0%*	*100.0%*	*100.0%*	*100.0%*	*100.0%*

(1) Includes EAGGF Guarantee transfers + Monetary compensatory amounts
(2) Include EAGGF Guidance, ESF, ERDF, Cohesion Funds and miscellaneous structural actions.
(3) Includes all EDF transfers and section B7 of the General Budget devoted to the external policy of the EU.
(4) Includes other European Union policies, financial compensation to member States and social benefits.
** Estimates.*

4.1.2 - Average weight of the different EUI expenses

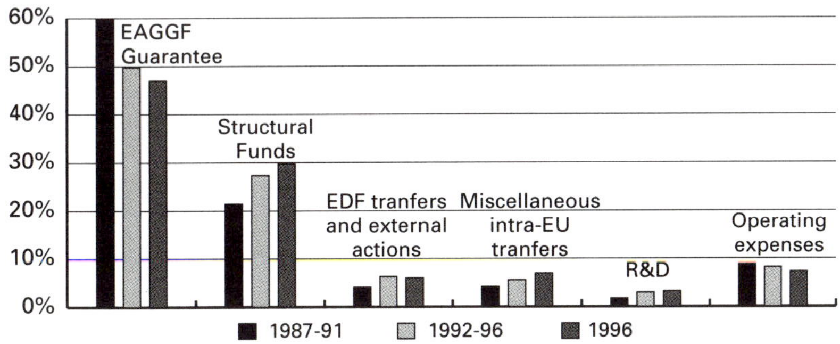

Source: EUROSTAT (balance of payments)

4.1.3 - Extra-EU transfers (ECU Mio)

Extra-EU transfers (ECU Mio)	92	93	94	95	96
EDF transfers (ACP)	1,734	1,117	1,541	1,564	1,296
%	*45.7%*	*30.7%*	*33.0%*	*31.7%*	*26.0%*
Asia and latin America	326	354	363	436	474
%	*8.6%*	*9.7%*	*7.8%*	*8.8%*	*9.5%*
Mediterranean basin	219	353	297	229	357
%	*5.8%*	*9.7%*	*6.4%*	*4.6%*	*7.2%*
CEEC and Ex-USSR	499	719	1,066	1,157	1,222
%	*13.1%*	*19.8%*	*22.8%*	*23.4%*	*24.5%*
Other	1,013	1,089	1,402	1,552	1,635
%	*26.7%*	*30.0%*	*30.0%*	*31.4%*	*32.8%*
Total	**3,791**	**3,632**	**4,669**	**4,938**	**4,984**

4.2 - EUI loans

Loans form the other instrument used by the EUI to implement the European Union policies. Of all the EUI, the European Investment Bank (EIB) is the main actor in this field. As for the Structural Funds, the majority of the loans has the purpose to ensure a better economic and social cohesion within the European Union. The development in value of the total amount disbursed by the EIB has followed a continuous upward trend from 1988 onwards. Actually, the total growth in value is of approximately 250% over the 1988-96 period. Member States are the main receivers of these loans, but loans vis-à-vis extra-EU countries amounted to 4.5 billion ECU in 1996. Moreover, loans vis-à-vis CEEC countries risen rapidely since 1992 as a preparation for the next enlargement of the Union.

Source: EUROSTAT (balance of payments)

4.2.1 - Loans of the European Investment Bank (EIB)

EIB loans *(Amount disbursed at 31 Dec. of the year in ECU Mio)*	88	89	90	91	92	93	94	95	96
Intra-EU	40,753	46,045	52,859	63,730	73,401	83,504	87,541	92,386	101,173
%	*96.4%*	*96.6%*	*96.7%*	*97.0%*	*96.9%*	*96.7%*	*96.5%*	*96.1%*	*95.7%*
ACP	631	630	656	709	811	923	899	901	934
%	*1.5%*	*1.3%*	*1.2%*	*1.1%*	*1.1%*	*1.1%*	*1.0%*	*0.9%*	*0.9%*
CEEC	0	0	0	28	147	300	579	956	1,378
%	*0.0%*	*0.0%*	*0.0%*	*0.0%*	*0.2%*	*0.3%*	*0.6%*	*1.0%*	*1.3%*
Mediterranean basin	896	998	1,146	1,247	1,354	1,511	1,611	1,699	1,972
%	*2.1%*	*2.1%*	*2.1%*	*1.9%*	*1.8%*	*1.8%*	*1.8%*	*1.8%*	*1.9%*
Other extra-EU	0	0	0	0	0	99	46	149	235
%	*0.0%*	*0.0%*	*0.0%*	*0.0%*	*0.0%*	*0.1%*	*0.1%*	*0.2%*	*0.2%*
Total EIB	**42,280**	**47,672**	**54,662**	**65,714**	**75,713**	**86,338**	**90,677**	**96,092**	**105,692**
%	**100.0%**	**100.0%**	**100.0%**	**100.0%**	**100.0%**	**100.0%**	**100.0%**	**100.0%**	**100.0%**

Apart from the EIB, the General Budget and the ECSC are providers of loans too. But, a downward trend is observed from 1993 onwards concerning the total amount disbursed by these two institutions. Nevertheless, particularly concerning the loans vis-à-vis CEEC countries, it takes a quite important place within the external policy of the European Union. Finally, most of these loans vis-à-vis extra-EU countries are guaranteed by the Guarantee Funds directly depending on the Commission.

4.2.2 - Other loans of the EUI

Other loans of the EIB *(Amount disbursed at 31 Dec. of the year in ECU Mio)*	90	91	92	93	94	95	96
Intra-EU (1)	7,116	7,159	5,457	7,897	7,042	6,621	5,115
%	*84.0%*	*75.0%*	*61.3%*	*63.7%*	*59.5%*	*60.4%*	*55.5%*
CEEC	350	1,045	1,873	2,823	2,925	2,327	2,019
%	*4,1%*	*10.9%*	*21.0%*	*22.8%*	*24.7%*	*21.2%*	*21.9%*
ACP	585	652	704	789	822	867	919
%	*6.9%*	*6.8%*	*7.9%*	*6.4%*	*6.9%*	*7.9%*	*10.0%*
Mediterranean basin	425	693	873	889	1,050	1,155	1,160
%	*5.0%*	*7.3%*	*9.8%*	*7.2%*	*8.9%*	*10.5%*	*12.6%*
Total Budget	8,476	9,548	8,907	12,398	11,839	10,970	9,213
%	*100.0%*	*100.0%*	*100.0%*	*100.0%*	*100.0%*	*100.0%*	*100.0%*
ECSC loans	#N/A	#N/A	7,676	7,690	6,986	6,174	4,656
Total Budget + ECSC	#N/A	#N/A	16,583	20,088	18,825	17,144	13,869

(1) It includes loans related to balance of payments assistance, Euratom and NCI.

Source: EUROSTAT (balance of payments)

5 - Competitiveness and labour productivity

5.1 - Share of OECD production - total manufacturing (%)

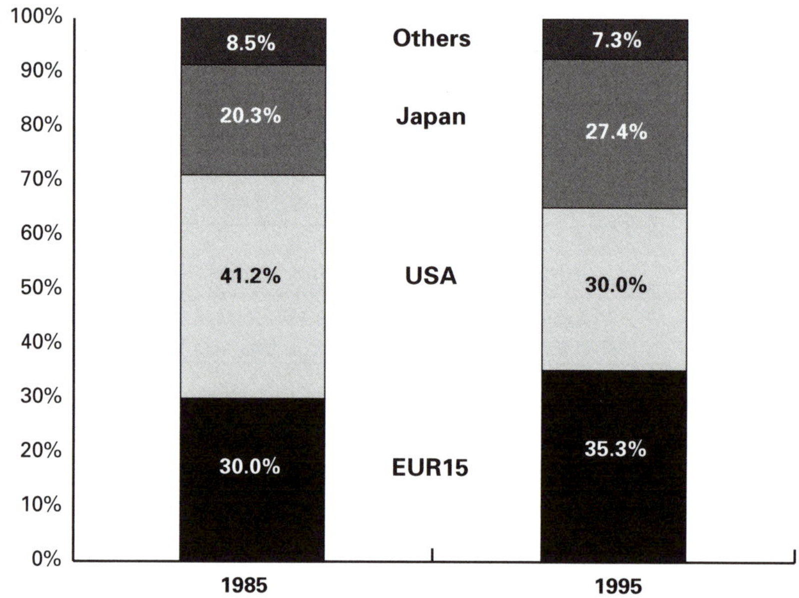

5.2 - Unemployment rate, as share of the total labour force

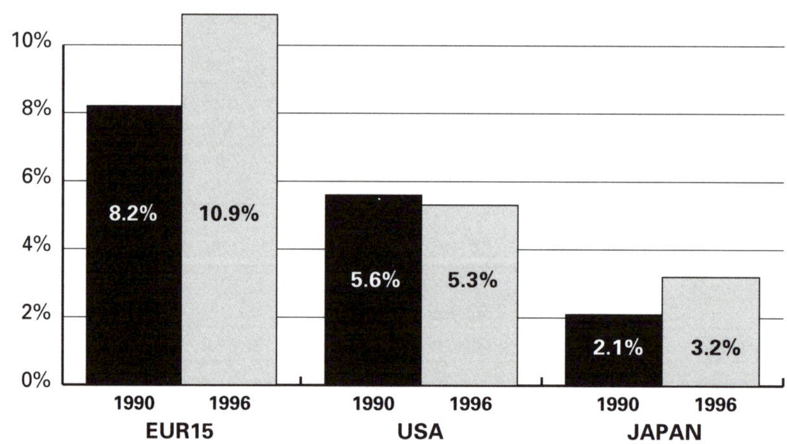

Source: EUROSTAT

5.3 - Labour productivity, level (at market exchange rate)

Source: EUROSTAT

5.4 - Labour productivity, value added per hour worked

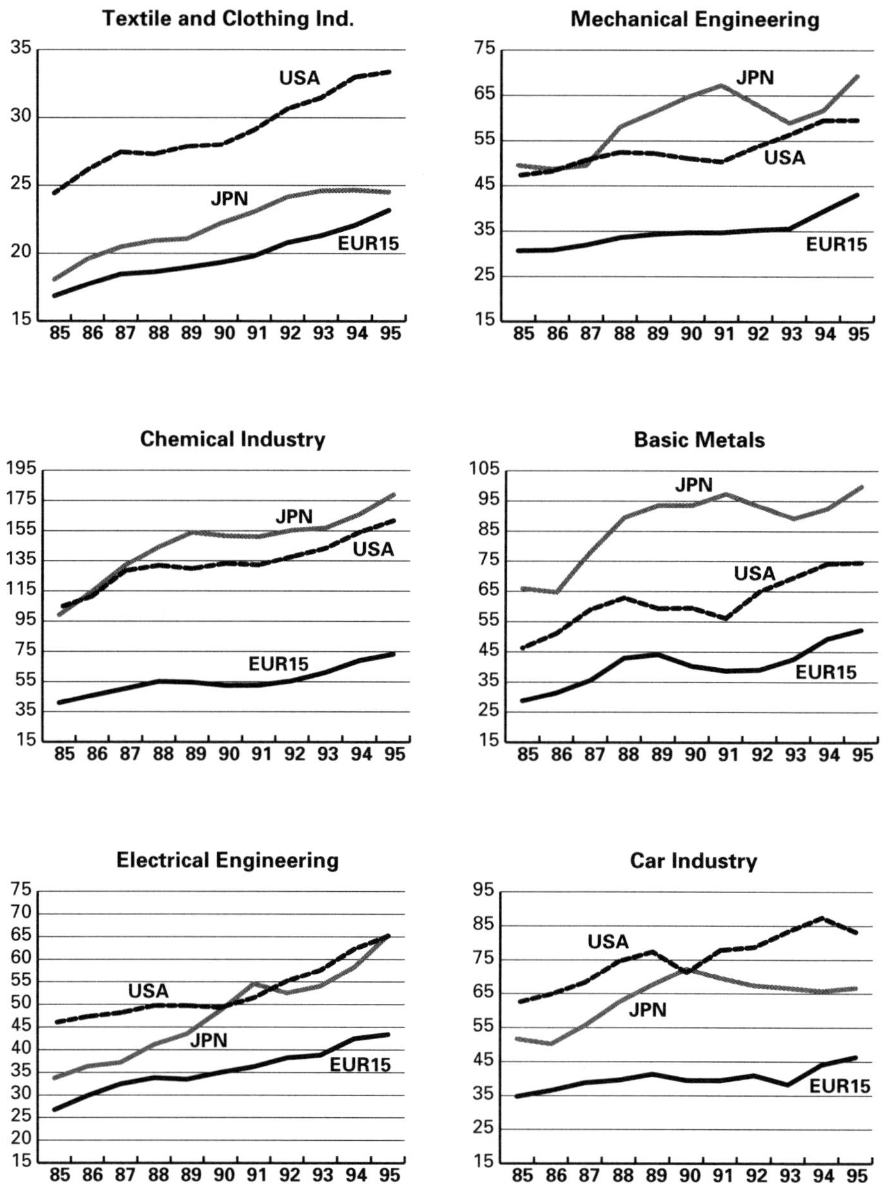

Source: EUROSTAT

5.5 - R&D per capita (current ECU)

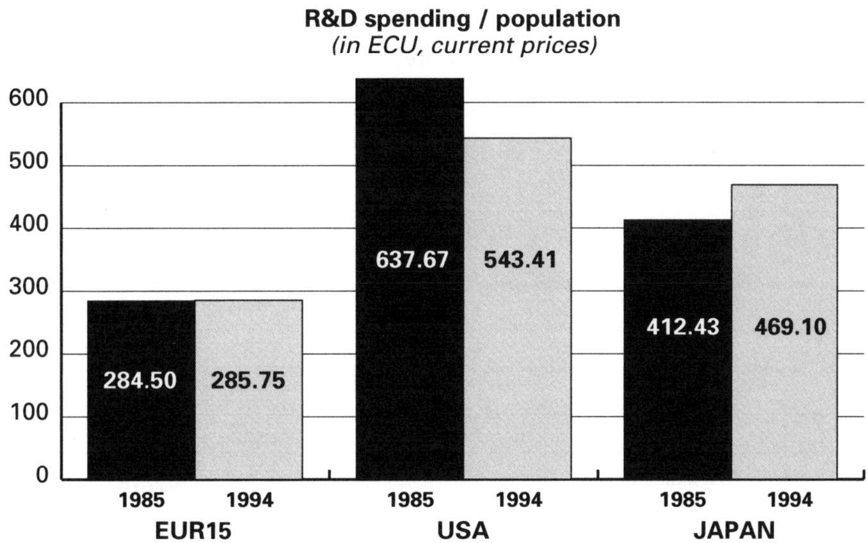

Source: EUROSTAT

5.6 - Per capita spending on information technology (ECU)

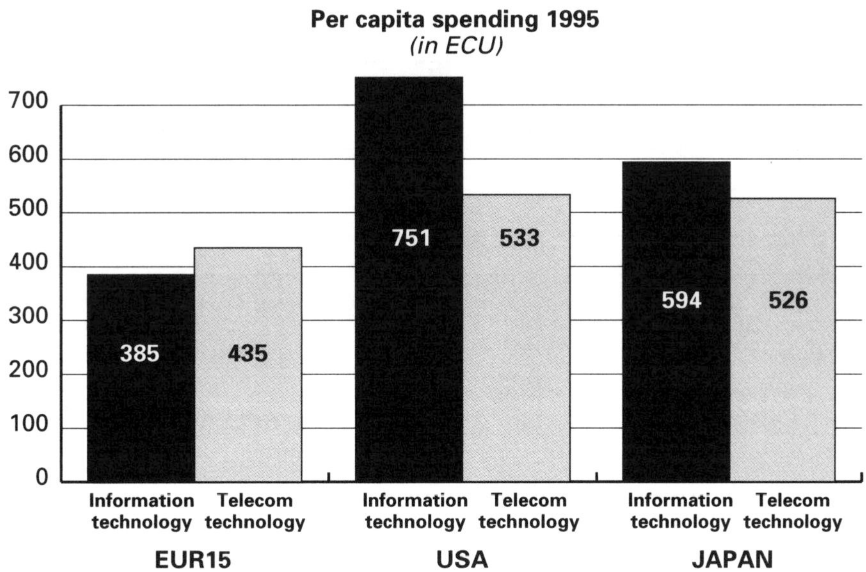

Source: EUROSTAT

6. Financial markets of the Union: capitalization, returns and pension funds. Section and text by Thomas Rabe (Cedel Bank).

6.1 - Financial markets and market capitalization

6.1.1 A - Comparing the financial markets of the European Union (EUR15), the likely euro countries (EUR11), the U.S. and Japan in 1995(A)

in billions of U.S. dollars unless noted otherwise

	Population (in millions)	GDP	Total Reserves Minus Gold	Stock Market Capitalization
EUR15	372	8,428	376	3,779
EUR11	289	6,805	285	2,119
USA	263	7,254	75	6,858
Japan	125	5,134	183	3,667

Source: World Economic and Financial Survey: International Capital Markets, IMF, 1997

6.1.1 B - Comparing the financial markets of the European Union (EUR15), the likely euro countries (EUR11), the U.S. and Japan in 1995 (B)

in billions of U.S. dollars unless noted otherwise

	Debt securities			Bank Assets	Bonds, Equities and Bank Assets	Bonds Equities and Bank Assets (in % of GDP)
	Public	Private	Total			
EUR15	4,810	3,864	8,673	14,818	27,270	324
EUR11	3,904	3,089	6,992	11,972	21,083	310
USA	6,728	4,323	11,051	5,000	22,908	316
Japan	3,448	1,877	5,325	7,382	16,374	319

Source: World Economic and Financial Survey: International Capital Markets, IMF, 1997

6.1.2 - Stock markets' size (domestic equities) (1996)

	Market capitalization in % of GDP
Austria	14.3
Belgium	45.9
Denmark	41.8
Finland	50.7
France	38.9
Germany	29.6
Greece	19.7
Ireland	49.7
Italy	21.7
Luxembourg	19.4
Netherlands	97.8
Portugal	23.7
Spain	42.3
Sweden	97.2
United Kingdom	14.9
EUR 15	32
U.S.	68
Japan	65

Source: Federation of European Stock Exchange and European Commission

6.2 - Differences in rates of return of equities compared to bonds

Nota: the premium normally associated with the return on equities over bonds depends very much on the level of the stock market at the beginning and at the end of the period over which comparisons are made.

Several different sources are given below. All sources show consistently higher return on equities.

6.2.1 - Annual real rates of return in domestic currency (1967-1990)

	Equities	Bonds
Denmark	7.0 %	3.4 %
France	9.4 %	1.0 %
Germany	9.5 %	2.7 %
Italy	4.0 %	-0.2 %
Netherlands	7.9 %	1.0 %
Sweden	8.4 %	-0.9 %
United Kingdom	8.1 %	-0.5 %
USA	4.7 %	-0.5 %
Japan	1.9 %	0.2 %

Source: E.P. Davis, 1995

6.2.2 - Annual excess returns of equities over bond markets in domestic currency (1981-1995)

Belgium	11.5
France	4.5
Germany	7.1
Italy	1.5
Netherlands	6.9
Sweden	15.5
United Kingdom	2.9
USA	2.9
Japan	1.5

Source: JP Morgan , FT/S+P Actions World Indices, Pragma Consulting

6.2.3 - Annual returns of equities on the U.S. market (1926-1984)

Small company stocks	9.10%
Large company stocks	7.10%
Long term government bonds	1.70%

Source: Ibbotson Associates Inc.

6.2.4 - Annual returns of equities and gilts on the UK market (1919-1993)

Equities	7.9%
Gilts (long)	2.0%

Source: BZW 1994

6.2.5 - Annual returns of equities and fixed income products on the Belgian market (1959-1994)

Equities	4.6%
Fixed income	2.3%

Source: Banque Degroof

6.3 - Demographics, pension funds and mobility of labour in the euro era

Demographics

In most European countries birth rates are decreasing: people are living longer and retiring earlier. The ratio of people at work to retired people is declining accordingly. At present, in the European Union there are four people of working age to support each pensioner. By 2040 there will only be two. Governments are trying hard to sustain state pension schemes which are based on the pay-as-you-go principle and are innovative in finding solutions. But measures such as increasing pension contributions or cross-subsidizing the state pension system with direct or indirect taxes only help for a while. In the long run such measures are counterproductive. They increase labour costs with detrimental effects on the competitiveness of the European economy and the ability and willingness of investors to create new employment in Europe.

Pension funds and investments

Several countries in Europe have introduced legislation to encourage supplementary funded pension schemes known as “pillar 2 schemes”. The European Commission has made a number of attempts to bring a “European dimension” to the debate. To this end, it has recently published a so-called Green Paper titled “Supplementary Pensions in the Single Market” in which it discusses three main themes: the importance of the rate of return, restrictions on investments and mobility of labour.

The Green Paper looks at how to improve the rate of return on investments as a means to reduce the contributions to pension schemes. It provides an interesting example which assumes that a supplementary pension aims at providing 35 per cent of the salary after 40 years working life. If the average return on investments is 2 per cent, the pension contributions are 19 per cent of the salary. If the rate of return doubles to 4 per cent, the contributions fall to 10 per cent. If it triples to 6 per cent, they fall to 5 per cent.

Investment performance is *inter alia* impaired by regulatory restrictions on the investment of pension funds assets. It is striking that only twelve months before the planned start of the EMU, some Member States still require pension funds to invest a certain percentage of their assets within a particular country or in government bonds. In Germany, for example, pension funds may not invest more than 30 per cent of their assets in equity (of which a maximum of 6 per cent may be in non-EU equities), 25 per cent may be in EU property and 20 per cent overall in foreign assets.

The most significant change resulting from the euro will be in asset allocation. To put this in the right perspective, in 1995, the total assets of pension funds and life insurers in the EU amounted to almost ECU 3.000 billion. Currency risk and regulatory requirements demand pension funds and insurers to cover their liabilities with investments in the same currency. A single currency will mean that they can match their liabilities with assets held anywhere in the "in-countries". Many institutions have already started organising their investment research on a pan-European basis because of the expected shift in investments. In the Netherlands, for example, the second biggest pension fund sector in the EU, domestic investment opportunities are limited. The funds are therefore highly interested in cross-border investment, also for diversification purposes.

But the introduction of the euro will not solve the problem of unjustified rules limiting investment in certain types of assets. The Commission proposes two options to overcome this: either to apply the provisions of the Treaty of Rome on free movement of capital and to start proceedings against member States who do not comply or to agree on a common set of necessary prudential rules. In the Green Paper, the EU Commission left open which option it will choose.

Mobility of labour

The third theme of the Green Paper is mobility of labour. For people wishing to use their right of free movement to work in other member States, non-portability of supplementary pension schemes is a real and significant obstacle, not least because of taxation. The European Commission intends to propose legislation which has two main objectives: to preserve the acquired rights for members of pension schemes who cease active membership because they move to a different member State and to allow workers temporarily seconded by their employer in another member State to remain affiliated to the existing supplementary pension scheme. The Green Paper lists a number of further obstacles to be removed. Most striking (in terms of reducing mobility) are burdensome qualifying conditions for acquiring supplementary pension rights. In Germany, for example, the vesting period is ten years.

For the European Monetary Union to prove a success (i.e. for it to be what economists call an "optimum currency area"), one of two things is required: either Member States should be affected by economic disturbances - so-called economic shocks - in similar ways, or there must be an adjustment mechanism without recourse to exchange rate policy instruments; this mechanism could be flexible wages and highly mobile labour so that workers move from declining areas to expanding ones. In Europe, labour is clearly not sufficiently mobile to compensate asymmetric economic shocks. This lack of mobility reflects differences in culture, language, educational systems and pension systems combined with the non-portability of pension rights.

The initiative of the European Commission deserves full support. Not only would it contribute to the solution of the problems surrounding the "demographic time-bomb", it would also help to increase mobility in the European Union and to bring the EMU closer to an "optimum currency area".

Thomas Rabe

6.3.1 - Contribution of each pillar to pensions*

Type of scheme		
Pillar 1:	pay as you go	88.8%
Pillar 2:	pensions funds, book reserves, insured plans	7.0%
Pillar 3:	personal options	0.9%
Others		3.3%

** EU average excluding Austria, Finland, Sweden*

Source: EUROSTAT

6.3.2 - Assets of life insurance companies (1995)

	Assets in bn Ecus	Assets as % of GDP
Austria	5	1.7
Belgium	13	6.3
Denmark	91	69.1
Finland	6	6.3
France	358	33.4
Germany	485	26.3
Greece	n.a.	n.a.
Ireland	18	40.1
Italy	43	4.9
Luxembourg	5	37.6
Netherlands	399	134.1
Portugal	3	3.9
Spain	28	6.4
Sweden	65	36.9
United Kingdom	1,282	146.5
EUR15	2,801	45.2

Source: EUROSTAT

6.3.3. - Pillar 2 : Coverage Level

	Coverage in % of total private sector employment	Characteristics	Supplementary pensions in % of total pensions - 1993
Belgium	31	Voluntary; funded; pension funds and group insurance.	8%
Denmark	80	Company funds, professional funds through collective bargaining (all funded).	18%
France	90	Quasi mandatory ; collective bargaining; pay as you go + voluntary top hat funded shemes.	21%
Germany	46	Voluntary ; partially book reserved (approx 56%), funded (44%) through Pensionkassen, Support Funds and Collective Insurance.	11%
Greece	5	Voluntary; mainly top hat; some limited funding.	n.a.
Ireland	40	Voluntary; funded ; pension funds and group insurance.	18%
Italy	5	Voluntary; mainly top hat in view of high levels of social security pensions; partially funded.	2%
Luxembourg	30	Voluntary; mainly book reserve type plans; a limited amount of funding exists.	n.a.
Netherlands	85	Company funds; industry-wide funds through collective bargaining; all funded.	32%
Portugal	15	Voluntary; pension plans (not funds) executed by recognised management companies and insurance companies; funded; mainly top hat in view of high levels of social security pensions.	n.a.
Spain	15	Voluntary; mainly top hat in view of high levels of social security pensions; partially funded; mainly book reserves: will now be phased out.	3%
United Kingdom	48	Voluntary; funded.	28%

Source: European Federation for Retirement Provision (EFPR). European Pension Funds 1996

6.3.4 - Assets of life insurance companies (1995)

	Assets in bn Ecus	Assets as % of GDP
Austria	5	1.7
Belgium	6	2.9
Denmark	65	49
Finland	6	6.3
France	317	30
Germany	379	20.5
Greece	n.a.	n.a
Ireland	n.a.	n.a
Italy	31	3.7
Luxembourg	5	37.6
Netherlands	138	45.6
Portugal	3	3.9
Spain	18	4.2
Sweden	65	36.9
United Kingdom	565	67.1
EUR15	1,604	24.9

Nota: Figures not completely comparable: owing to different national valuation rules, investments can be valued at purchase prices, as in Germany, or at current price, as in the U.K. EU total includes only member States listed.

Source: EUROSTAT 1997.

6.3.5 - Distribution of pension funds assets (as % of total assets)

	Equities	Fixed income products	Real estate	Short term placements	Foreign assets
Belgium	36	47	7	10	n.a.
Denmark	22	65	9	4	7
France	14	39	7	40	5
Germany	11	75	11	3	6
Ireland	55	35	6	4	n.a.
Italy	14	72	10	2	25
Netherlands	30	58	10	2	25
Portugal	18*	57*	5	19	n.a.
Sweden	32	47	8	13	12
U.K.	80	11	6	3	10
U.S.	52*	36*	4	8	10
Japan	29*	63*	3	5	n.a.

** estimates*
Source: Royal Institute of International Affairs, UBS and EFRP

6.3.6 - Life insurance assets (as % of total assets in 1994)

	Domestic equities	Foreign equities	Domestic fixed income	Foreign fixed income	Real estate	Other
Denmark	20	5	66	-	3	6
France	19	-	69	-	8	4
Germany	5	n.a.	76*	n.a.	5	14
Italy	7	5	70	5	12	2
Netherlands	12	2	71**	4	6	6
Spain	2	n.a.	55	n.a.	10	33
Sweden	23	n.a.	61	n.a.	7	9
U.K.	49	12	24	3	9	3

Nota: Split between domestic and foreign assets unavailable for Germany, Spain and Sweden

** includes loans (61%)*
*** includes loans (50%)*
Sources: Comité Européen des Assurances, OECD Insurance Statistics Yearbook 1987-1994

6.3.7 - Main national regulations on pension fund portfolio

Denmark	A maximum of 40% may be invested in "high risk assets" - these include domestic equities, foreign equities and unlisted securities. Also 80% currency matching requirement. In case of EU currency, up to 50% of liabilities can be covered by assets denominated in ECU. No self-investment.
France	At least 50% to be invested in EU government bonds, less than 33% in loans to sponsors.
Germany	Maximum 30% EU equity, 25% EU property, 6% non-EU bonds, 6% non-EU bonds, 20% overall foreign assets, 10% self-investment limit.
Italy	No pension law for self administered schemes but investment policy determined by the board of directors and usually restricted to government bonds, bank deposits, insurance policies and property.
Netherlands	5% self investment limit; prudent man rule.
Spain	5% limit in securities issued by any one enterprise. 90% of assets must be invested in quoted securities, bank deposits, property or mortgages. 1% must be in current accounts or money market.
Sweden	Majority to be held in bonds, debentures and loans.
U.K.	5% self investment limit; prudent man rule.
USA	Prudent man rule.
Japan	Minimum 50% in bonds, maximum 30% in equities, 20% in property, 30% in foreign.

Source: European Commission, "Supplementary Pensions in the European Union", 1997.

6.3.8 - Main national regulations on life insurance companies

Denmark	40% combined limit on domestic equity and foreign equity, 10% limit on unlisted securities, 10% combined limit on mortgages and loans.
France	65% combined limit on domestic equity, unlisted securities and foreign equity, 40% limit on property, 10% combined limit on mortgages and loans.
Germany	Maximum: 30% domestic equity, 25% property, 6% foreign equity, 5% foreign bonds, 10% unlisted securities, 50% combined limit on mortgages and loans.
Italy	Maximum: 20% domestic equity, 20% unlisted securities, 20% foreign equity; 50% foreign bonds, 50% property, 50% mortgages, 0% loans.
Netherlands	10% combined limit on unlisted securities and mortgages, 8% limit on loans.
Spain	No specific limits.
Sweden	25% combined limit on domestic equity, unlisted securities and foreign equity, 25% combined limit on property and mortgages, 10% limit on loans.
U.K.	10% combined limit on unlisted securities, mortgages and loans.

Source: Policy issues in insurance, OECD, 1996

PROMETHEE and Ernst & Young associates profiles

Albert Bressand (editor) is managing director and co-founder of PROMETHEE. He is a member of the board of international economists of *TIME magazine* and of the editorial boards of *Politique Internationale* in Paris and of *The International Economy Magazine* in Washington. As a fellow of the World Economic Forum, he has been chairing a number of panels on international finance and on "digital age" issues at Davos. Having worked previously at the World Bank after taking his Ph.D. at Harvard and engineering degrees from Ecole Polytechnique and Ecole Nationale des Ponts et Chaussées, and having served as economic adviser to the Foreign Minister of France, he now focuses on issues at the interface between these three realms of economic, political and technological changes.

Catherine Distler is deputy-director and co-founder of PROMETHEE. Her main publications build on her engineering studies in telecoms to reach into the broader world of networks; they include *La Planète Relationnelle* (Flammarion, Paris 1995 with Albert Bressand), *2100 Récit du Prochain Siècle* (Paris, Edition Payot with Thierry Gaudin), *La Déréglementation dans les années 1990* (Paris, PROMETHEE, 1988) and *Global Highways: The Future of International Telecommunications Policy* (Chatham House, London with Vince Cable).

Joachim Epperlein is an audit partner with the German practice of Ernst & Young. He specialises in the insurance and banking sectors. He sits on the steering committee of the international banking and insurance group of Ernst & Young and is a member of the banking committee of the Institute of Auditors in Germany.

Patrick Gounelle is executive chairman of the French firm of Ernst & Young in Paris. He has 25 years experience in various fields such as audit and consulting, due diligence, and major deals. He also serves on various Ernst & Young international steering groups.

Hans de Haan is an audit partner with Moret Ernst & Young in Amsterdam. He is chairman of its banking group and Euroteam, and also acts as an advisor to the treasury management group. He is responsible for co-ordinating the audit of major international financial institutions in the Netherlands and abroad. He served on a committee to prepare an international accounting standard on financial reporting of financial instruments for the IASC.

Kenneth Hay is an audit partner with Ernst & Young in Luxembourg. He has 20 years experience in the banking and financial services sector. He is serving a number of the firm's prestigious financial services clients in the country. He is a member of the IRE (Institut des Réviseurs d'Entreprises) banking committee.

Lionel Lavigne is a consulting partner with Ernst & Young in Paris. He co-ordinates the euro activities of the firm, both for France and for Europe. Also in France, he is responsible for payment systems and cash management. Before joining Ersnt & Young he held a variety of finance roles for major corporations.

Bernard Nivollet is a consulting partner with Ernst & Young in Paris and national director of its financial services practice. He is also in charge of the European risk management network of the organization and a member of its international banking and financial services steering committee. His main area of expertise is risk and value-based management

Jean Saint-Geours is Vice President of PROMETHEE and Chairman of the ThinkNet Commission. He has been chairman of COB (Commission des Opérations de Bourse), chairman of important French banks such as Crédit National, Crédit Industriel & Commercial, General Manager of Crédit Lyonnais, and also chairman of SEMA-METRA International and President of SLIGOS. Known also for his books on economic and social issues as well as his novels, he serves as chairman of "La Cinémathèque Française".

Ivan Wagner is a partner with Atag Ernst & Young in Zurich. He is chairman of the banking and financial services group of Ernst & Young both in Switzerland and worldwide. He developed the banking consultancy services in Switzerland and has been co-ordinating Ernst & Young's consulting activities for this market segment at the European level.

FOR ADDITIONAL STATISTICAL INFORMATION

LUXEMBOURG
Eurostat Data Shop Luxembourg
Tel.: +352-43 35 22 51
Fax: +352-43 35 22 221
E-mail: agnesn@eurostat.datashop.lu

BELGIUM
Eurostat Data Shop Bruxelles / Brussel
Tel.: +32-2-299 66 66 - Fax: +32-2-295 01 25
E-mail: piera.calcinaghi@eurostat.cec.be

DENMARK
Danmarks Statistik - Eurostat Data Shop
Tel.: +45-39 17 30 30 - Fax: +45-39 17 30 03
E-mail: bib@dst.dk

FRANCE
INSEE - Eurostat Data Shop
Tel.: +33-1-53 17 88 44
Fax: +33-1-53 17 88 22
E-mail: datashop@dg75iisa.insee.atlas.fr

GERMANY
Statistisches Bundesamt - Berlin
Eurostat Data Shop
Tel.: +49-30-23 24 68 67
Fax: +49 30 23 24 64 00

ITALY - Roma
ISTAT - Eurostat Data Shop
Tel.: +39-6-46 73 31 05/02
Fax: +39-6-46 73 31 07/01
E-mail: dipdiff@istat.it

SPAIN
INE - Eurostat Data Shop
Tel.: +34-1-583 91 67 - Fax: +34-1-579 71 20
E-mail: datashop@mundiprensa.es

SWEDEN
Statistics Sweden - Eurostat Data Shop
Tel.: +46-8-783 48 01 - Fax: +46-8-783 48 99
E-mail: infoservice@scb.se

UK
ONS Sales Office - Eurostat Data Shop
Tel.: +44-171-533 5676
Fax: +44-171-533 5689
E-mail: gloria.ryan@ons.gov.uk

USA
Haver analytics - Eurostat Data Shop
Tel.: +1-212-986 9300 - Fax: +1-212-986 5857
E-mail: eurodata@haver.com

Eurostat Homepage - http://europa.eu.int/eurostat.html

INDEX

ABN AMRO, 32, 172-183, 194, 225
access to funds, 215
ACP, 12
Adenaueur Konrad, 217
AEX, 108
AFB (French Banking Association), 123
Agence France Presse, 163
Airbus, 121
Aktion Finanzplatz, 77
Akzo Nobel, 111
Albert Michel, 233
Alcatel, 45
Allais Maurice, 125
American Airlines, 58
AMEX, 111
Amsterdam Exchanges, 102-103, 107-109, 112, 114
Amsterdam Summit, 204, 208, 227
APEC, 175, 226, 229
ASAP (Amsterdam Special Action Plan), 204
ASEAN, 32, 229
ASEM, 12
Asset Management, 166, see chap. X
Association of Credit Institutions and Investment Firms (AFECF), 61
AXA, 166
Banc One, 166
Banque de France, 22, 239
Barclays,166
Barings, 125-126
Bayerische Hypotheken und Wechselbank, 85
Bayerische Vereinsbank, 84
Beese Carter, 62,67
Big Bang, 40-43, 49, 235
Blair Tony, 158
Bocquet Dominique, 233
Bomans Luc, 27, 31, 130-139, 222, 244
bond culture, 59
Bond Indices, 212,
Bourlanges Jean-Louis, 233
BOVESPA, 50
Bracchi Antoine, 35
Bretton Woods, 18, 20, 21, 78, 84
Breuer Rolf-E., 13, 26-27, 29, 94
British Airways, 58
Brock Horace, 73
Bundesbank, 86, 252
Butler, Sir Michael, 233
BZW,166,
CAC 40, 108
CAC, 43, 47, 52
CBOE, 111
CBOT, 111-112, 120
CCF bank, 220
Cedel Bank, 27, 32, 105, 140-155, 200, 225, 288
Central European Bank, 59
Chambre Syndicale des Agents de Change, 125
Chancelier Khol, 230
Chandler Alfred, 223
Chateaubriand, 7
Chicago Mercantile Exchange (CME), 43, 50, 57, 59, 111-112, 165
Citibank, 160, 179
Clearing and Settlement, 35, see also: Cedel, Euroclear, SICO-VAM, 98, 143
Clearing, 21, 57
Club Europe,184, 186, 191,
"Club Med." countries, 22, 185
Coal and Steel Community, 20, 33, 145
COB, 62, 67, 220, 239-242
Cogema, 125
Collas Philippe, 31-32, 118, 184-194
collateral, collateralization, 213, see chap. VI – VII
Comex, 111
commitment, 67
Common Market, 33
Conseil des Marchés Financiers (CMF), 220-221, 239-242
contact, 66
contract, 67
Cooper Richard N., 30
corporate bonds in euro, 215
cost of executing trade, 48
Crédit Lyonnais, 166
credit risk, 21
Crédit Suisse, 85
credit valuation, 212
cross-membership, 56, 57
CSD, Central Securities Depository, 32, 130, 135, 137-138, 143, 153
culture financière, 47
Davidoff Didier, 62
Dean Helen, 62
debt-rating agencies, 212
dematerialization, 42, 43, 143
derivatives markets, see chap. III, chap. V, 209, 216
Deutsche Bank,13, 179, 182, 223, 238
Deutsche Börse, 46, 50, 56-58, 62, 68-87, 94, 105, 113, 121
Deutsche Telekom, 51
Dexia, 210
Dillon Round, 30
Dinne Martine, 62
Distler Catherine, 67, chap. XII
Doumayrou Benedicte, 62
Dresdner, 166,
DTB, 56, 94, 97, 104-105, 119-121, 124, 160
Dubrœucq Paul-François, 62
DVP, 133, 143
EDF, 224, 235
Elf, 192
Elkins/McSherry, 47, 48
EMI, 133, 154, 251-253
EMS, 21-23, 25, 30, 70-71, 78-79, 147, 214, 215, 250
EMU, 10-11, 13, 15-16, 20, 132, 136, 147, 157-160, 212-213, 250
enlargement, 203, 218
entrepreneurship, 146, 207, see also EURO NM
Epperlein Joachim, 35, 39, 69
equity culture, 59, 78-79, 87
ERM, 21, 25, 234
Ernst & Young, 34, 35
Euratom, 20
EUREX, 88, 90, 94-95, 97, 109, 115, 121
EURIBOR, EUROLIBOR, 123
EURO NM, 51, 55, 107, 109, 226
Euro X, 158-159
Eurobond, 32, 79, see also chap. VI, 142, 199
Euroclear, 27, 32, 62, 105, 130-139, 181, 225-226, 228

Eurolist, 51
Euronext, 50-54, 56, 58-59
European Central Bank,10, 69, 168, 213, 230-231, 233
European Investment Bank (EIB), 28-29, 196-218
European Investment Fund (EIF), 208
Euroquote, 51
EUROSTAT, 7, 224, chap. XIII-XIV
fair price, 63
federalism, see Overview, chap. XII
FIBV, 62-63
financial geography, see chap. I, III, IV, VIII
fiscal policy and tax-reform, 73, 79, 212
Fischer Jörg, 25-26, 88-101, 104, 119, 225
Fombellida José, 62
Fondation Alphonse Weicker, 29, 82, 199, 232
Forex (Foreign Exchange markets), 214
France Telecom, 51, 252-253
Franchet Yves, 32, 230, 234, 244-255
François-Poncet Jean, 233
Frankfurt-Europlace, 52
FTSE, 108-109, 111
Fukuyama Francis, 230
G7, 12, 29, 31, 227, 228
Gardiner Michael, 35
GATT, 30, 175, 229
Geiger Albert, 35
GL, 121-122
Glass Steagall Act, 33
Global Credit Support Service see Cedel, 140, 143, 153
GLOBEX, 66, 124, 163-164, 226
Glos Michael, 230
Goldman Sachs, 189,
Gounelle Patrick, 35, 117
governance, 28, 31, 66, 73, 149, 228
Group of Thirty (G30), 130, 137, 228
Groupement d'Intérêt Economique Européen (GIE), 52
Groupement Informatique de l'Assurance (GIA), 226
GTS (Global Transaction Services), 180
GUN (Global Universal Network), 179, 182-183
Guynn Randall, 62, 135
Haan Hans de, 35, 103, 173, 180
Hambros, 166
HAVAS,163,
Hay Kenneth, 35, 141, 197
HBC,179
Hong Kong Shanghai Bank (HSBC), 166
hub, 65-66
Humbrecht & Quist, 208
Hunziker-Ebneter Antoinette, 35
Hurstel Pierre, 35
I-tech, 66
IASC, 220-221, 234-235
IATA, 126-127
IBCA, 142
IBIS, 56
IBM, 214, 215
ICSD, International Central Securities Depository, 137-138, 141, 144, 153
IMF, 3, 175, 227, 253
infoculture, 65
infostructure, 65, 67
infrastructure, 65
Institutional Investor, 47-48
interdependence, 28, 31
Internet, 34, 222, 224
Investment Service Directive (ISD), 33, 97, 103-104, 161, 229, 231
IOSCO, 235
ISO 9000, 251-252
issuance technique, 213
J.P. Morgan, 212
Karsenti René, 28-29, 168, 196-218
Kassenverein, 62
Keohane Robert, 229
Kirby Antony, 62
KLM, 111
knowledge engineering, 150
Krotov Victor, 221
La Serre René de, 35, 62, 220-221, 227, 235, 239-242
Lamers Karl, 230
Latin Union, 19
Lavigne Lionel, 35
learning process, 255
legal continuity, 211
Liberty, 144
LIBOR, 123, 216
Liffe, 104, 112, 119, 120, 124
Limbourg Nadine, 62
linking machines, 65, 224-225
Lloyds Bank, 166
London Stock Exchange (LSE) and London, 42, 46-47, 52, 63, 84, 95-96, 98, 99, 105,-106, 108, 111, 118, 122, 124, 156-157, 159-161, 168, 188,189-198, 214
Lord David Simon,159
Loumeau Philippe, 62
Lufthansa, 58
Lussi André, 27, 31, 140-155, 182, 207, 222
Luxemburg Employment Summit, 248, 250-251
Maalouf Amin, 218
Maastricht criteria, 32, 74, 78-79, 87, 110, 174, 192, 203, 253-254
Maastricht Treaty, 10, 18, 19, 22, 59, 74-75, 103, 110, 147, 231, 232-233, 244, 249, 253
Marez Oyens Gerrit de, 62-63
market making, 63
Marks Karl, 78
MATIF, 43, 62, 88, 95, 104, 105, 116-139, 165, 237
Mattern Franck, 72
Mazières Bertrand de, 35, 221, 227, 234, 239-242
McKinsey, 80-81, 84
McSherry voir Elkins
Mediterranean, 201, 218, 192
MEFF, 62, 124, 162
Mercosur,175, 249
Merrill Lynch, 163
Möller George, 26 ,102 - 115
Monnet Jean, 23, 145, 217
Monnet method, 23, 24, 230, 244, 248-249, 255
Montreal exchange, 112
Morgan Guaranty Trust Company, 137-138, 228
Morgan Stanley Dean Witter, 166, 167
Mouillon Christian, 35
mutual recognition, 33, chap. XII
NAFTA, 30, 32, 175, 226, 229
NASDAQ, 63, 99
network life cycle, 65-66
Network Markets Study Group, 62-67

network of networks, 64
networked market, 62
Neuer Markt, 55
Neuflize Schlumberger Mallet, 177
New York Stock Exchange (NYSE), 38, 47, 50-51, 89, 99, 114
Newman Dan, 7, 35
Nivollet Bernard, 35,185
NMAX, 55, 107
Non-participating member states, 96, 211
NSC and NSC system, 51-53, 55-58, 121, 124-125, 226
NSM bank,177
Nye Joseph, 229
OAT, 123,186,
Odier Bungener Courvoisier, 177
OECD, 226-227, 229, 253
Ohmae Kenishi, 228
Oller José Luis, 62
operators, 66-67
Opt-out, 212,
Ostry Sylvia, 226
OTC over the counter, 67, 106, 118
Outsourcing, 139
Paris Europlace, 39, 77
PEA (Plan d'Epargne Actions), 191
Péguy Charles, 7
Penn Jeremy, 62
pension fund, 28, 73, 77, 82, 149, 168, 188, 191, 210
pension system, 247, 248
Peters Denis, 35
Peugeot, 57
Pfauwadel Gérard, 26, 32, 62, 116-139,199, 241
Philips, 111
PIBOR, 123, 216
Plazza agreement, 29
price discovery mechanism, 62-63
PTS (Private Trading Systems), 31, 66-67, 107
R-tech, 62
Rabe Thomas, 35, 144, 288
Raufast Jean-Charles, 7
relationship management machine, 65
RELIT, 43, 47
remote membership, 210
Renault, 57
REPO (repurchasing operations), 213
reserve currency, 217
Reuters, 66, 156-168, 163, 225
Richard Pierre, 210
Risk taking, 27, 74, 81, 97-98, 174, see chap. V, VI, VII, X, XI
Rossignol Bruno, 35, 43, 54-55, 61
SABRE, 223
Saint-Geours Jean, 35, 62, 67, 220-221, 234-238
Santer Jacques, 9, 23
SBC see UBS
SBF-Bourse de Paris, 25, 38-61, 62, 105, 116, 119, 125,161
Schäube Wolfgang, 230
schéma de place, 44
Schengen Treaty, 224, 230
Schuman Robert, 15, 217
Schumpeter Joseph, 74
Schuster Stephan, 35, 223
Schwab Charles, 193, 194
SEAQ International, 31, 107
Securities and Exchange Commission (SEC), 50, 62, 67
Security (economic), 151-2
Seifert Werner, 27, 32, 59, 68-87, 119, 207, 226
Seiters Rudolf, 230
Shell, 111, 114, 222, 224, 226
SICAV, 125
SICOVAM, 39-40, 43-44, 137
Sidney exchange, 112
Siemens, 45
Simex, 112
Société Générale Asset Management, 32, 118, 166, 184-194, 225
Société Générale, 187, 189,
SOFFEX, 91, 92, 94, 95, 97, 124
Soros George, 22
sovereign debt issuances, 213
Stability and Growth Pact, 59, 87, 132, 204, 208, 227, 230-231, 249
Standard and Poors, 142
standards and accounting standards, 76, 218
statistics, chap. XIII-XIV
STET, 51
straight-through-processing, 152
strategic alliances, 31
strategic option, 25
Strauss-Kahn Dominique, 162
Streit Clara, 72
strip, 213
SuperCAC, 43, 47, see also NSC
supervisors, 67
supra national issuers, see chap. XI
swap, swaption, 199, 209, 214-216
SWIFT, 62, 173, 181
Swiss Banking Corporation, 85
Swiss Confederation, 88
Swiss Exchange, 46, 49, 57, 90, 92, 94, 98
systemic risk (and technical), 31
T-tech, 66
T.S. Eliot, 7
TARGET, 63, 133, 181, 198-199, 233
TAURUS, 52
TEN (Trans European Networks), 208
Thatcher Margaret, 71-72, 244, 246
Théodore Jean-François, 25, 31, 38-61, 119, 198, 225-226, 241
Thomas Law, 191
Thomson Financial Services, 62
Toffler Alvin, 7
Treaty of Amsterdam, 11, 12
Treaty of Rome, 20, 30, 196, 200
Twain Mark, 22
UBS, 85,167
Unilever, 111, 114
United Airlines, 58
Uruguay Round, 30
Van den Brink Dolf, 31, 32-33, 83, 172-194
venture capital, 207
Villeneuve André, 26, 32, 124, 156-168, 226, 230
Voth Jürgen, 72
Wagner Ivan, 7, 35, 89
Walras auctioner, 62
Werner Plan, 20, 174
Wicks Sir Nigel, 251
Winterthur, 85
World Bank, 200, 214-215
World Economic Forum, 144
WTO, 32, 178, 226, 229
Xetra, 226